DOWN HIGHWAY ONE

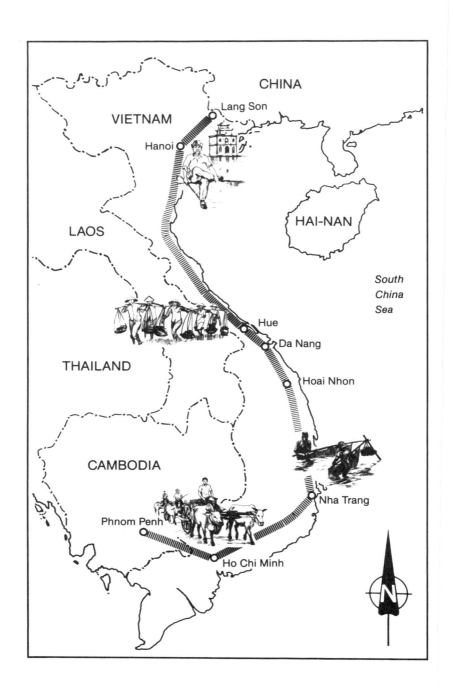

Down Highway One

Journeys through Vietnam and Cambodia

Sue Downie

Illustrated by Venn Savat

ALLEN & UNWIN

© Sue Downie 1993

Cover photographs: author's collection

First published 1993
Allen & Unwin Pty Ltd
9 Atchison Street, St Leonards NSW 2065 Australia

National Library of Australia
Cataloguing-in-Publication entry:

Downie, Sue.
  Down Highway One: Journeys through Vietnam and
  Cambodia.

  ISBN 1 86373 322 1.

  1. Cambodia—Description and travel—1975— . 2. Vietnam—
  Description and travel—1975— . I. Title.

915.96044

Set in 10/12pt Cheltenham
by Graphicraft Typesetters Ltd, Hong Kong
Printed by Eastern Printing Company Ltd, Bangkok

Contents

Acknowledgments

I am indebted to hundreds of people who, over the past four years, have made this book possible. I am especially grateful to those who helped in 1988 and 1989, when travelling and working in Vietnam and Cambodia was not as easy as it is now.

In Vietnam: The Press Department in Hanoi and Ho Chi Minh and the Foreign Economic Relations Bureau in Danang, with a personal thanks to Ho The Lan, Nguyen Quang Dy, Tran Ngoc Thach, Phan Thanh Hao, Bui Huu Nhan, Truong Hao and Tran Dinh Nguyen; also Ian Lincoln (without whose help I would not have made it to Phnom Penh in August 1988), Graham Alliband and Sean Kelly.

In Cambodia: The Prime Minister's Office, especially Cham Prasidh, and the Press Department, especially Chum Bun Rong and Sun Saphoeun; Jennifer Ashton and John Nichols, Onesta Caprene, Grant Curtis and Susanne Wise, Neville Henry, Lyndall McLean (for her bed and electricity regulator!), Rob Walker and Marian Brown (for the use of their bungalow) and Eva Mysliwiec. A special thanks to Margaret Bywater who acted as courier and encourager. Thanks to the numerous people who carried computer discs, films and reports out of Vietnam and Cambodia for me, to Alan Boyd and Dominic Faulder for dispatching them around the world, and to Mike Stead for providing sanity and a sanctuary in Bangkok.

Mike Morrow and others at Asia 2000 helped in the early stages —my thanks to them. Thanks also to the newspapers and magazines which allowed parts of articles to be reprinted including *The San Francisco Chronicle* (California), *The Australian, The Daily Telegraph* (Sydney), *The South China Morning Post* (Hong Kong), *The Straits Times* (Singapore), *Asiaweek* and *Asia Magazine*.

A special thanks to those who read the manuscript or parts of it at various stages and numerous times, especially Rina Paas who never tired of reading printouts; Ian Lincoln, Colin Mackerras and John McAuliff for their comments and corrections on the final manuscript, also Jean Yeates and Bill Oats; and those who read chapters: Bui Huu Nhan, Pham Thanh Hao, Tran Dinh Nguyen; Pung Peng Cheng, Ros Kosal, Wendy Foley, Francois Grunewald, Sally Ryder and Brigitte Sonnois; and in the final stages: Dorothy Kentwell, Cindy Burns and Robin Biddulph.

Sue Downie
Phnom Penh

Preface: Being there

One of the longest and most historic roads in Southeast Asia is Highway One, which runs from the China border in the north, down the length of Vietnam, and until 1990 into neighbouring Cambodia ending in Phnom Penh. Since the end of the American–Vietnam War in 1975 some aid workers, journalists and diplomats had travelled by road from Hanoi, either south to Ho Chi Minh City (old Saigon), or north to the border town of Lang Son, but no-one had traversed the *full length* of Highway One: 2100 kilometres from Lang Son to Phnom Penh.

Travelling Highway One had been a long-term dream of mine. It began with the Vietnam War when in 1975 as a student half a world away, I traced on a large map the daily movements of the North Vietnamese as they advanced southwards down the Ho Chi Minh Trail and Highway One, finally taking Saigon in April of that year.

Even after Vietnam finally opened its doors to Western media, only a small number of journalists were allowed to visit, and my 1988 approval for a journalist visa came only after repeated requests, although permission for subsequent visits was given more easily.

Travelling Highway One in Vietnam posed logistic, rather than security, problems, but in Cambodia the civil war meant there was no guarantee the Phnom Penh Army had full control of the section of Highway One from Ho Chi Minh to Phnom Penh. At least one Western aid worker had travelled between the two cities in a Government car, but the idea of a Westerner going by public bus was initially considered 'outrageous', and I was almost expelled from Cambodia for doing so.

I set out in July 1988 from the China border with a hired car and a Foreign Press Centre guide. On the second leg, from Hanoi to Ho Chi Minh, I had a guide who lived in Ho Chi Minh and had fought the French and the Americans. We were accompanied by his wife and five-year-old son, a driver who had never done the trip before and didn't speak a word of English, and a mini-bus stacked with 20 tyres and 15 batteries—not because we anticipated that many breakdowns but because they were cheaper to buy in the north than in the south. We were a travelling circus. The last part of the trip only took a day but was probably my most interesting day on Highway One. I travelled by public bus from Ho Chi Minh to Phnom Penh—the first foreigner to do so since the end of the American–Vietnam War—accompanied by taped Western music, dozens of uniformed soldiers and numerous live chickens.

The shape of Vietnam—long and thin, not unlike Italy—meant Highway One passed through 15 of the country's 40 provinces, from the beautiful mountainous northern regions, through the very poor central provinces, to the beaches and forests of the south; it then turned northwest through the southeast corner of Cambodia where it crossed the Mekong River and ended in the capital, Phnom Penh.*

It was a fascinating, exhausting and sometimes dangerous trip that slowly revealed the real face of Vietnam and Cambodia, giving an overall picture of life and death in two of the world's poorest countries. The daily hardships, the grinding poverty, bureaucratic inefficiencies, the unexpected liberalisations, the expectations of the cadres (government officials) and secret wishes of the people were slowly uncovered, layer by layer, as we headed south. The atrocious condition of the road often made travel agonisingly slow; the dust, heat, bureaucracy and language barrier added to the frustration. But one month and more than 2500 kilometres later, I had 20 hours of taped monologue, dozens of interviews, more than 1000 photos—and a glimpse of life in Vietnam and Cambodia today.

Eight months later I returned for another two months to report and gather more interviews and photos for the book, and in that short interim I noticed considerable changes in both countries. In 1990 I spent four months reporting in Vietnam and Cambodia, again travelling Highway One, then took up residency as a correspondent in Phnom Penh.

In Vietnam in 1988 and 1989 I was given almost complete freedom to go where and when I liked and to photograph anything. At no point did guides or the authorities refuse my requests to interview people or to visit sites (except the then controversial Soviet base at Cam Ranh Bay), and at no time did they suggest visiting something or someone they wanted me to include in my news reports or the book. However, the political climate changed in 1990 and Westerners—particularly Americans and journalists—were limited in where they could go.

---

* My first trip down Highway One was in 1988, and by 1992 place names had changed, forested mountains had been cleared, Vietnam had 17 (not 15) provinces and Highway One continued to the southern tip of Ca Mau, not Phnom Penh, hence I write in the past tense.

The reverse was true in Cambodia. On the first visit I was not allowed to use a cyclo (trishaw), to visit homes or to go to the provinces. Eight months later I was able to do all three. In 1990 I not only visited families but lived in a Cambodian home, and six times my guide tried to persuade me to visit a province! Although the Press Department said it was acceptable for me to interview anyone, the Ministry of Communications was not quite as liberal and refused my repeated requests to meet a train driver and a Mekong River boat operator, saying I was 'a strange person for wanting to interview the ordinary people'!

On the first trip to Vietnam and Cambodia I had a Government-appointed guide with me almost every day for four weeks. But on return visits, both Governments said I was free to make my own arrangements, and a guide/interpreter was only allocated when requested. Many aspects of life in both countries were changing rapidly. In 1991 I shrugged off my Press Department guide, employed a Cambodian journalist as my assistant and operated independently.

When inside Vietnam and Cambodia, I saw a different image from that portrayed in the West especially in 1988 and 1989. To build this picture, between 1988 and 1992, I interviewed more than 500 people, a proportion of whom appear in this book. Not everyone will agree with what some of these people have said, but they are entitled to their opinions and I am simply recording their expressions. Like the people I met, I have not dwelt on the past—the French or American eras. This is Vietnam and Cambodia today, as I saw it, in the mountains, the rice fields and the cities. I didn't go looking for the good or bad, but recorded life as I found it.

Author's notes

A note on currency: All dollars are US dollars, as that is the second currency in both countries, and the currency that sets the blackmarket rate. Both the Vietnamese *dong* and Cambodian *riel* have been subject to spiralling inflation and huge discrepancies in the official and blackmarket rates, making it difficult to put a value on goods and services.

Khmers in Kampuchea, or Cambodians in Cambodia? The country had been known as Cambodia to English-speakers (and Cambodge to the French) until the Khmer Rouge came to power in 1975 when it became known as Democratic Kampuchea. The Heng Samrin administration took over in 1979 and adopted the name the People's Republic of Kampuchea (PRK) which was changed in 1989 to the State of Cambodia: Kampuchea was used only from 1975–89. I have used Cambodians for two reasons: first, some people associate Khmers with Khmer Rouge (the Communist guerillas); and second, the Khmer people are only one of several races living in Cambodia—admittedly, the largest.

A note on names: I have not used Mr and Mrs, as the Vietnamese and Cambodians don't. Vietnamese are known by their last name—the first name is the family name—and women do not change their name after marriage. Similarly, Cambodians are generally known by their last name, although some are known by both, for example, the Prime Minister is never Hun, nor Sen, but Hun Sen. Cambodians sometimes split two names into three, for example the President may be Heng Sam Rin, but outside the country he is Heng Samrin. The Vietnamese often split place names—Ha Noi, Da Nang, Hai Phong—but for familiarity and continuity I have adopted the Western nomenclature. However, Ho Chi Minh, having a Chinese name, is referred to as Ho.

A note on ages: Vietnamese have little concept of time, and generally ages and birthdays are not important to them—I was constantly amused by the number of people who didn't know how old they were. During the war there were more fundamental necessities than keeping records, so many of the younger generation don't know when they were born. In addition, many parents faked their children's birth dates by several years, to avoid their conscription into military service. Many Cambodians add another year to their life at Khmer New Year (April), regardless of when they were born. In addition, Vietnamese and Cambodians consider they are one year old when they are born, so 12 months after birth they turn two. To further add to the confusion, some of those accustomed to Western ways, automatically take a year off when asked how old they are. All this means it is difficult to ascertain someone's age so I have simply used the age they gave me.

History at a glance

Vietnam

Vietnam owes its character to a rich heritage of religion, distinct culture and tradition of national independence. Its history can be traced back to 1879 BC when the legendary Hong Bang dynasty reigned over the then Kingdom of Van Tan, what we now know as northern Vietnam.

The Chinese ruled what is now northern Vietnam for more than 1000 years through a succession of emperors from 11 BC to 939 AD when the first Viet state, called Dai Co Viet, was established.

The Cham Empire, which dates from 192 AD, ruled over much of what is now southern Vietnam. The Cham people were influenced by culture from India and to a lesser degree Indonesia. Although Cham culture and agriculture were well developed, the Chams were unable to withstand the Viets who pushed south and finally conquered them in the 1400s.

The Golden Age was during the Le Dynasty which lasted almost 400 years, beginning in 1418 when the national hero Le Loi routed the Chinese from the north and established his capital in Hanoi. It was a period of great progress; agriculture, commerce, arts, crafts and literature flourished. Eventually two powerful families divided the country: the Trinhs ruling the north (known as Tonkin) and the Nguyens controlling the central and southern regions (Annam and Cochin China) from their new capital in Hue. In 1802 the Nguyen emperor Gia Long unified the country and established the Imperial Court in Hue from where the emperors ruled until the last, Bao Dai, abdicated in 1945.

The French first came to Vietnam as missionaries during the Golden Age. After years of conflict, they took Cochin China by military force in 1863 and within 10 years ruled Tonkin and Annam, administering the three regions separately. The French built roads, railways, ports, churches, schools and hospitals; established huge rubber plantations; and opened new export markets.

But they were hated by the majority of Vietnamese who were exploited and became second-class citizens in their own country, subservient to their wealthy colonial rulers.

The communist movement began as an independence struggle, led by Ho Chi Minh who wanted to evict the French and saw Marxist/Leninist philosophy as the answer. He founded the Communist Party of Indochina in Hong Kong in 1930, then set up the Viet Minh guerilla force in 1941 and began a national uprising against the French. The opportunity for revolution came during World War II when the French in Indochina were taken over by the Japanese.

World War II temporarily put an end to French rule in Vietnam. Thousands of French soldiers and civilians were imprisoned by the Japanese, although the French had limited power to continue running the country. When the Japanese surrendered in August 1945, the nationalists in the north led by Ho Chi Minh established a Revolutionary Government in Hanoi and declared Vietnam an independent republic. Under the armistice, Britain was to disarm the Japanese south of the 16th parallel, while China was responsible for the Japanese in the north. The Chinese recognised Ho Chi Minh's call for independence and his Revolutionary Government. But in the south, Britain allowed her ally France to return to power, rather than hand over to the communists in Hanoi.

The Indochina War began in September 1945 when Saigon erupted in violence as several Vietnamese factions attempted to gain control and the French tried to re-establish their authority. Fearing the Chinese would remain in the north indefinitely, Ho Chi Minh's government allowed the French to return under certain conditions. However, peace was short lived. Fighting between French and Vietnamese forces broke out in 1946 and continued for eight years in the north and south until the French were defeated in May 1954 at the battle of Dien Bien Phu in the remote northwest of the country.

After the French conceded defeat and agreed to grant independence under the July 1954 Geneva Agreement, the country was divided north and south of the 17th parallel: the north under Ho Chi Minh's Democratic Republic of Vietnam, and the south under the Republic of South Vietnam led by emperor Bao Dai and the pro-American Prime Minister Ngo Dinh Diem. It was to be a temporary division until reunification and nationwide elections could be held the following year. But Diem, supported by the US, refused to go to the polls, paving the way for the beginning of the American–Vietnam War.

United States involvement in Vietnam began with military support for the French during World War II, and later economic aid to the Diem Government in Saigon. American military and economic aid, amounting to billions of dollars, continued throughout the 1950s and 1960s while successive South Vietnam governments fought the National Liberation Front (Viet Cong) and resisted North Vietnam's attempts to reunify the country. American advisers had been in South Vietnam since 1945 and the US Navy since the early 1950s. The first troops arrived in 1965. After the Paris Peace Agreement of 1973, American troops withdrew but military advisers remained and billions of dollars were poured into South Vietnam until Saigon fell on 30 April 1975, ending 30 years of war and reunifying the country under a communist government in Hanoi.

During the American–Vietnam War three million Americans served in Vietnam and 57 939 lost their lives; an estimated 600 000 Vietnamese died and another three to four million—roughly 10 per cent of the population—were wounded.

After reunification Vietnam began rebuilding its economy and infrastructure but suffered enormous setbacks. The US refused to re-establish relations or help with post-war rebuilding. Vietnam invaded Cambodia in December 1978 and drove out the Khmer Rouge. As a consequence, in 1979 China attacked along Vietnam's northern border and Vietnam was also subjected to a trade and aid embargo imposed by the US and supported by other Western countries and ASEAN (the Association of Southeast Asian Nations). The embargo crippled Vietnam's economy. Living standards only started to show signs of relative improvement after 1989–90, helped by economic reforms, and a new foreign investment policy.

Cambodia

The French ruled Cambodia, as they did Vietnam and Laos, from the 1880s until 1953 when France granted Cambodia independence. When King Sisowath died in 1941 the French appointed 18-year-old Prince Norodom Sihanouk to the throne. Fourteen years later Sihanouk, in order to form a political party, abdicated in favour of his father. He won a landslide victory with large support from peasants while urban intellectuals opposed him.

Sihanouk renounced US economic and military aid and forced the closure of the US aid missions in 1963. He then allowed North Vietnamese troops to establish sanctuaries inside Cambodia during the American–Vietnam War. In retaliation the US began air raids against communist bases inside Cambodia in 1968, forcing two million people—one-third of the population—to abandon their fields and seek sanctuary in Phnom Penh. In 1970, while Sihanouk was abroad, the National Assembly replaced him as Head of State with Defence Minister General Lon Nol. In Beijing, Sihanouk joined with the Khmer Rouge (Cambodian reds) and made a public appeal to Cambodians to fight against Lon Nol. For the following five years resistance forces, with Sihanouk as a figurehead, fought the US-backed Lon Nol Government, until 17 April 1975 when the Khmer Rouge took control of Phnom Penh.

The Khmer Rouge emptied the cities and forced millions of people into hard labour in its attempt to establish an agrarian-based society. Sihanouk returned to Phnom Penh to be Head of State, but was put under house arrest by the Khmer Rouge. More than one million people are estimated to have died of disease, starvation or execution during the Khmer Rouge period, which has become known as the 'killing fields' era for the hundreds of mass graves that were later found all over the country. The Khmer Rouge, led by fanatical Marxist Pol Pot, was driven out by the Vietnamese who launched an across-the-border invasion on Christmas Day 1978.

The Phnom Penh Government was set up on 7 January 1979 with the help of the Vietnamese, and was therefore not recognised by ASEAN or any Western country. The Khmer Rouge regrouped along the Thai border and in June 1982 formed a coalition with Sihanouk and forces loyal to a former Sihanouk Prime Minister Son Sann who in 1979 had established the US-backed non-communist Khmer People's National Liberation Front (KPNLF). Together these three factions fought the Government politically and militarily until 23 October 1991 when the Government and three resistance factions signed a peace agreement in Paris, paving the way for Sihanouk to return and the United Nations to set up a transitional authority pending UN-supervised elections.

The China border to Hanoi

We reuse the needle until it's blunt.
Hoang Van Cong, provincial health worker

Northeast Vietnam is breathtakingly beautiful, with incredible escarpments and azure distant mountains. Sheer rocks rise like skyscrapers from the rice fields—bright green with crops, or rich brown from being freshly tilled. In the distance, a 300-metre precipice ends abruptly in a stony creek. The otherwise window-pane smooth precipice is interrupted by vegetation clinging precariously to narrow ledges and tiny crevices. It embodies, all too dramatically, the ruggedness of the region—an appealing mixture of beauty and isolation, subsistence and survival.

Against this rugged backdrop, weather-worn women work the fields barefoot, with loose black trousers rolled thigh high turned into a pair of shorts. Young boys attend buffaloes, massive and clumsy as they turn the fields with primitive ploughs, or graze freely beside the rivers. Children, pigs and hens roam through the villages and along the creeks. Rivers and streams, flanked by bamboo, palms and banana trees, wind through green valleys dotted with villages of earthen brick-and-tile homes. The air is fresh and invigorating; the tranquillity engulfing.

Highway One begins in these hills, 200 kilometres northeast of Hanoi. Technically it starts in the wide, dusty main street of Lang Son town, just 14 kilometres south of the China border, and 2240 kilometres by road from Ca Mau on the southern tip of Vietnam. The northern border is the most mountainous part of the country, and many aspects—geology, climate, fauna and flora—are similar to southern China, although vastly different from the lush green plains of the huge Red River Delta 100 kilometres to the south. This is one of the coldest parts of the country, with temperatures averaging 14°C in January (compared with 26°C in Ho Chi Minh, the southern capital). While the rest of the country experiences two seasons—cool and dry, and hot and humid—the north has a real winter, with temperatures as low as 4°C, early morning frosts, and occasional snow.

The mountains of the northern provinces are home to many ethnic minorities, or hilltribes, who are noted for their colourful dress and traditional lifestyle. The Viet people are Vietnam's main race and it is they who give the country its name. They live in urban and coastal areas and make up 88 per cent of the population. Of the 53 ethnic groups, six (the Tay, Zao, Nung, Ngai, H'mong and San Chay people) live in Lang Son province, many in poor conditions and in remote areas. They build small wooden houses on stilts, cultivate rice, maize and tobacco, and wear dark blue clothes, often brightly and beautifully embroidered.

Lang Son, the provincial capital, is a nondescript town, an outpost halfway to nowhere, 150 kilometres from the coast and flanked by mountains to the north. To the southeast is the South China Sea, and beyond that the Philippines archipelago. To the southwest is the largely uninhabited jungle and mountains of Laos. East, north and west is China which bears down on Vietnam like an enormous impervious cloak.

The north of Vietnam, originally known as Au Lac, was dominated by the Chinese for 1000 years until 939 AD when it became an independent state, Dai Viet, ruled by royal dynasties. Fighting between Vietnam and China is centuries old, and was revived in 1979 when China attacked Vietnam's northern provinces. Intermittent clashes continued until 1989, leaving Lang Son and other northern towns battle scarred.

When I first visited Lang Son in July 1988, Vietnam and China were still engaged in their border war. I arrived by car from Hanoi with a Foreign Press Centre guide, Hao, and a driver. Hao was 37, but to Western eyes she looked 27, and had been a press guide for 'some years'. Like most Vietnamese in her position, she didn't like to give away too much too soon, and I learnt very little about her during the four-hour drive from Hanoi.

When we arrived we were received by the People's Committee which administers the province (similar to a municipal or county council) and arranges visits and interviews for foreign guests. The Committee was housed in a series of low, pale yellow buildings which looked all but deserted, although someone had made a half-hearted attempt at encouraging a garden. The toilet—my first in rural Vietnam—was as uncared for as the garden. Unsure whether to hold my nose or trouser hems, I paddled in and out in record time, while Hao and the young driver tried to conceal their amusement.

We were eventually greeted by the province's Vice-President, Nang Lam, in a large airy reception room which had hanging on its wall a huge painting of former President Ho Chi Minh looking down on us from a 30-degree tilt. Lam apologised for keeping us waiting—I later learnt that our arrival was unexpected, as a message sent from Hanoi two days earlier had failed to arrive. Yes, interviews could be arranged, but first lunch, he said, gesturing to the verandah outside, where a delicate wooden stand held a white enamel basin of water, above which hung a small clean cotton towel. It was almost Victorian, and very refreshing.

Conscious of the low hygiene standards in rural areas and wary that local cuisine might not agree with a Westerner's more delicate constitution, Hao had thoughtfully brought a lunch of pressed rice and pork—eaten with fingers and dipped in copious salt, sugar and lemon juice—which to my surprise, Lam and his assistant shared with us. I don't know where or what the driver ate, and judging by Hao's lack of concern I assumed he took care of himself.

I had asked to visit a typical commune, so after lunch Lam and his deputy took us to Maipha, one of 222 communes in the province. After a short dusty drive from Lang Son, we came to a wide valley where commune members grew wet season rice. The bare hills had been stripped for firewood. A row of shabby single-storey buildings functioned as the school, health centre and administrative office, where the commune leaders received us. There was little formality—one official slipped off his sandals, slouched across three chairs and spent most of our visit idly pulling grey hairs from his head—but ritual remained. In order to make tea, the commune secretary, an easy-going man of about 50, poured water from a flask into the teapot, then used the water to rinse six tiny handleless cups. He added tea to the pot, refilled it with water, filled the cups and placed one in front of each of us.

Our hosts explained that there were 2900 commune members divided into five agricultural units. Each shared land, implements, labour, produce and profits. Lack of irrigation meant they produced only one crop of rice a year which was supplemented by small crops of cereals, tobacco, maize, sweet potatoes, peas and nuts. After a portion of the rice harvest was given to the Government as tax, each family received an allowance of rice. If there was any surplus it was exchanged for consumer goods or sold on the blackmarket. However since 1983 Maipha had been hit by a series of floods and droughts which had destroyed the rice crops. The commune had received only limited supplies from the Government and so was forced to buy extra rice on the blackmarket. 'In 1986, it was 30 dong a kilo on the blackmarket, but in the crisis time it was 960 dong. Now it's 650,' the official said, moving his chair away from the wall to reveal a water mark. 'In 1986, the flood came up to that line. The dam and pumping station were destroyed. Then last year we had a drought and lost 60 per cent of the crop and we had serious food shortages.'

In a drafty, poorly-lit room, health worker Hoang Van Cong took from a rickety wooden cupboard a stethoscope, a blood pressure wrap, two syringes and a spatula. This was the health clinic, and these were his tools—a pitiful example of provincial health care. 'We reuse the needle until it's blunt,' he said. Despite lack of facilities and supplies, he was endeavouring to fight respiratory infections, lung disease, diarrhoea and malnutrition. 'Sixty per cent of the people are malnourished and it's increasing', he said. As part of the national strategy to immunise children under five against the preventable childhood diseases—polio, measles, tetanus, diptheria and whooping cough—he had managed to vaccinate all except nine of the children before supplies ran out.

Back in Lang Son town we passed piles of rubble and half-demolished buildings. These were a stark reminder that in February 1979, China and Vietnam were at war. Most buildings damaged during this brief encounter had been rebuilt by the time I visited. Many dark, smokey, Chinese-style houses had been replaced by modern, brick homes, giving Lang Son a new look. Other buildings—including a hospital—had remained in ruins, awaiting funds.

Before dawn on 17 February 1979 the first of 85 000 Chinese soldiers had begun to stream across the 1600-kilometre border which winds westwards from Lang Son through the mountains to Laos. By the time Lang Son fell 16 days later, 80 per cent of its buildings had been reduced to rubble. But before that day's end China began to withdraw, saying it had achieved its aim, which paramount leader Deng Xiaoping said was to 'teach Vietnam a lesson' for invading Cambodia and ousting the Khmer Rouge. Western analysts now say China did not voluntarily withdraw but was forced to retreat after a decisive counter attack by Vietnamese forces which were largely made up of northern militia, rather than the regular army.

The 16-day war left about 10 000 Chinese soldiers and probably another 10 000 Vietnamese soldiers and civilians dead, and five provincial capitals, including Lang Son, in ruins. The two countries closed the border and ended official trade. Vietnamese and Chinese troops regularly clashed along the border, until early-1989 when Hanoi and Beijing finally declared a truce, withdrew their troops, re-opened the border, and began a new relationship which reshaped regional politics and paved the way for a peace settlement in Cambodia. During the decade of conflict many northern villagers supplemented their living by smuggling goods across the border. They brought from China mainly consumer items, cloth, clothes, food and Chinese beer. And they sent back to China geckos (lizards) and traditional herbs used for medicine, turtles, chickens and salt, along with jewellery and antiques sold by families in need of cash.

On the northern side of Lang Son, I was taken down several dirt streets and along an overgrown path to a square brick house. There I was warmly greeted by Hoang Dinh Trang, a retired teacher, who led us into his tiny two-room home. It took almost 10 years after the Chinese invasion to save enough from his small pig-rearing enterprise to build a new home.

Trang, whose ancestors had come to this region in the 11th century, was 62, and his wife Van, 54. They had six daughters before their only son was born in 1979. (It is not unusual in Vietnam for 40-, 50- or even 60-year-old men to father children.) In families where tradition is strong, a son is regarded as essential, as is the case in other Asian communities. 'The Vietnamese have a saying,' Hao, my guide explained. 'Ten daughters means nothing but one son means everything; if they have daughters it means they have no children. Polygamy is illegal [since 1958], but the husband of a barren woman often asks a second wife to have a son for him.'

Trang offered generous glasses of exceedingly strong homemade wine. 'My brothers sacrificed their lives in the army, and two nephews were killed in Laos and Cambodia, so it was important that I have a son to continue the family. Now I have a son and a grandson and they are very precious. During the war we saw a lot of people killed and we thought we needed more children but since 1980 life has been more stable and there is no need to have so many. If family planning was available when I had children I would obey the law and have only two. I have too many, it's too crowded,' he said.

From 1980, in an attempt to hold down Vietnam's staggering population growth, the Government set a limit of two children per family. This was encouraged rather than enforced through free contraceptives, abortion and sterilisation for both men and women. Disincentives included a delay in pay rises for government employees who had more than two children and, in some cases, dismissal. Enforcing family planning was particularly difficult in Lang Son province. Supplies of contraceptives were irregular, and it took some women three days to walk from their village to the family planning clinic. Hilltribes shunned contraception, married young—girls often started childbearing in their early teens—and had large families.

The mountains northwest of here, in neighbouring Cao Bang province, were the temporary home of nationalist leader Ho Chi Minh before he became President in 1945. They were also the birthplace of the Viet Minh, the revolutionary army which overthrew the French, and later (when known in the south as the Viet Cong) defeated American forces.

After almost 30 years in exile, Ho returned to Vietnam in January 1941 and established his headquarters in caves near Pac Bo village, only a kilometre from the China border. With the help of Vo Nguyen Giap, who had studied guerilla and revolutionary warfare in China, Ho built a small band of revolutionary fighters who made up the Viet Nam Doc Lap Dong Minh Hoi (the Vietnam Independence Allied League).

During World War II when Japan occupied Vietnam, the Viet Minh provided intelligence information to the US Office of Strategies Services (OSS), the precursor to the Central Intelligence Agency (CIA), which had a base in the southern Chinese city of Kunming. In return, the guerillas received arms and supplies, and training for their small but growing army. It was a short-lived alliance, and 20 years later Ho, Giap and their communist followers were fighting the Americans rather than collaborating with them. Ironically, when an OSS team visited the Pac Bo mountains in 1945, an American medic probably saved the life of Ho who was suffering from severe malaria, dysentery and other tropical diseases. One OSS officer reportedly described him as a 'pile of bones covered with dry yellow skin'.

Heading south from Lang Son, we passed a stream of people coming into town, some on foot, others on bikes, many lugging cane baskets laden with produce. Women carried heavy loads on the end of bamboo poles which bounced gently as they trotted along barefoot. In rice fields, dozens of people toiled, heads down, bottoms up, conical straw hats bobbing, their backs always arched towards the hot sun. Young boys, dressed only in shorts, scampered behind buffaloes or stood by while they grazed. Other beasts lay in half-ploughed water-logged fields, chewing cud and flicking flies. Into this otherwise peaceful setting hurtled an old army-style Landrover followed by a thundering antiquated bus crowded to bursting point with people and produce, the roof stacked high with bicycles, baskets and boxes. Drivers dodged chickens as well as pedestrians and cyclists.

Most of Vietnam was poor, but Lang Son province especially so. Many ethnic minorities were farmers, eking out a meagre existence by growing vegetables which they sold at local markets or sent across the border to Chinese traders. The hills were steep, the amount of usable land small and the prices for produce minimal.

Some fields were terraced for rice, others grew tobacco, and on higher ground eucalypts and pines had been planted. A crop of late season rice was being harvested; men were cutting straw with sharp sickles and practised ease; and women bundled and carried loads up steep slopes to the highway. Pigs roamed through rice and tobacco plots, and a young girl herded ducks along a path between fields, gently guiding them with a cloth tied to the end of a long pole. Two naked skinny boys bathed in a nearby river. A pair of furrow-faced crones contemplated the scene with a detached amusement. Some old women flashing dark ochre-coloured teeth, stained from eating the nut of the areca palm, waved at us—it was a rare sight for them to see a car from the south.

A large piece of furniture was transported on bamboo lengths balanced between two bicycles, and a live pig was carried stretched out on its back in a cane basket strapped to the back of a bicycle. Young boys pushed trailers loaded with short, freshly-cut logs destined for household stoves. Cyclists pedalled silently by or pushed bikes up inclines, some almost disappearing beneath cut grass stacked high in large baskets strapped to bicycle sides.

Further south, rugged scrub-covered hills had been cleared of forest but they were not terraced and offered no crops nor forest plantations. Erosion had cut ugly jagged paths down many gullies. Small neat piles of firewood appeared every few kilometres along the highway. As forests were progressively cleared for firewood and farming, the supply of wood for fuel diminished and cutters were forced further into the hills.

Although this route was known as Highway One, it was a highway in name only. It was more like a D-grade road—narrow and potholed with disintegrating edges. About 20 kilometres south of Lang Son we came upon a road sign warning us to 'Slow down, windy road', and indeed the highway began to snake its way through low steep hills. Numerous boulders were scattered on the road, put there, I was told, by bandits to slow the traffic. But my driver assured me night-time highway robberies were not common. The area was hauntingly isolated.

The skeletal remains of abandoned railway carriages suggested that a train had been stopped abruptly—by war? Nothing more remained than empty rusted shells, with wild grass reaching to the windows. They resembled the discarded jackets of giant insects.

A scarecrow stood limply in the middle of a small rice field in a spurious attempt to deter birds. A group of farmers spread rice straw across the highway to dry, then raked and tossed it with long forks. The dry straw would be stored, to be used later for roofing or as fuel for cooking. Men doing roadside mechanical work laid a large sheet of metal across our path forcing us to drive over it: an accepted method for flattening sheets.

Women working the fields often wrapped a cloth around their head to protect themselves from the sun, the colour identifying them with a particular ethnic tribe—white for H'mong women, navy blue for Thai and light blue for Tay.

Stopping to take photos of children, I was suddenly struck by the penury. I had seen it from the comfort of the car—the dirty torn clothes, bare feet, matted hair, bloated bellies—but now I was beside it, feeling it, smelling it, and it became real. A woman, grey-haired and impassive, watched from a distance as the children jostled and joked. They touched my freckly arms, and I let some look through my camera lens, but the sadness of one boy's eyes bore right through me.

Further on the highway was spanned by a long high railway bridge resembling a giant centipede on long legs. The line only took trains from Ho Chi Minh as far north as Lang Son, although it was once possible to travel from Saigon to Paris, via Peking and Moscow, a journey of about two weeks. I had long dreamt of making the trip, rattling up the coast of Vietnam, through the mountains of southern China to the wintery north, and across Siberia to Prague, then south to Paris. (In 1990 repair to the northern section began, and cross-border travel was expected to resume in 1993.)

We stopped at Dong Mo market 38 kilometres south of Lang Son where most sellers and buyers were women. The market was a sea of bobbing conical hats as shoppers, in black trousers and loose cotton shirts, moved between baskets of produce, perusing, feeling for ripeness and bargaining. Sellers squatted on the ground surrounded by wares displayed in baskets or on mats. Leafy vegetables, pumpkins, bananas, Chinese pears and bound hens were on offer. Others sold sweet cakes and sticky rice, woven hats and baskets, clothes and cloth. Sandalled feet padded past piled produce, and crumpled notes were exchanged for crisp green vegetables.

Uncertain eyes followed me as I moved down crowded aisles. At one point a young boy in red shorts slunk sideways through the mass of black trousers, clutching a live hen, never taking his eyes off me—probably the first Westerner he had ever seen. Many older women showed enamel teeth when they smiled. Traditionally, northern rural women painted their teeth with black enamel, as this was a criterion of beauty.

Numerous cafes or little restaurants with rows of low tables and small stools offered lemon juice, iced tea, sweet soup with green beans and 'black drink' or *thach*, made by boiling herbs and algae which set into a block of soft black jelly to be drunk with sugar, ice and water to lower blood pressure. At a walk-in State-run store opposite the market, women were frantically pushing and clamouring to buy some highly sought-after supplies, which I finally discovered were large pale blue blocks of soap made from cow fat and salt.

Heading south again we passed remnants of the American–Vietnam War—the twisted remains of a bombed iron bridge half submerged in a river, a neat cemetery with small squat white headstones. Some houses had still not been rebuilt 20 years after being bombed, and occasionally part of a brick wall or a pile of rubble protruded above the scrub.

The first American bombs were dropped on North Vietnam on 5 August 1964 during the Tonkin Gulf affair. Three days earlier the US destroyer *Maddox* and three North Vietnamese patrol boats had become involved in a 20-minute skirmish just off an estuary of the Red River Delta, each side claiming the other had provoked the incident. In the following 48 hours 'freak weather', an 'over-eager' young sonar operator and trigger-happy White House advisers, including Defence Secretary Robert McNamara, led President Lyndon Johnson to believe the *Maddox* had been attacked a second time. Just before midnight (4 August, Washington time), Johnson declared on national television, 'Repeated acts of violence against the armed forces of the United States must be met not only with alert defence, but with positive reply'. As he spoke, US Air Force bombers were on their way to four North Vietnamese patrol boat bases and an oil depot. In later years, it was revealed 'with almost total certainty' that the second attack did not occur. Nevertheless, the war in North Vietnam, although undeclared, had begun.

In the next nine years the US Air Force caused massive destruction in North Vietnam, hitting six industrial cities, 28 of the 30 provincial cities, more than 350 hospitals, 1500 infirmaries, 3000 schools and 1000 churches or temples. According to Vietnamese data, five million square metres of houses were destroyed, not including many thousands of thatched huts, 40 000 farm animals were killed, and all road bridges, sea and river ports, and power stations seriously or completely destroyed.

The stated intention of US Air Force commander General Curtis LeMay, was to 'bomb them back to the Stone Age'. The heaviest attacks were made between 1965–68 and in 1972. The most devastating—and decisive—came during Christmas 1972, when President Richard Nixon decided to use brute force after the Paris peace talks deadlocked. In 12 days of unrelenting air raids, day and night, the US dropped 36 000 tons of bombs, more than the total for the previous two years. Parts of Hanoi and the port city of Haiphong were reduced to rubble, although the damage was far less than American broadcasts asserted. A few days later, on 8 January, the North Vietnamese returned to the negotiating table and within three weeks a cease-fire agreement was signed. Although American troops began withdrawing, the fighting continued for another two years.

Hao, who until now had only talked of work-related matters, explained that some families from Hanoi had moved north to areas such as Lang Son when the American bombing had escalated in the north. They had been allocated caves to live in as protection. She told how her family stayed in a house at night and a cave during the day for about a month before returning to Hanoi.

Doing 80 kilometres an hour along the only straight stretch of reasonably good surface, dodging people and potholes, made me nervous. We passed a road-repair gang sitting on the verge, and later went through a surprisingly sophisticated cutting—surprising, because everything in these northern provinces appeared comparatively primitive, from coal-fuelled buses to buffalo ploughs.

The hills to the south were undulating and uncultivated, covered with wild bush—the epitome of remoteness. We reached the halfway point between Lang Son and Hanoi later that day. Hills and scrubland gave way to vast flat expanses of rice fields dotted with conical hats and working buffaloes. It was wonderful coming down out of the hills onto the plain at dusk: a powder-blue sky with white puffy clouds and just a tinge of pink, and the fertile fields with shades of green and a touch of yellow. This was the beginning of the plain of Bac Bo, or the Red River Delta, often referred to as the second 'rice bowl' of Vietnam, the first being the vast Mekong Delta in the south.

Rice is the staple diet and main crop in Vietnam. This part of the country has two rice harvests, one in April and the other in November (March and October according to the Vietnamese or lunar calendar). In early January and June the rice is planted in dense beds in open air nurseries or in a small corner of a rice field, and six to eight weeks later transplanted by hand into larger fields in neat well-spaced rows. Four months after transplanting the crop turns yellow like a ripe wheat crop and is ready for harvest. Passing through the area at transplanting time, we saw women bundling up seedlings, while men and beasts ploughed waterlogged fields. Buffaloes were everywhere: grazing beside the road, wallowing in muddy fields, or dragging 10–20 prong ploughs

controlled from behind by a farmer. To haul water from canals to fields, pairs of workers—often . young girls—pulled on a rope strung between them with a bucket in the centre.

Unlike the mountain areas, a sense of urgency existed down in the delta. Everyone worked faster, crisper. Women trotted along at a no-nonsense pace balancing baskets of seedlings on poles which gently swayed in a sing-song motion. I felt like getting out and joining them, but wondered if I could keep up with their pace.

After the French left in the 1950s, the North Vietnam Communist Government carried out a policy of land collectivisation. (However, land in the south remained privately owned, much of it by rice barons who lived in Saigon and grew fat on the rent of peasants, and even after reunification in 1975 southern farmers resisted collectivisation.) In the 1980s, for the first time in 30 years, northern families could decide how and when they worked the land, rather than being dictated to by a collective. As a result production increased immediately, and in 1989, for the first time in decades, Vietnam exported rice, becoming, virtually overnight, the world's third largest exporter behind the USA and Thailand.

The road dissected these flat fields with the railway line on one side and a long row of acacias on the other. Taking advantage of a straight flat section, much to my horror, my driver, like a madman, raced a train to a bridge used by both rail and road traffic. The boom gates were already down and a row of trucks were queuing on the other side, but we edged under both gates and crossed over. It was one of those inimitable dual purpose rail–road bridges, where vehicular traffic waited for a train, then drove on the train tracks across the single lane bridge. This type of bridge was common in Vietnam, but sometimes traffic was held up for hours waiting for trains. We were forced to stop at a second bridge, but pedestrians and cyclists slipped around the end of the boom gate and walked or cycled along the track, regardless of the danger of being hit by an oncoming train. Immediately after the train passed, the gates were lifted, and I had the unnerving experience of driving over a single lane bridge directly behind a train.

Highway One was the only proper road. Smaller dirt roads and cart tracks led off to nearby villages and unseen towns. Closer to Hanoi, side roads became more frequent, and some were even sealed, but none bore signs, so deciding whether to turn left or right at a junction required experience or local assistance. Without stopping, our driver called to a roadside seller who headed us towards Hanoi.

Houses were mainly built of earth-coloured brick—soft looking, roughly made and left unclad. These insubstantial homes were no more than little lean-tos with thatched roofs. One, with a huge '1986' painted above the door, looked 20 years old, such was the quality of construction. Most were one- or two-storey, although some closer to Hanoi were three- or four-storey terraces.

Here, amid the fields and flurry was what Hao described as 'the cradle of Vietnamese culture', for Ha Bac province in the Red River Delta was the site of Vietnam's first kingdom. The delta, the heartland of the north, fans out in a triangle, from Viet Tri northwest of Hanoi to points north and south of Haiphong, from the highlands of northwest Vietnam to the Tonkin Gulf, covering 15 000 square kilometres. It is among the most densely populated parts of the country; home to more than seven million people, most of whom are involved in growing rice. The lifeline of the delta is the 1149-kilometre long Red River which flows from the mountains of southern China, through the highlands, then slowly meanders across the vast flats southeast of Hanoi where it divides into six branches before depositing an awesome 122 billion cubic metres of water a year into the blue-green waters of the Tonkin Gulf.

As we approached Hanoi at dusk, the road became congested with pedestrians carrying loaded baskets on their shoulders; bicycles laden with goods; and still others pushing or pulling carts; and amongst all this, crowded buses and trucks which should have been pensioned off long ago. An alarming number of buses and trucks had only one working headlight, and they had an unnerving habit of turning it off just before passing an oncoming vehicle. The explanation: a shortage of light bulbs!

Activity on the highway at night was as great as during the day, and in many ways more interesting. Dodging barefoot boys, broken bicycles, bouncing baskets and blind trucks, I felt both like a nervous grandmother and an excited child seeing a new world for the first time.

Shut off from the outside commotion in our mobile cocoon, Hao and I developed a sense of togetherness, and we began to talk. We talked about the Vietnamese family unit, of marriage and divorce, the post-war shortage of men, the increase in premarital sex and the still-strong social stigma of being a single mother. These were subjects not readily broached with Westerners, but as a guide and interpreter, Hao was one of the few Vietnamese exposed to Westerners and was therefore more open to discussion and more liberal in her thoughts.

Hanoi: city of bicycles and trees

I didn't think of them as people who play instruments and dance and sing!
Vance Gainer, former American serviceman

I was struck by Hanoi's charm, especially its grand colonial buildings, many reminiscent of those in provincial France: yellow-washed walls, green wooden shutters, magnificent circular court-yards, grand staircases and tiny attic windows. Hanoi, it seemed, had barely changed since the French departed. Magnificent old trees embellished the main streets like ancient custodians, reach-ing over the streets so that they almost touched in the centre.

In the leafy cool of early morning I watched as thousands of cyclists peddled by in an ambience of casualness. Many carried a pillion, perched uncomfortably on the rear luggage rack or front bar. Sometimes children balanced on handlebars or were tucked in woven cane carriers strapped to the rear. Other cyclists had bags or baskets of green vegetables protruding from the top, or bananas and pumpkins tied to racks. Live ducks hung upside down from handlebars. As they cycled along, young men wrapped an arm around a companion's shoulder, laughing as they went. There were almost no cars, just thousands of bicycles each weav-ing a perilous path through the myriad. It was strangely quiet, as a whispering sea of two-wheelers drifted past effortlessly. As in the countryside, women wore trousers and conical hats. Men donned pith helmets still made as they were in colonial times, and many wore clothes made from army fabric. The sheer number of cyclists and their uniformity of dress was daunting. At inter-sections, traffic unravelled itself in a baffling display of ingenuity. Cyclists appeared not to look left or right, but continued straight ahead with an unconcerned air. Into this dishevelment stepped brave pedestrians who—either by instinct or years of experience —worked their way through the confusion. I watched a blind man cross a busy intersection—he held out a short white stick and walked across, hoping everyone would avoid him, and miraculously they did.

The only real form of public transport was the cyclo, a three-wheel carriage powered from behind by a man sitting astride a bicycle frame—the reverse of the traditional Chinese trishaw. Like bicycles, cyclos were used to carry produce as well as people. It was not unusual to see a cyclo laden with huge baskets of melons, or sacks of rice, being lumbered along the street with a woman riding atop. Cyclo drivers cruised the streets waiting to be hailed by a hand signal or the jerk of a head.

The streets were not only used by pedestrians, cyclos and bicycles, but also for selling, cooking, washing, building, eating—everything imaginable. Groups of men sat on small wooden stools drinking tea from tiny cups. A woman cooked on the footpath, and not far from her, a man relieved himself against a urine-stained wall. Two women sold beer from a barrel surrounded by half a dozen stools on the footpath beneath a shady tree. Bicycle repairers worked, not in a shop, but on a street corner. Barbers placed two chairs on a footpath and hung a mirror on a wall. Old women washed clothes in large metal bowls. On the mid-level of a three-storey terrace, a woman opened large green shutters to water a pot-plant-crowded verandah enclosed by ornate wrought-iron lacework. This could have been in a large town in southern France. But the French left Vietnam in 1954 and this was now the capital of one of the poorest countries in the world, where many of the city's three million people lived in sub-standard housing and wondered where their next meal would come from; where people repaired and recycled everything possible because there was no alternative; where a shop doubled as a living room and a bedroom; where women squatted on the ground behind pathetic bunched bananas waiting for buyers.

Nestled in the centre of Hanoi's old quarter I found Ho Hoan Kiem (the Lake of the Restored Sword). Surrounded by lawn and aged trees, it is the pivotal point of the city and regarded by the Vietnamese as 'an emerald jewel set in the heart of the city'. According to legend, after King Ly Thai To successfully defended northern Vietnam against Chinese invaders in the 15th century, a golden tortoise rose from the lake and took the King's sword—the Vietnamese inverted version of King Arthur receiving his magical sword from the Lady of the Lake.

On a small island at the southern end of the lake stood the old three-tiered Turtle Pagoda, which, although dilapidated, had a mystic air, especially when shrouded in lake mist. On an island at

the northern end was the Ngoc Son temple and to reach it I walked across the exquisite red arched The Huc Bridge which threw magnificent shadows onto the lake, giving a fairytale touch to an already romantic setting. Painted dragons adorned the temple walls, and the carved wooden doors were painted bright red and yellow.

The lake and surrounding park were a playground for young and old alike. In the early morning, the energetic jogged the lake's circumference and the infirm rested on concrete seats at the water's edge. At dusk, young men and women gathered on the grass to talk and laugh and smoke. And on Sundays, families sprawled across the lawns enjoying their day off, while cigarette and sweet vendors moved among them calling attention to their wares.

On my first night in Hanoi I dined not with Hao but with a Press Centre guide who I had met earlier. Ignoring the pleas of half a dozen eager cyclo drivers wanting to take me to a Western restaurant, and determined from Day One to uphold my motto of 'when in Rome do as the Romans do', I cajoled the young guide to come with me into an establishment claiming to be a 'resturant'. It consisted of a large dimly lit room with a scattering of wooden tables and chairs where men bent over bowls of soup. I ordered some, smelt it, then decided Romans were not always right! A fat rat wandered across the floor, stopped to look at the diners who were intruding on his domain, then scurried off to the darker recesses of the restaurant as if on important business. After our 'meal' I left the guide to cycle home to his wife while I wandered down to the lake.

I walked along a footpath, between trees, past people and benches, barely able to see in the darkness. I almost bumped into people, and was several times startled by a bicycle appearing from the darkness. It was very unsettling but also intriguing; I never quite knew what would happen next. (When I returned eight months later, lakeside lamps were ablaze and the whole area well lit, but the magic of the pre-lamp atmosphere was somehow destroyed.)

Beside the lake lovers embraced in the darkness; girls lounged on the grass beside their bicycles; men played cards in tight-knit circles under dimly-lit street lamps; women sold cigarettes and chewing gum from baskets sitting on the ground, each lit by a tiny candle. Two men holding hands strolled around the lake. Public displays of affection between the sexes are rare, but it is accepted and common for men to hold hands. As in Thailand, girls hold wrists or link fingers as they walk or cycle together.

At the northern end of the lake, houses appeared to be built on top of each other like Lego blocks. Some were quite dilapidated while others retained ornate features including arches, carvings and awnings which dated from early in the century. Rising from atop the pile was a jungle of TV antennas. Below, in the faint light and haze which hung around the lake, stood three of Hanoi's antiquated trams, like prehistoric transporters resting beside their watering hole. (As amusing as they were, the cumbersome drab old trams were a distinct characteristic of Hanoi, and I was sad to see them relinquished in 1990.)

Leaving the lake, I stumbled down Hang Gai Street—dark, narrow and crowded. I had been told that a certain shop in this street changed money on the blackmarket, but when I found it and ventured through the narrow doorway, a short woman sitting behind the counter shook her head. Two doors further on, I bought a silk blouse for 7000 dong ($2.50) from a woman who offered to change one US dollar for 2800 dong. I wandered next door and bought a hat. The woman there offered an exchange rate of 3150!

By 8.30 in the evening the streets were virtually deserted, and walking back to my hotel I felt a little apprehensive, even though it was only two blocks and was along what must have been the only fully-lit street in one of the safest cities on earth. I passed a woman sweeping the main street in the pitch black with a huge broom which she methodically swayed back and forth. It was eerie, and reminded me of something out of a Hitchcock movie.

The Press Centre had booked me into the Thong Nhat, the old French-built Metropole Hotel designated for Westerners. The $45-a-night suites, with high ceilings and expansive windows, over-looked Ngo Quyen Street, and from the ornate colonial balconies it was possible to peer down through tamarind trees and watch the city pass by. At dawn, the streets were swept while bullocks hauled carts to market and cyclos lumbered past with piles of baskets or bricks. An old wood-burning bus rattled past. Then came the morning pedal traffic, quietly, rhythmically, as if floating with a current. Giant leafy trees and silent bicycles made this a peaceful city—certainly a contrast to neighbouring Bangkok with its traffic jams, constant horn-tooting, stifling pollution and high-rise glass towers. Hanoi's bicycles will eventually be replaced by motorbikes, then cars, and in 20 years this once-silent slow-moving city will no doubt have a bustle and bizarreness to rival Bangkok's.

Vietnam was a haven of coincidences, as I discovered on my first morning. Over breakfast, I mentioned to another journalist also staying at the Thong Nhat that I wanted to talk with Western aid workers. He suggested a woman called Margaret Bywater who was staying at the Government Guest House. I found her without difficulty, but when she handed me her business card, I almost dropped it. According to the address, her office was the building where I had once studied music—the first Westerner I spoke to in Vietnam worked in the same street as my old school, 8000 kilometres away!

During my first two days in Hanoi, while the Press Centre arranged a schedule of interviews based on my list of requests, I was free to explore the city. I set off in a cyclo—a carefree, although sometimes bumpy, mode of transport—with a driver who spoke limited English. Riding in a Hanoi cyclo was like travel-ling in a three-sided wooden box with wide arm rests. It made me feel like the sacks of rice I frequently saw transported in them. For 20 000 dong ($6.40) a day, Hung, my driver, peddled tirelessly, smiling and nodding, whether or not he understood what I said.

East of the Lake of the Returned Sword is the Song Hong (literally, the Pink River, but known in English as the Red River) which every year between May and September floods the plains outside Hanoi, but is prevented from inundating the city by a dyke. Along its riverbanks stand one- or two-storey flimsy houses, threaded together by narrow muddy paths. North and west of the lake is the old French quarter: a collection of tightly packed terraces on narrow streets. Elsewhere were colonial buildings with green wooden shutters, stone fences, magnificent circular courtyards, grand staircases, and tiny green framed windows set in red-tiled roofs.

When the French took control of Hanoi in 1883 it was a major trading and cultural centre. King Ly Thai To chose the site back in 1010 and named the settlement Thang Long, meaning City of the Soaring Dragon, because he thought he saw a golden dragon rise into the air. Vietnamese hero Le Loi, who evicted the Chinese in 1418, called the city Dong Kinh, which Europeans adapted to Tonkin. Later the name Tonkin was used to include the whole northern region. The city's position inside a bend of the Red River gave it the name Hanoi—Ha meaning river and Noi meaning inside.

With no guide books (the first since French times appeared in 1989), exploring the city required local knowledge resulting in a fair degree of hit-and-miss. Nevertheless, I managed to find the Thien Tien pagoda where the 11th century hero Ly Thuong Kiet is said to have defeated Chinese invaders; the house where Ho Chi Minh wrote the Declaration of Independence; the old French Lycée, the prestigious French high school now used as government offices; and the former home of the French commandant, now the office of the Communist Party's daily newspaper *Nhan Dan*.

It was impossible not to find Hoa Lo Prison, better known as the 'Hanoi Hilton', an eyesore occupying a whole block near the city centre. Its six-metre-high walls topped with barbed and electric wire were in stark contrast to the elegant colonial buildings surrounding it. The French-built prison is where American pilots shot down over North Vietnam were held—and tortured—during the war.

Riding down tree-lined Hai Ba Trung Street, my cyclo driver leant forward, tapped me on the shoulder and exclaimed, 'America! America!' He pointed to a pair of high wrought-iron gates where a plaque proclaimed *Mat Tran To Quoc Vietnam* (Municipal

Fatherland Front of Vietnam). Between spindly cyprus trees was a pale green double-storey building which had been the US Consulate until 1954. With conscious irony, when the National Liberation Front, better known as the Viet Cong, was formed in 1960, it took over the old Consulate as its Hanoi headquarters, and then spent the next 15 years fighting its former occupants on the battlefield.

Hanoi's markets were a hotchpotch of hustling, bustling, babbling women who bought and sold household, personal and dietary necessities amid apparently acceptable disorder and repetition. Small-scale entrepreneurs were pawns of capitalism, satisfying the needs of a socialist system that didn't recognise, but accepted, private enterprise.

At the large Cho Dong Xuan (known to foreigners as the Covered Market) all the stalls seemed to sell the same products: rows of cottons, pencils, toothbrushes, bright coloured materials, plastic sandals, jeans. There was an abundance of cooking implements, lamps, bicycle parts and dozens of boxes crammed with an assortment of nails, screws and metal bits and pieces. Screw-drivers were sold next to dried fish, and denim shirts next to raw limp meat. It was smellier, dirtier and less organised than similar markets in Asia, and I was relieved to leave.

At the Cho Hom market, women offered pink roses, green vegetables and shiny fresh white noodles sold from baskets covered by broad leaves to hinder flies. Live chickens lay on the ground, their legs bound. There were no supermarket checkout bags here. Women put purchases in well worn cane baskets, or tied them in bundles and carried them by palm-leaf string. The usual 'wrapping paper' was banana leaves cut into small squares and expertly folded into neat parcels.

We passed an open air comic book library where men paid a few dong to hire a squat stool and a comic. Readers, all men, sat hunched over their books, all facing the same way like a group of students in an outdoor class. One young man was obviously amused by the contents of his read and shared his delight with a friend. Both erupted into peals of laughter, but the other readers remained unmoved. At the next stall an old man with cracked glasses sold lottery tickets offering a one-million-dong first prize.

It was unusual to see people wearing glasses. Many could not afford to buy them, others considered them unnecessary, and some older people equated glasses with intellectuals, which did not equate with communism. One Western ambassador later told me how one weekend he was stopped by the embassy's police guard who gingerly removed the diplomat's glasses. Placing them on his own nose, he expressed obvious delight at clearly seeing the streets of his capital for the first time. The spectacles were returned and the ambassador continued on his way reflecting on the realisation that all around him were policemen, drivers, cyclists and pedestrians who must have a very blurred vision of the world.

At the end of Dien Bien Phu Street, past the War Museum with its giant aged tower and old citadel walls, I found Ba Dinh Square with the National Assembly (parliament) on one side and Ho Chi Minh's mausoleum on the other. On Saturday nights thousands of young people gather to meet or ride around this huge square: an open space in an otherwise huddled city.

Ba Dinh Square has been a focal point in Vietnam's history. On 2 September 1945 thousands of people waving Viet Minh banners and portraits of nationalist leader Ho Chi Minh converged on the square to celebrate the Viet Minh take-over following the Japanese surrender. Here they heard their new president proclaim Vietnam's independence and the foundation of the Democratic Republic of Vietnam.

I sat on the steps of the parliament overlooking the vast square and imagined the ageing bearded Ho addressing the crowds. He began by quoting from the American Declaration of Independence: 'All men are created equal. They are endowed by their Creator with certain inalienable rights, among these are Life, Liberty, and the pursuit of Happiness.' He went on, 'The Declaration of the French Revolution made in 1791 on the Rights of Man and the Citizen also states all men are born free with equal rights, and must always remain free and have equal rights. Nevertheless, for more than 80 years, the French imperialists, abusing the standards of liberty, equality, and fraternity, have violated our Fatherland and oppressed our fellow-citizens . . . deprived our people of every democratic liberty . . . enforced inhuman laws . . . built more prisons than schools . . . mercilessly slain our patriots. They have drowned our uprisings in rivers of blood . . . fleeced us to the backbone . . . devastated our land . . . robbed us of our rice fields, our mines, our forests, and our raw materials . . . reduced our people to a state of extreme poverty . . . [and] mercilessly exploited our workers.'

I imagined the crowds listening in awe to the man they had never seen before. He told them the French had fled, the Japanese capitulated and Emperor Bao Dai had abdicated. 'Our people have broken the chains which for nearly a century have fettered them and have won independence for the Fatherland . . . We, members of the Provisional Government of the Democratic Republic of Vietnam, solemnly declare to the world that Vietnam has the right to be a free and independent country.'

Total independence, however, was not achieved until 1975, six years after Ho Chi Minh died. His embalmed body lies in a monolithic 20-column stone and marble mausoleum, reminiscent of Mao Zedong's in Beijing. Every three months, Soviet experts come to re-embalm Ho's body which is viewed by thousands of Vietnamese each week. When I visited, it was guarded by four stiffly-uniformed soldiers with white gloves. I found the chilling temperature, the incredibly austere atmosphere and Ho's insipidly reconstructed face repulsive, yet I lingered, intrigued.

Nearby, I came upon a small temple, and in the dim interior discerned a man sitting with his back to me reading a magazine. His shirt pulled up to his armpits, he had nine long needles protruding from his spine, each with a small red patch at the base of the needle where it entered his skin. As my eyes adjusted to the light, I realised there was a man dressed in monk robes who was inserting or removing needles from the legs, heads, hands or noses of a number of people. The atmosphere was almost mediaeval.

Along an open corridor, which fronted a garden of small neat trees, was the main temple with three shrines side by side. In the dim light one woman prayed, bowing from the waist with the palms of her hands pressed together at chest height. Another lit sticks of incense and distributed them to various parts of the temple, leaving a trail of sweet scent and scant smoke which quickly dispersed. I sat for a while engulfed in tranquillity, and drifted into a past world as if drawn by mystical ancestral powers.

That night, my second in Hanoi, I walked to Restaurant 202—at the time, one of only three restaurants where Westerners ate. Footpaths swarmed and swayed with people—this was living room, playground, classroom—and open doors emitted smells of frying fish and singed chilli. A bookshop sprawled onto the footpath, and a quick peep inside revealed a bedroom in the loft, shadowy figures, drapes, furniture, faces, glowing coals, and the unmistakeable smell of open-pot cooking. Next door, a woman slept on the counter of a shop. A man in white shorts bathed on the footpath, rubbing himself with vigorous concentration, then washing away the suds by scooping bucketfuls of water from a communal well outside a shop, totally oblivious to the passing pedestrians.

A group of card players sat in a circle and flicked long narrow cards with Chinese-looking characters onto the ground with force, almost vehemently. Flick, flick, as if whipping someone. Terse words were exchanged, and the only woman player roared laughing. Flick, flick. The circle and its onlookers became intense. A final assault with the cards, then everyone went into ecstasy or anguish, and instant analysis.

At Restaurant 202, the first room was crammed with bikes, and the second looked like a laundry. Unappetising smells greeted patrons as they passed the kitchen and mounted the stairs to the restaurant. The menu was in English and French; the patrons were an assortment of Vietnamese and Western; and the food a blend of both cuisines. As always, it pays not to look in the kitchen—the food was excellent in taste and presentation.

The following morning, I persuaded the Press Department that even for my official work a cyclo was the best way to see and feel the city, and that it was not necessary for me to have the $30-a-day black Government Volga (with kitsch frilly white curtains on the rear window) which was assigned to all visiting journalists. Instead, I took my round-faced smiling cyclo driver with his lop-sided green army hat and cycloed around the city, while Hao, my guide, cycled beside me on her bicycle.

For my first official interview in Hanoi, I was shown into a large high-ceiling room with a row of tall windows. The shutters were partly closed to reduce the sun, and a shoulder-high fan made a gallant effort to cool the room. I was seated at the end of a long table, bare except for four tiny china cups turned face down, and a blue and white tea pot. There was nothing else in the room except a telephone on a small corner table.

The austere setting was in contrast to the warm welcome given by Professor Nguyen Thuy Hoang, Director of the National Institute of Hygiene and Epidemiology, and his offsider. Both offered very enthusiastic handshakes. As with all official receptions throughout Vietnam, business was to be conducted under the gaze of Ho Chi Minh whose portrait always hangs from the walls. Generally, interviews started with about 90 seconds of nervous, grinning chit-chat, then it was down to business. Two hours later, Professor Hoang and I had touched on Vietnamese–American relations, anti-smoking campaigns, prostitution and AIDS.

For lunch, Hao took me to a local cafe for *pho*, or noodle soup, the most common dish in Vietnam, made with rice noodle, egg noodle or vermicelli, to which is added pieces of beef or chicken, chopped shallots and a mixture of unidentified spices. The 'kitchen' consisted of a well-worn concave chopping bench above which hung several cooked chickens, a glass-fronted cabinet displaying tomatoes, peppers and shallots, and two huge pots, one simmering with stock, the other bubbling with noodles.

Diners sat on stools at low wooden tables, such that their knees were higher than their bowls of soup. Although it was undignified, I decided it would be easier to take a corner of the table and do the splits—and was pleased to see Hao adopt the same technique.

This was definitely not the Ritz. Patrons spat their chicken bones onto the floor, to be chewed by a sickly black dog which moved lethargically from table to table seeking human rejects.

On each table dozens of once-black wooden chopsticks that now resembled the chewed ends of pencils, were crammed upright in a tin. Draped over the top was a small dirty rag used for wiping the implements before use. I opted for my shirt, and wished I'd brought my own, plastic, chopsticks. Despite the surroundings, the meal was delicious—tasty and immensely satisfying, with no after-effects!

Outside, a tea lady poured hot drinks with a casualness borne from years of repetition, ignoring a man with a wispy black beard who flirtingly played Western songs on an old guitar. Several men drew on long bamboo waterpipes and slowly released puffs of tobacco smoke.

After lunch, Hao granted my request to meet renowned artist and musician, Ta Tan, now a retired professor living in a two-room home. The front room—his office, studio, lounge room and private gallery—was crammed with his drawings, paintings and sculptures. A few minutes after the introductions, the electricity supply was cut and the ceiling fan came to a standstill. Just as the room was becoming unbearably hot, the power resumed without a comment from Ta Tan; I concluded that it must have been a regular occurrence.

'I'm worried about people like Michael Jackson,' Ta Tan explained as he refilled our tea cups. 'We are Vietnamese, we cannot be Western, but some people copy Western singers in their songs and clothes. I like to listen to modern music, but I will continue composing traditional folk music because inside I am traditional, and the most precious thing is to preserve our music for future generations.'

Ta Tan supplemented his government pension by selling his exotic sculptures made from tree roots, and vivid and exuberant silk paintings depicting classical village dances. 'This one,' he said, moving across the room, 'is of musicians who go to the home of a wealthy man to play for him, and if he is happy with them he beats the drum.' I wanted to buy two but didn't have enough dong with me. To my surprise, Hao handed over the money, saying I could repay her later. (On another occasion, I unexpectedly had to give someone $220, but didn't have that amount in dong. Without hesitation, my guide pulled one million dong from his shoulder bag, explaining that he was carrying it from Hanoi to Danang for a friend and as long as I changed dollars to dong in the next three days he was happy to lend it to me.)

Later that afternoon Hao and I met Le Van, Deputy Director of Aid-recept, an independent commission which co-ordinated all aid received by Vietnam. He was anxious to get technology and know-how from the West. 'When we need a fish it is better to give us a fishing stick than a fish,' he said with a grin. He talked of the present food shortages which had forced the Government to make its first international plea for help. He blamed pests, drought, long winters, typhoons and flooding, but he didn't mention mismanagement, inefficient farming methods or poor distribution practices. He neglected to say that while seven million people in the north were said to be facing starvation, farmers in the south hoarded rice because the Government would not offer market prices.

I visited Tarique Farooqui of Unicef who also talked of food shortages and warned that the level of malnutrition could leave hundreds of thousands of children with impaired physical and intellectual development. 'If they continue on this rate for four months they could be crippled. For some of these children, survival could be a consideration, not just development,' he said.

Across town, the Ministry of Agriculture's Director of Production, Tran Viet Chy, warned that about 40 per cent of the newly planted summer rice crop was not under water due to a lower than average rainfall and lack of electricity and fuel to drive irrigation pumps. I ended my first day of interviews with a feeling of gloom.

Supper that night was at a lake-side cafe with some Westerners, including two Americans who said they visited regularly, despite the trade embargo which among other things forbade travel agents selling tickets to Vietnam. The cafe was crowded and we cramped around a low round table to eat Vietnamese ice cream (made from condensed milk) served in small aluminium cocktail bowls. Loud music crackled from an ageing Sony. The cafe was a real jewel in the middle of an otherwise dark shuffling city. It seemed as if half of Hanoi's youth had turned out to drink coffee and beer and to enjoy themselves beside the lake. Congestion was no deterrent.

Later, we strolled along the lake to one of Hanoi's few discos. On the first floor of the Bo Ho Hotel, small groups of people sat at low tables in a large darkened hall. Ceiling fans spun frantically but made no impact. Warm Coke was served but it did little to quench the thirst. Those not dancing watched the band and in particular its female singer who belted out Vietnamese songs to upbeat music, supported by an energetic guitarist with long hair, exceptional in Vietnam. In the second set, in a display of versatility, he swapped his black electric guitar for a highly-polished saxophone. His co-guitarist had slightly curly hair and sported a thin moustache, both of which are unusual for Vietnamese men. The dancers swirled and spun and jived, dipping and twisting, as the band played a mixture of disco and old-time dance music. Among the dress- and trouser-clad women three in particular caught my eye: a very shiny silver pair of extremely tight pants, one mini skirt, and a pair of shorts. One girl, sitting on the edge of the crowd, was obviously grossly intoxicated, another rarity in Vietnam.

When I returned eight months later, young people were sitting on fashionable cane and wood chairs at white-clothed tables, each with a short-stem carnation and a sprig of greenery in a stylish little vase. The hall was well lit, the drinks cool and the fans more efficient. A year later, the whole hotel was being revamped.

I first came to Vietnam to prepare reports on the health situation, based on interviews with health workers and administrators and visits to some of the country's 20 000 hospitals and clinics. My visit to the most famous hospital, Bac Mai, on the western outskirts of the city, was memorable. Outside the hospital I watched appalled as a bullock lay flat on his side, still attached to an old wooden wagon stacked high with bricks. His head was limp, his eyes glazed. 'He just collapsed,' said a newspaper seller, who turned back to his stand, as if he had seen it all before. In a country where human rights are not always respected it's too much to expect animal rights to be considered important.

Bac Mai was built by the French in the mid-1930s as the country's first civilian hospital, and was partly destroyed by the US's 1972 Christmas bombings of Hanoi. Surgeon Vu The Ngoc, who had just returned from treating war victims in Angola, showed me where an unexploded bomb had dropped through the middle of the theatre roof during surgery.

In the emergency ward, men almost naked lay alongside scantily covered women. One young man had his arms and legs strapped to the bed, restraining his jerking movements as he reacted to the effects of pesticide poisoning. A woman, loosely covered with a dirty cloth, had Japanese encephalitis and was suffering from a brain haemorrhage. Next to her, a girl was recovering from a hospital-performed abortion, which is an accepted part of family planning in Vietnam.

In the women's ward, patients wearing identical stiff cotton pyjamas sat or lay on old iron beds, a rattan mat as their mattress. The high iron bedends stood closely, side by side in two facing rows down the length of the long room, creating a corridor and a fenced-in feeling. In the children's ward, the pathetic thin bodies of babies lay limp, almost lifeless, on mats beside their mothers. The room was overcrowded, but clean. Upstairs, a group of doctors gathered for their lunchtime bowl of noodles while an antiquated kidney machine kept alive a 44-year-old man who lay motionless in a large, virtually empty, ward. It was an eerie, almost macabre, scene.

At the Maternity Hospital, near the city center, the Deputy Director, Dr Do Trong Hieu, said they had already used up their annual quota of medical supplies. 'We use our scalpel blades until they become blunt. Sometimes we run out of catgut and have to borrow from other institutions,' he said. 'We are short of everything, and we must buy one at a time, we can't afford to buy in bulk. The ceiling leaks when it rains. The sewerage and drains are very old and very, very bad. Sometimes we don't have electricity, or water for washing our hands,' he said, pointing to a theatre completely bare except for an antiquated operating table and old sink. Across the courtyard, nine premature babies shared six donated humidicribs, none of which had the necessary oxygen supply or monitors attached.

'We ask patients their occupation and if they are rich we explain our difficulties and ask them to pay some of the bill,' said

Hieu. The Maternity Hospital was one of several hospitals that unofficially started charging patients long before the Government directed them to do so.

At the National Institute of Nutrition, Hao and I sat with the Deputy Director, Dr Ha Huy Khoi, and ate yoghurt—the Institute's specially-developed nutritionally-rich yoghurt. He explained that the Institute encouraged families to produce their own vegetables, fish, poultry and other animals to provide a more balanced diet, through a system known as VAC (the Vietnamese acronym for garden, pond, animal husbandry). 'It's a closed eco-system. Waste from the pigs gives fertiliser to the garden, waste from the garden is fed to the fish and fish nourish the man.'

By 6.30p.m. on the second day of five interviews a day, I realised the only time I had felt dirtier, grottier and sweatier was the previous night! I was in need of a break, and the Billabong Bar at the Australian Embassy was the place to go to on a Friday night in Hanoi. It had the city's best selections of imported music, beers and wines. An American script writer, a Hong Kong architect, the Thai Ambassador, a Bangkok-based journalist, swimming in-structors, someone's aunt on holiday—they were all there.

Apart from a wealthy American–Vietnamese seeing her home-land for the first time in 30 years, the indigenous population were conspicuous by their absence—this was the Westerners' domain, an oasis of wine and song in the middle of austerity; a sanctuary where they could buy $5 worth of drinks tickets and forget about the inefficiencies, inconveniences and ineptness of their daily life here.

I left the music, bright lights and clatter of the bar, and was pedalled back to the hotel through the empty midnight streets, under the dominance of huge leafy trees. The night was cool and black, and completely silent except for the rhythmic squeak of the cyclo's turning wheels—a moment in time. Riding along tranquil, wide streets lined with ironwood trees planted by the French 100 years ago, past once-grand French residences, it was easy to forget the depth of hatred the Vietnamese harboured during almost a century of colonial rule. However, I was reminded of it the next morning when I visited the Fatherland Front.

Here, Nguyen Tuc, Chief of the Economic and Social Department, gave me as a parting gift a copy of *The United National Front in the Vietnamese Revolution*. As far as I could see, the younger gener-ation appeared to have no animosity towards the French. How-ever, Government and party publications still referred to 'the French aggressors' or 'French imperialists'. Nor were Americans spared the poisoned pens of officialdom. Reading the book later in my hotel I soon recognised the tone: 'The US imperialists . . . set up

the Ngo Dinh Diem puppet administration representing the US subservient reactionary feudalists, compradore capitalists and militarist bureaucrats'. Propaganda terms such as these were not limited to Government literature. One middle-aged Vietnamese whom I spent two weeks with, always referred to the South Vietnamese regime as 'the puppet government', in casual conversation and when interpreting, whether or not that was the phrase used by the other person.

The book Tuc gave me had been published before the revised constitution deleted references to enemies and 'aggressors'. 'We suffered a lot in the past, but we forget it and build a new solidarity,' Tuc said. 'If we don't have normalisation (with the US) it's not because of us. We have the right to blame the Americans for what they did during the war—they caused a lot of suffering to the Vietnamese people—but we must look forward instead of back.'

With thoughts of normalisation I headed down Dien Binh Phu Street, past Chi Lang Park, dominated by a megalithic impression of Lenin, and up the broad sweeping staircase of a colonial masterpiece, where I found Foreign Affairs spokesman Bui Hung Phuc waiting to pour tea and answer my questions on foreign policy. 'We want to develop relations with all countries, including the US. How soon that happens is up to the US, it's their decision,' he said, sitting forward on the hard wooden chair typical of most Government reception rooms. 'Of course we would welcome normalisation with the US but for the last few decades we have lived without them. We don't have to have relations with them to survive.'

On the way to the Olof Palme Hospital, my cyclo developed a puncture and was attended to by a young man whose curbside 'workshop' consisted of a metal bowl of water (for pinpointing leaks in inner tubes), a rudimentary kerosene fire for sealing leaks, and a collection of tools. The new tyre cost a mere 700 dong (23 cents) and it was assumed I would pay.

During the roadside repairs, I inspected the nearby Intershop, a Government-run store stocking hard-to-come-by Vietnamese and imported goods. There were numerous lookers but few buyers. Above the rows of plastic sandals, toilet paper, piles of cloth, and kitchenware, several styles of shirts hung on coathangers from the ceiling. The most expensive item was a treadle sewing machine, quite small, for 250 000 dong ($83). This was 1988 and civil servants earned 20 000 ($6.60) a month. On the same shelf beside the sewing machine were nylon carry-bags for 2000 dong, small soaps for 1200 and toothpaste for 1000. Men's underwear, bras, T-shirts, handkerchiefs, shirts, ties, jackets and towels sat with washing powder, small gas burners and pots. As was the vogue in socialist countries at the time, goods were displayed on shelves behind the counter or under glass tops, where they could not be handled. When I returned two years later, 'luxury' items such as these were being freely sold all over the city.

The hospital—built by Swedes and named in honour of their assassinated Prime Minister, Olof Palme—was on the western outskirts of the city, about 7 kilometres from the lake. Here I found the motherly Professor Nguyen Thu Nhan, Director of the Institute for the Protection of Children's Health. She was concerned about the shortage of paediatric doctors and nurses, the lack of funds for health education, the ever-present problem of malnutrition in children and the increase in hygiene-related illnesses.

'Fifty per cent of children under three years have malnutrition, and we are trying to encourage mothers to breastfeed up to 24 months, then teach them about weaning foods. We can reduce the number of children with malnutrition if we can increase the knowledge of mothers,' she said.

Next I met Professor Bui Thung, a jolly man who directed the Rehabilitation Institute where thousands of war victims were treated and helped back into a productive life. We struck up an instant rapport and joked our way through controversial subjects, with me seeking unofficial answers but not quite getting them. He said more than 60 000 Vietnamese (0.1 per cent of the population) had lost an arm or leg. Half were veterans and half civilians— victims of war and accidents. Many who survived the American –Vietnam War and Vietnam's ten-year involvement in Cambodia were accommodated at 40 institutions throughout the country.

He talked frankly of amputees reduced to begging, regarded with disdain in the north although prevalent in Ho Chi Minh. 'The government provided 300 dong a month plus accommodation, but because of inflation 300 dong was not enough, so they had to go out on the street. Now we have to give them more money so this will never happen again.' While he poured a fresh round of tea, I calculated that 300 dong was one-tenth of a packet of imported cigarettes.

Later, I visited a rehabilitation centre just outside Hanoi where 150 of the 170 inmates were in wheelchairs. They each had a single room with a bed behind a screen and a single cooker in a corner acting as a kitchen. Thirty-year-old Vu Duc San, who had been there since early 1981, said he preferred living with other paraplegic soldiers than in his home village. 'Here, I'm with friends who have been through the same ordeal and understand me. In my village I could not work and I would be a burden on my family, and there would be some stigma.' He described to me how in December 1977, his regiment was the first to respond to a Khmer Rouge attack on a Vietnamese village, in what was known as the Tay Ninh Massacre. After forcing the Pol Pot army back across the border, his unit remained inside Cambodia for more than a year. 'If they fought, we fought, and there was fighting all the time.' During an ambush in February 1979, a bullet grazed San's spine, rendering him paraplegic. He was still angry and bitter, he said, 'because I was so young'.

Vietnam's invasion of Cambodia officially began on Christmas Day 1978 and ended on 30 September 1989, although units such as San's were operating in the country before, and some allegedly remained or returned after the final pull-out. With one million soldiers, Vietnam had the fourth largest army in the world, and at one point 200 000 were across the border. Cambodia cost Vietnam dearly, in financial and human terms; 50 000 soldiers were killed or wounded and Vietnam became subject to an international trade and aid embargo imposed by the US and variously endorsed by other Western and Asian countries. In addition, China 'punished' Vietnam by invading along the northern border and breaking trade ties for a decade. Vietnam became isolated politically and economically from all except the Soviet–Eastern bloc, and Moscow is said to have sent an average of $1 million a day to Hanoi. Sweden and Finland were the only Western countries giving bilateral (government to government) aid. Others provided minimal amounts through United Nations and voluntary agencies.

I returned to Vietnam for April–June 1989, arriving on 5 April, the day Foreign Minister Nguyen Co Thach announced that the last Vietnamese troops in Cambodia would be withdrawn by 30 September the same year. In an impressively well-orchestrated move, a colleague and I were taken by a Press Department guide from the airport directly to a press conference at the Ministry of Foreign Affairs. We were whisked into front seats at a Ministry of Foreign Affairs building, where several other journalists and dozens of diplomats were already assembled. This was my—and possibly Thach's—first press conference in Hanoi. He sat before us on a raised platform with a bank of microphones and his translator, a tall attractive woman whose English translation he frequently corrected. He told us that if the Cambodian peace settlement failed and the 'murderous Pol Pot clique' returned to power, the US and other countries supporting the Khmer Rouge would be blamed, and Vietnam reserved the right to return to Cambodia.

Thach had done more than anyone else to rebuild bridges between Vietnam and the West and to resolve the Cambodian problem, and I was impressed by what I had seen of him publicly. A few days after the press conference, I met him in a reception room at the Ministry of Foreign Affairs. The sixth-ranking member of the Communist Politburo, he was distinguished in a tie and Western-style suit yet surprisingly casual. He talked easily (in a language he had begun to learn only in middle age) of his love of art and his years in jail, which had begun at the age of 17 soon after he left school to join the anti-French resistance. 'I have a low education—no MA,' he laughed. 'I like drawing and in jail I drew almost all my jailmates.' Thach, probably the best-known Vietnamese after General Vo Nguyen Giap, openly criticised China just as Hanoi and Beijing were moving closer to ending their decade-long conflict and normalising relations, and consequently he was dropped as Foreign Minister in 1991 to appease the Chinese.

I later spent almost two hours with General Giap in the immense reception room of the former Bac Bo Palace. He talked of his childhood, his role as commander of the Viet Minh forces which defeated the French, and of the North Vietnamese forces in their defeat of the Americans. He compared the much more evenly matched 13th century feudal wars to the technological wars of the 1960s and 1970s: 'the Americans had every kind of weapon except nuclear weapons, so we were far inferior in terms of materials'. He talked of Vietnam taking a greater role in the international arena and compared economic reforms here and in the Soviet Union. 'Vietnam is independent-minded and we should go our own way. *Perestroika* is a Russian word which should be applied to the Soviet Union. In Vietnam we adopted *doi moi*.'

The Government's new policy of *doi moi*, or 'renovation' was responsible for much of the change I was seeing in 1989. At the end of the American war, Vietnam kept its doors closed to the capitalist world, but the Sixth Party Congress in December 1986 decided to open them again, although it was more than a year before the first results were seen. Although the US embargo was still in place, the country's shattered economy was slowly starting to improve. More private enterprises were opening, people were starting to bank their savings in significant amounts, and buildings were being constructed and repaired. Several restaurants had opened in Hanoi, including the Piano Bar, where the hostess sisters played classics on violin and piano as guests dined on crab, quail and crème caramel. A cyclo driver estimated there were now 1000 cafes in Hanoi, double the number two years earlier. And I saw my first poster of a Western pop group: WHAM.

Despite the embargo, businessmen from the West and Asia began establishing export deals and joint ventures with the Vietnamese Government. Hundreds of others came to assess the situation so they would be ready to move in once the embargo was lifted.

American veterans also began returning in noticeable numbers from 1989 onwards. For anaesthetist Dr Vance Gainer, coming back to the country he had fought in was like completing a circle. 'This is where I did my growing up, and it was great to come back, but there was no catholicism. Some people had bad experiences in Vietnam during the war and I had bad experiences, but I dealt with that a long time ago.' He found his stereotypes vastly different to reality. 'In the south during the war you saw a conglomeration of farmers, bar girls and VC [Viet Cong]. I didn't think of them as people who play instruments and dance and sing—only as shadowy and without form, because that's what we were told. This time I saw them in a completely different light. A night at the Opera House [in Hanoi] was one of the most enlightening evenings I've had. I was real sad to be leaving.'

'The past is done,' said another veteran, New Jersey plastic surgeon Dr Art Brown who returned with Operation Smile, a volunteer medical team which did 107 cleft palate operations in Hanoi in a week. 'We have to get on with things today and forever—and at every level of Government in Vietnam that is reiterated. It's unfortunate that a small minority [of Americans] are still bitter and are still looking at Vietnam as it was 20 years ago. One of the Vietnamese surgeons and I were trying to work it all out. He just said, "people are people and governments are governments".'

Many veterans were surprised at the warm reception they received and the lack of bitterness. Over a cold Heineken, former Air Force communications technician Bruce D'Agostino recalled how on his first evening in Hanoi, he met a young dancer who talked freely of how her father and brother were killed in the 1972

US bombing raid. 'She said, "that's life, that's war",' he said. 'In 1967, if anyone had said you would be disco dancing in Hanoi with a girl whose father and brother were killed by B52s, I wouldn't have believed them. It was great to come here without being a GI and to go out with girls who are not prostitutes.'

Returning to Hanoi in March 1990 after nine months away, I barely recognised the city. It now boasted colourful streets, crowded shops, landscaped parks, painted fences and street lamps— although there were still only two sets of traffic lights in the capital of a country that had 65 million people. Shops and markets were flooded with consumer goods, imported mainly from China, Japan, Singapore and Thailand.

In one year, Hanoi's standard of living had improved more than anywhere else in the country. *Doi moi* included encouraging private enterprise and giving farmers land control, and the results could be seen everywhere. Agricultural and manufacturing production had increased, many more consumer goods were available, the quantity, quality and variety of food was better, and the overall appearance of the city and its inhabitants had improved considerably. There were many more motorbikes and cars, clothes were brighter and more modern, shops offered everything from videos and imported beers to reject kitchenware from China.

In the past, I had sometimes found it difficult to consider Hanoi a city. It had a population of around 4 million in 1988 but it didn't look or function like a capital. Shops were drab and few, public transport virtually non-existent, and cars a rarity. Hanoi reminded me of an overweight conservative old lady who shuffled along in a diligent manner, unconcerned by her dishevelled appearance. In 1990, the old lady began a major transformation. The emergence of video shops, same-day photo processing and slick Toyota Celicas helped transport Hanoi out of the 1940s in a matter of months rather than decades.

But with the changes some of the magic had faded. It was no longer the city of romantic shadows that I had known in 1988. Motorised transport now shattered the tranquillity; fruit bags once made from the pages of magazines had been replaced by plastic ones; and the inimitable old wood-fuelled buses had been relegated elsewhere. And despite the obvious consumer-oriented changes, schools, hospitals, offices and other Government-run institutions remain in a neglected state: schools without textbooks, hospitals without syringes and offices lacking typewriters.

But even so, Hanoi was still a captivating place. On that first night back, in March 1990, I again walked around the lake, now landscaped and lit, to the Hang Gai Street money changers who were now displaying plastic toys and trendy T-shirts. Part-way down a darkened Ly Quoc Su Street, I wandered into the dimness of a temple tended by black-clothed women; withered maidens with black head scarves and betelnut-stained teeth. None of them spoke a word of English so I ventured a few words in Vietnamese. They took me by the wrist and, through a mixture of sign language and exaggerated expressions, told me about the temple.

They poured copious cups of tea then sat me on the floor where they had spread a mat which was then laid with bowls of soup, cabbage and meat (of unidentified source) and plenty of rice. I was given terrible old wooden chopsticks which had been used by who knows who. We sat and ate and grinned at each other, and watched worshippers come and go as they brought temple offerings of cigarettes and fruit—bananas, mangos, little oranges—some with money stuck between them. At the end of our meal, a younger woman produced a metal bowl with steaming hot water and pink soap, and suggested I wash my hands, which I did although no one else did. Finally, we said farewell and I returned once more to the street, as if returning from a dream, wondering where I'd been and what I'd done in the past hour.

This once beautiful old French town, which had been sadly and steadily falling into a shabby decaying city, was now starting to take on a new lease of life. After decades of abuse and neglect, old buildings were being repaired and extended, and fences painted and gardens revived. But as the city sprouted, brick and concrete Czechoslovakian-designed accommodation blocks were being built, causing Western architects to survey the scene with concern. 'If the Vietnamese can preserve what's here now, they will have one of the best tourist attractions, but it needs a lot of careful planning and gentle persuasion,' lamented Bangkok-based building consultant David Abotomey, who had been working with the authorities to develop a preservation plan for the city.

Although most villas remained neglected, some had been returned to their former glory. Two examples were the British and Australian embassies. The latter was a trio of magnificent colonial buildings with ornate balconies, wooden shutters, stucco moulding and tiled arches. With shades of former colonialism, 120 people who had lived in and around one building, were now rehoused elsewhere to make way for the ambassador's residence. I went with some friends from the Australian Embassy—a secretary who was over six feet tall and towered over her Vietnamese colleagues, and a gay teacher and his young Vietnamese boyfriend—to the Gala 90 concert at the nearby Soviet-built

Cultural Palace (which should have been called the 'Concrete Palace'). Expecting a 1970s-style variety show, we were instead entertained by a raunchy disco singer storming the stage in skin-tight multi-coloured pants and a skimpy 'boob-tube', tossing her long hair and handling a microphone with suggestive motions.

Our raunchy singer turned out to be 26 years old and had been singing for just four years. 'I prefer Western songs because they have more energy. Vietnamese songs tend to be romantic and often sad. I buy cassettes, listen to them under my headphones, write down the words then get my English teacher to check it. Then I start singing them,' explained Ngoc Anh, the diminutive Saigon-born singer. I noticed that she wore a gold ring on each finger and learnt that she earned in one night what a civil servant earned in a month. Some people were getting rich in Vietnam.

Other Vietnamese became dong-millionaires by selling consumer goods to a public who had been starved of such luxuries for more than 40 years. Three weeks after the Government sanctioned private enterprise, the Dinh brothers opened stores in Hanoi and Ho Chi Minh, and within six months they had a monthly turnover of 18 million dong ($5150). Beneath bright lights and polished glass, their Hanoi store stocked imported electrical goods, watches, cosmetics, perfume and fashionable clothes from Thailand, Hong Kong and Japan—and colourful men's underwear from Australia. Dinh Dhai Hong, 34, who sported a thick gold chain and four rings, including a large diamond creation and a flashy Omega watch, told me that the Hanoi store was so successful that the family had closed the Ho Chi Minh one and reinvested in a second shop in the north.

By early 1990, inflation was down from an annual rate of 700 per cent to about 20 per cent. The price of gold, often as much as 30 per cent above international rates, was closer to the world rate than it had been for many years. The gap between the official and blackmarket exchange rate was the narrowest ever.

However, *doi moi* brought problems. Corruption was more evident, the gap between rich and poor was widening, unemployment was as high as 20 per cent in some urban areas, and many factories operated at only half capacity—the Vietnamese blamed a shortage of materials and parts, but omitted to mention mismanagement.

I went back to the Olof Palme Hospital to find out Professor Nguyen Thu Nhan's opinion on the latest changes. 'There is now freedom and food is sold everywhere on the streets, but there are no controls so sometimes food stays in the heat all day, and there has already been an increase in dysentery.' Californian plastic surgeon Bryant Toth told me that there was an increase in vehicle accidents. 'From a medical point of view, it is becoming a dangerous city. It's like giving children toys—they've never had motor vehicles, and the city is not designed for motor vehicles.' He and two colleagues came several times a year—using their own funds—to operate and help train Vietnamese surgeons. They had just completed 40 operations during two weeks in Ho Chi Minh and Hanoi. 'Provide these doctors with the opportunity and the materials to work with, and you end up with very efficient surgeons more rapidly than in any other country because they are very industrious, clever, bright people.'

There was no doubt the city had become a more hazardous place for cyclists who still made up 95 per cent of commuters. Lines had been painted on the road to separate incessant horn-tooting cars from the cyclists they terrorised, and during peak-hour, traffic officers stood on old gendarme stands controlling intersections with whistles and sticks.

I was planning to stay in Hanoi for some time, so decided to get a bicycle. Buying and riding a bicycle in Hanoi was a unique experience. A friend took me to a State-run store where I paid 150 000 dong ($33) for a Vietnamese bicycle with Chinese parts. 'Ones with Vietnamese parts fall apart,' she said. The first thing you do with a 150 000-dong bike in Hanoi is take it to a bicycle repairman. His job is to see that it is street-worthy. Mine wasn't, so it was wheeled back to the store and swapped for another. He then screwed and fiddled, twisting wrenches and spinning wheels with the ease and speed of an expert, and after 20 minutes he had it running smoothly. Nevertheless, I had to take it back to him three times in the next three days.

I found negotiating intersections on the bike easier than it appeared as a pedestrian. There were no rules, no lights, few bells, and remarkably, no yelling. Everyone plotted a course well in advance, then silently, politely, slowed down or accelerated to weave through the maze.

One Sunday morning, I cycled with a friend to Hang Hanh, a famous noodle street and the place for Hanoi's trendies to have Sunday breakfast. There was more gold jewellery and flashy clothes being worn here than anywhere else in the city. The fashionably-clad consumed large quantities of bottled Chinese beer as well as noodle soup with chunks of compressed chicken, pork and blood products.

A few days later the nation was to celebrate the 100th anniversary of Ho Chi Minh's birth—19 May 1890. The night before the big anniversary, Communist Party leader Nguyen Van Linh told a special commemorative gathering at the National Assembly that their former leader was 'a model communist', and said Vietnam was committed to a continuation of Maxist–Leninist communism.

While Linh was addressing the austere gathering, Cardinal Trinh Van Can, Vietnam's highest-ranking Catholic, retired to his room adjacent to St Mary's Cathedral saying he felt tired. A few hours later he died of a heart attack. Ho Chi Minh and Cardinal Can had each fought for what they believed in, one leading a communist movement, the other heading a powerful religious body which opposed communism. Can was ordained in 1949 while Ho was leading his Viet Minh guerillas against the French 'imperialists' who were supported by the Catholics. Can became a bishop in 1963 when Ho's war against the American 'imperialists' began in earnest, a war that ended with the closing of many Catholic churches and the imprisonment of priests.

I had attempted to meet Can, but it was too late. The morning after he died I went to the Archbishop's House next to St Mary's Cathedral and found four young seminarians guarding his body which was draped in red. A large portrait of the 69-year-old Catholic leader hung from the wall above.

Can had led an estimated 7–8 million Catholics, and as news of his death spread, mourners came from all over the country, arriving by train or in overcrowded, dilapidated buses bearing banners professing their faith. Thousands of men, women and children, all wearing long white head bands, gathered for three days in the vast square in front of the cathedral. Vendors sold ice creams and religious paraphernalia including black beads and

fans. Boys amused themselves fighting on the sidewalks or squirting young girls with water pistols.

When the body was finally taken to its resting place, in the cathedral floor, thousands of people lined the streets, or perched on balconies, fences, trees and rooftops. A group of distraught women wailed uncontrollably as they shuffled behind the coffin decorated simply with white plastic flowers. The sheer size of the crowd, the consistency of dress and stunning bright robes of the 22 bishops was a spectacular sight. It was the largest Catholic gathering in post-war Vietnam and a reminder to the Communist Government that Catholicism was still strong.

The two big Cs—communism and Catholicism—lived in an uneasy balance. The Government had given the Church more concessions in the previous three years, but Catholics still did not enjoy total freedom. 'Now we can go where we want to, repair churches and do our pastoral work more easily,' said one priest, but like all others interviewed, he would not comment on continuing restrictions, nor give his name.

During 1990 there was considerably more liberalisation in the media and the performing arts. Through a regular newspaper column, signed simply 'NVL', Nguyen Van Linh had been urging 'openness' in all areas and not just in the economy. Slowly, film producers, novelists, playwrights and editors began to embrace *doi moi*. Newspapers began running comment columns, editorials, letters to the editor, and regularly exposed individual cases of corruption, nepotism, incompetence and unfair practices.

General Secretary Linh had personally told a conference of artists, directors and editors, to 'write with the pen straight'—to reflect reality and tell the truth. Novels, poems, plays and films began presenting the less-than-attractive side of life, and delved into previously taboo subjects. The story of a man taking money illegally, his wife having an affair, and the eventual breakup of his family, may not sound extraordinary in other countries, but in Vietnam in 1990 it was novel. 'We show reality—life as it is—which was not done before,' said Pham Thuy Chi whose Youth Theatre produced *Fifteen Days Against Trial*. Their production of *My Life* dealt with adultery, prostitution, murder and corruption—subjects which three years earlier would have been unthinkable to present in public.

Films began to include political comments, and to criticise social 'negatives'. One controversial example was *Girl on the River* by self-taught writer–director Dang Nhat Minh. A romantic film about a boat girl (prostitute) who saved the life of a revolutionary soldier who after the liberation turned his back on her prompting her to marry a South Vietnamese soldier. It was the first film to depict a South Vietnamese soldier as the hero, and a revolutionary as the antihero. It also portrayed what many people believed: that senior government officials—all former revolutionaries—were ignoring the common people who had helped them achieve victory. But after a highly acclaimed first screening, the film was banned. Communist Party leader Linh and his colleagues realised that 'openness' had gone beyond the bounds of official comfort. Other films and several books were also officially criticised or banned.

By late 1989 the move towards liberalisation was being turned back. As director Minh said, 'The leaders were encouraging criticism, but when they started getting criticism themselves they began closing the door again'.

This closing down—some say clampdown—soon became evident in all areas. As the wall came crumbling down in Berlin, the communist flag went up in Vietnam. The more liberal the Soviet Union and the Eastern bloc became, the higher the flag was hoisted in Vietnam. 'Socialism is the way ahead', resounded through the halls of Hanoi's bureaucracy. While the rest of the world championed democracy in the socialist bloc, Vietnam was battening down the hatches and distancing itself from these events and at the same time building bridges with the largest communist power, China. Vietnam's communist leaders were prepared to take the economic chapters out of Mikhail Gorbachev's book on *glasnost*, but they closed the book when it came to the section on political reform.

The communist hardliners made it clear that they had no intention of allowing full democracy nor a multi-party system. 'Other countries have a multi-party system and it's good for their country—and we don't criticise their right to do that—but we have our own circumstances which are quite different,' assistant Foreign Minister Le Mai told me. 'The Vietnamese people are very anxious to maintain political stability so they can continue to have better economic conditions. If they look around the world, they see that where there is a multi-party system, political stability is lost.'

In 1990, before he was sacked, Foreign Minister Nguyen Co Thach was voicing more liberal views than his colleagues, and urging political as well as economic reform. 'They are two sides of the same coin and one is not possible without the other', he often said, but at the same time argued that if political reform came too quickly, the economic success train could run off the tracks.

More *doi moi* and democracy were expected after the 1990 meeting of the Central Committee. Instead, the committee re-affirmed the Communist Party's commitment to socialism and sacked outspoken liberal Tran Xuan Bach from the Politburo. So began a crackdown which led to the arrest of prominent anti-government figures, including prominent Catholic priest Father Chan Tin, and the expulsion of several Westerners, including an American businessman accused of being a CIA agent, an American English language teacher working in Hanoi who was charged with inciting anti-communist feeling by distributing English language newspapers to her students, and a French Vietnamese scientist for allegedly being in possession of secret government documents.

Many agency workers, academics and businessmen who had frequently visited or lived in Vietnam were given 'a hard time' by the bureaucracy, as were some journalists wanting to travel outside Hanoi. I spent 11 physically and emotionally draining weeks in Hanoi waiting for permission to travel down Highway One to gather more material for this book. After battling with the bureaucracy I was eventually allowed only to make a bumpy five-day trip from Hanoi to Hue and back. More than 400 foreign journalists applied to be in Ho Chi Minh for the 15th anniversary of the 'fall of Saigon' (30 April) but in the end only 10 were allowed, and I wasn't included. I and several colleagues had earlier been allowed into the country but were then asked to leave. The Government feared demonstrations on 30 April. On the eve of the anniversary the Party's newspaper, *Nhan Dan*, said attempts to disrupt public order and security would be squashed by the army if necessary, a warning that raised images of Beijing's Tienanmen massacre which had occurred less than a year earlier. It was the first time Vietnam's leaders had publicly recognised the possible existence of an opposition movement.

Two main opposition groups caused concern: The Club of Former Resistance Fighters (known as The Club), an organisation of southern veterans from the French and American wars who were disillusioned with the Party's performance; and the lesser known Poets by the River, which was based in Danang and disseminated information through poems. Its leader, jailed since 1988, managed to smuggle out poems which were sometimes read on the BBC's Vietnamese-language program.

In 1990 the Government was concerned—some said paranoid —about subversive activities from three groups: liberals within the country calling for political reform; Westerners, especially Americans suspected of inciting anti-communist feelings; and overseas Vietnamese. They were particularly worried about Vietnamese living in America, France and Australia, who returned as tourists, businessmen or to visit relatives, and brought with them ideas for change. Authorities had evidence that overseas Vietnamese worked with underground movements, particularly in Ho Chi Minh, Danang and Hue. A group of 30 overseas Vietnamese arrested on the Vietnamese–Cambodian border west of Dalat in June 1990, were said by the authorities to have been trained and armed by the CIA in Thailand. The 'paranoia' was not totally unfounded. During three months in 1990, the Post Office uncovered 3000 different anti-government documents mostly printed in France and the US, and sent to individuals and organisations mainly in the south. Some called the masses to arms, others pointed to political changes in Eastern Europe.

Vietnam was caught between maintaining its stronghold on

communism, and losing international credibility and thereby much-needed foreign currency. It had worked hard at re-establishing links outside the socialist bloc, and as a result hard currency was starting to flow in. In the two years 1988–89 more than $1 billion had been invested by foreign companies, and an incalculable amount brought or sent by overseas Vietnamese.

Initially most foreign businessmen found operating in Vietnam extremely difficult. By 1990 efficiency had improved, although still fell short of international standards. 'When I first came here, I was dealing with former military people used to taking orders and not making decisions themselves. They had no impetus, no drive, no commercial sense,' said Hong Kong-based Frank Skilbeck who acted for several European, Australian and Asian companies. 'Slowly they have improved, partly because they have been exposed to people like us.'

Several aid agencies returned after 1989. On his first visit in 1990 Tony Jackson of Oxfam UK was surprised at the industriousness of the country. 'My impression, from the press in Britain, was that Vietnam is 65 million people trying to leave the country as boat people. Instead, it's 65 million people growing rice, smashing rocks, moving sand, making bricks, burning lime, and transporting all the above. It's an incredible burst of energy. Some people want to leave, but the image in the press is that everyone is fleeing this hopeless country, and it's just not true.'

During my last morning in Hanoi I visited a departmental head and his assistant who had helped solve an administrative problem for me. Vietnamese sometimes gave presents, such as fruit, to officials—a politer version of 'tea-money'—and on the advice of a Vietnamese friend, I took mangos. The director slipped off his sandals, stood on a chair, lit an incense stick and offered the fruit to Buddha before bidding me farewell. My last task before leaving was to buy some silk for a friend in Phnom Penh. Already half an hour late, I hurtled down Hang Gai Street—no one hurries in Vietnam—with a $70 bundle of the finest silk in Vietnam strapped to the back of my bicycle. Somehow the front wheel became tangled in a tram track. I managed to stay afloat, but only just. Having lost control of the pedals, I developed the wobblies, and acquired a huge bruise on my right foot; I cycled the rest of the way feeling like a blob of jelly.

Hanoi to Hue: down the Mandarin Way

You can't use a stadium to grow rice.
Disgruntled farmer

The longest and most arduous section of Highway One was the 1700 kilometres from Hanoi to Ho Chi Minh. Before I set off in July 1988, numerous hardened foreign residents warned me that the road was bad, and one encouragingly suggested I cut my trip short and fly out of Danang if the going became too rough.

Outside Thong Nhat Hotel, waiting to take me south, was a van with a guide from the Press Centre in Ho Chi Minh. Nhan looked about 50, wore white tennis shorts—exceptional in Hanoi—and was noticeably better dressed than his northern colleagues, as were his wife and young son whom, I was surprised to find, were to travel with us. The van was Japanese, blue and stacked high with tyres and batteries. Ben the driver, a 37-year-old father of six, was much darker and stockier than any Vietnamese I'd seen. While Nhan and his family squeezed in the back with the spares, I rode with the driver.

The exceedingly wide Pho Giap Bat Street, the main route south, abruptly turned into a goat track at the city boundary. As elsewhere in Vietnam it was crowded with animals, foot-traffic, cyclists and vehicles. Most new cars and buses were Japanese, underscoring the fact that Japan had been for 10 years Vietnam's largest non-COMECOM trading partner, with two-way figures amounting to about $10 million a year. The occasional new-looking square-fronted trucks bore Soviet names. Older vehicles looked as if they were held together by string and staples. Necessity made the Vietnamese, like many people in developing countries, master repairmen who somehow manage to keep vehicles going beyond their normal life expectancy.

Instinct dictated I wear a safety belt, even though I found it hot and uncomfortable and no one else did. The dust, heat and noise of Hanoi had been draining and after 10 days hard work, smiling at people had become tiresome, as did being treated like an object of curiosity. Out in the countryside my spirits were revived. The mountains were magnificent, the sky blue and the fields green. In the late afternoon it was cool, fresh and peaceful.

Far more people were in the fields here than north of Hanoi. Young girls scooped water up into baskets to irrigate fields. Men and women, in water up to their knees, cut bricks from mud and stacked them on the bank to make mud brick islands where simple thatched huts would later be built for watchmen to shelter in while protecting fish and rice seedlings from ducks.

I watched a girl with clipped hair tease a young man leaning on his spade, and wondered about her private life. Would she marry for love or convenience, or to meet parental expectations? Everything in Vietnam seemed so public—bathing, breastfeeding, urinating. What opportunity had she for private courting? How could she find a secluded space in this country of 65 million people?

Bright yellow and red strands of recently-dyed bark hung on fences and strands of wire before being made into mats. Taken from the *day* (jute) tree, the bark is soaked in water, mashed, then pressed through a machine to produce threads. Roadside ponds grow *muop*, a green vegetable used in soup. It floats on the surface, held in place by bamboo poles resting on the water.

A row of old *xa cu* (teak) trees followed the road. Tall and majestic, they continued for miles into the countryside, broken only by towns where small flimsy stalls lined the roadside. Noodle shops were always numerous, and open-fronted stalls sold everything from crystallised MSG to vegetables and soap.

Coming through Thuong Tin village, two years later, I found the small muddy open-air market had been replaced by a covered mart with a bright orange tiled roof. Under the government's policy of encouraging private enterprise, the local authorities had built modern rows of stalls which they then leased to retailers. By 1990 economic liberation was evident, but at the next town, Phu Xuyen, political freedom was not—as I discovered when I stopped to talk with a farmer.

My translator and I sat on a bank for more than half an hour talking with 70-year-old Viet while he grazed his two cows. He hoped to earn more money this year to buy new clothes, he said pointing to his sandshoes held together by cloth 'laces'—green in one and red in the other—and patched so many times that little of the original material remained. One lens of his glasses was cracked and half the other was missing. He was happy the government had now allowed farmers to lease land from the State to work individually rather than in a collective, but he was angry that good agricultural land was being taken for non-farm use. He became very agitated, waving his hands and shaking his head. 'They have taken rice fields to build a football field and stadium, but you can't use a stadium to grow rice.'

I asked did he have any other complaints about the authorities. Instantly, a man stepped forward from the small crowd of people who inevitably gather around a Westerner, and demanded that the interview stop. From my position on the ground, I looked up and took in good shoes, tailored trousers and a white shirt, pen in pocket—a sure sign of authority. My heart sank. It was the last question for my last interview in Vietnam, and it almost cost us a night in detention.

My guide argued determinedly, waving permit papers but all to no avail. We were taken to the police station and held until the Hanoi authorities (presumably the Interior Ministry's secret police) verified that we had permission to be in this district. After sitting in silence for almost an hour, the chief, wearing a white shirt with *two* gold pens and gold-rimmed glasses, returned and said we were free to go.

On my first trip down Highway One, the Dong Van area featured houses of brick with rendered fronts but unclad sides. Roofs were tiled or thatched. White tombstones, each topped with a small neat cross, sat in the middle of a rice field like white dots on a green cloth. The American bombings of North Vietnam were not restricted to Hanoi, and some towns, such as Dong Van and the next, Oue, were razed. Although no more than 13 years old, most buildings looked considerably older, due to poor construction. Cafes were deserted and the schools appeared desolate. A small white horse grazed beside the road and his scrawny, bony body left me with a hollow feeling. The whole place had an eerie, daunting atmosphere.

When we stopped soon after, a well-organised Mrs Nhan (I didn't know her name) produced refreshing damp cloths, a knife to cut fruit and a cool drink from a thermos flask. When handed the blue plastic mug of lemon drink I was unsure whether it was to be consumed in total or shared. Five-year-old eyes studied me with veiled curiosity. I mentioned that a friend had suggested I travel with a damp cloth in a plastic bag, but I had not seen a plastic bag in Vietnam. Nhan's wife, who spoke no English, immediately brought out a plastic bag, moistened my cloth and placed it inside. Nhan and his son relieved themselves beside the van.

Urinating in public was a standard practice. Cyclists would alight from their bicycles, answer nature's call then continue on their journey without a sideways glance. In the open fields, women would stand with one leg of their baggy black trousers rolled up—no toilet paper, no squatting, no embarrassment. I later saw men do the same rather than pulling the front of their trousers down.

Roadside cafes were numerous, as were signs saying '*Com Pho*', Vietnamese for rice and noodles. Some offered *Com Pho Bun*, adding vermicelli made from arrowroot to the menu. According to a Vietnamese friend, *com* was referred to as 'wife' as it was an everyday staple, and *pho* represented the lover, to be enjoyed less frequently. Many cafes hung pork or cooked chickens from the eaves of their thatched roofs. Hanging meat in the open air was the norm, although some Vietnamese friends said they never ate from such stalls for fear of dysentery, and seeing swarms of flies at some, I tended to agree.

In 1990 I was curious to find out more about these roadside cafes. As we drove slowly along a row at Ha Nam, I spotted one run by a young woman wearing make-up, a stylish haircut and fashionable clothes, which meant not only might she be interesting to talk to, but also the cafe's hygiene might match her tidy appearance. Twenty-year-old Vu Thi Mai talked while serving us iced coffee. Her customers were locals and travellers, and she worked 5 a.m. to 10 p.m., making mainly rice and noodle dishes prepared in the back corner of the cafe where pots simmered on wood-burning fires.

The cafe consisted of an uneven concrete floor and a low bamboo ceiling from which hung a single light bulb. The front was open and the rear partly walled off. On the walls were calendar pictures of young Vietnamese girls in traditional *ao dai* dress—no bikinis here. A tiny blue fan with invisible spinning blades cooled us.

The shop had been allocated to her parents because her father was a war veteran. Now it was her business and home she said pointing to a bed folded against the wall. In the back of a food display cabinet were her clothes and personal possessions. As jewellery was not often seen in the countryside, I was intrigued by hers, which included earrings, necklace, a sapphire ring and one of plain gold. She explained that she had worked hard to buy the gold ring. The rest of the jewellery was from her grandmother who went to Thailand in 1954 as part of the revolutionary movement but hadn't returned. Her grandmother made her money running a pig farm and she occasionally sent gifts to her family in Vietnam, Mai explained.

Her brother Minh joined us. He was still waiting for a job after being discharged from the army two years before. He had served his compulsory three-year national service as a truck mechanic. Now he wanted to be a driver, but that required a six-month course costing 1.5 million dong. In the army he received 700 dong (23 cents) a month, and was given no pension on leaving. He was not bitter, he said, just dejected.

Northwest of Ha Nam was the huge Soviet-built Hoa Binh hydro-electric scheme, the largest in Southeast Asia. The project was begun in 1979, and ten years later it employed more than 35 000 people under the direction of Soviet advisers. The aim was to harness the power of the Red River's largest tributary, the Da River, so as to provide much-needed electricity, as well as a water supply for the Red River Delta in the dry season, and conversely, to control flooding in the Delta at other times.

The Red River Delta extends to the south as far as Ha Nam Ninh Province, and as we traversed this tiny province, Highway One ran along the top of a long, straight dyke designed to prevent flooding from a tributary on our left. Rice straw was stacked high beside the road to dry before being used to feed cattle and to thatch roofs of houses and sheds. Between the piles, flax grew to the road's edge, forming an almost continuous row of alternating flax and straw—like driving down a corridor with two-metre-high grass walls. As traffic was light and the road offered a flat hard dry surface, it was used by villagers as a work place to dry rice, corn, chillies, cassava and potatoes. Often small stones marked a 'fence' around the produce being dried.

Highway One cut through the southern side of the delta with the river about 30 kilometres to the east, and mountains to the west. The road was rough, not with large potholes and dips, but with continuous bone-rattling corrugations. While travelling, I could not turn and talk to Nhan in the seat behind without risking neck dislocation from the jolting, so conversation was limited, but I discovered he had two older daughters in Saigon (as he still called it) plus his five-year-old son who was with us. Nhan was 61, which was hard to believe: he looked 10 years younger, a characteristic which I later learnt was common with Vietnamese. Reticent by nature, he slowly revealed he had helped in the struggle against the French. As a 16-year-old, he had carried supplies on foot and by boat from Thailand, through Cambodia to Vietnam, and later joined the Viet Cong to fight the Americans. (Months later, I learnt he had also been involved in the 1968–73 Paris peace talks. He had also gone to Phnom Penh in January 1979 to help the Cambodian administration establish a Ministry of Foreign Affairs.)

With the dyke behind us, we followed a huge dark ridge which rose precipitiously from the rice fields and made a striking backdrop for a large stone church. To visit the church, we drove down a narrow dirt road strewn with straw, past little ponds where pigs wallowed to a tight cluster of old brick and tile houses separated from each other by stone paths—suggestive of a village in rural China. A group of men were building a pond, lining it with large grey rough cut stone. One called 'ullo' to us with the drawl of someone not used to the word. The other men stopped and chattered among themselves, gazing all the while.

The church yard was partly covered in dry straw, and speckled hens scratched about, pecking randomly. Village children gathered around while I took photos. Some stood in front of the camera and then, laughing, dashed away in a split second. A woman in a soiled cream top with a silver cross around her neck and a bunch of keys in her hand, offered to open the old wooden door. Inside the church, with its high gothic ceiling painted white a long time ago, the only sound was of birds chirping. There was a musty smell, bird droppings on the pulpit, and an air of abandonment, but the key-lady said a bishop came once a month from Hoa Binh to conduct a service which filled the wooden pews.

Catholics first came to Vietnam as missionaries in the 1600s and Ha Nam Ninh became a strong Catholic area. In the 1990s it was still predominantly Catholic, with very few Buddhists. Many families who moved to South Vietnam in the 1950s to avoid the communists were from this area. The heart of Catholicism in the north was just 40 kilometres away at Phat Diem (renamed Kim Son) where stands the largest cathedral in the country. It was also there that the Americans placed dissidents to operate against the communists after the 1954 Geneva Agreement.

On the road again, Nhan kept to himself and his family unless asked a question, yet he was a treasure of information. He explained that the magnificent range to the west was named Vinh Ha Long Tren Dat, Vietnamese for 'Ha Long Bay on Land', because the rocky outcrops resembled the precipitous islands of Ha Long Bay east of Hanoi; that Hoa Lu had been the 10th century capital (legend has it that after winning a battle the king returned to the capital and put his sword in the ground; a phallic stone now stands in the spot and is believed to be the sword's remains); that the next town, Ninh Binh, marked the southern boundary of Tonkin, the name given to northern Vietnam during the French rule; that excavation work in this and the previous province (Ha Nam Ninh and Ha Son Binh) revealed extensive evidence of Bronze Age settlements dating back 3000 and 6000 years, respectively.

Old trucks and overcrowded buses rattled down the highway with wares stacked high. As they passed, I glimpsed tired faces, tanned arms, suckling babies, wispy beards, and normally dignified women with weathered looks. (From 1989, Government bus companies began selling off their old vehicles which were then bought by private operators, renovated and put into service, offering cheap fares on short routes.) We stopped at a manually-operated rail crossing while an old steam train trundled by with open doors and empty carriages. Later at another crossing an aged diesel rumbled past, but unlike the steam train it was crowded to capacity with several people on the roof. This was a Ho Chi Minh to Hanoi train which took three days and three nights—longer than the journey did before 1945. Nhan said they stopped no more than a few minutes at main stations, and passengers had to take all they needed for the journey, including food and drink, or buy from platform hawkers. Highway One seemed preferable.

A long wooden boat with a pale canopy drifted down a river, its slender oars casually dipped into the water by a hatless woman standing astern. Boats with cream-coloured cloth sails lolled like lilies on the wide river. It was as still as a mill pond. (By 1990, cement had replaced wood as the hull for many boats.) This area was rich in limestone, and slow burning kilns produced a soft red glow, with white clouds of steam rising lazily from their peaks. As dusk approached, the mountains faded and country smells became pungent. I again wondered about private lives. Who lived in those little thatched houses that offered only rudimentary protection from the elements? What and how did they cook, where did children ssDid men help with household chores as the Women's

Association official in Hanoi told me they did? What did they talk about in their lamp-lit caverns, with no radio or newspaper to enrich their thoughts. We were but a flash in their lives, and we drove on without answers.

We followed the lowlands for several hours, then left the delta and ventured into the hills. The going became considerably rougher and the van almost came to a standstill going up one long incline. Flatter sections of road had large corrugations, setting the van in a seesaw motion, like a rocking chair in top speed. Sometimes the dips were so deep we virtually had to stop to negotiate them. Roadside activity at night was not much different from day, making night travel difficult. The few vehicles on the road obviously knew the route, overtook us at full speed and disappeared into the darkness. Our driver Ben had never done this trip before so he was cautious. We passed a row of roadside cafes, each with a single light and I thought of a line of miners with lamps trudging home for supper.

Only four hours from Hanoi and my neck and shoulders were already aching. I found sitting in the front of a flat-nose van with nothing between me and the road except the windscreen, and straining into the darkness, was physically and mentally stressful and I started to doubt whether I could endure another nine days of this.

It was pitch black and I had no idea where we were except somewhere in the hills. Crickets could be heard in the distance. Then began a tropical downpour. For the first time we closed windows and resorted to air-conditioning. Then huge frogs came out, bouncing across the road.

In the darkness, we crossed the famous Ham Rong (Dragon's Jaw) bridge where the US Air Force is said to have lost more than 60 planes while trying to destroy it and hence break the communist's vital north–south supply lines. One of the first US aircraft downed by the North Vietnamese army was shot down by artillery guns stationed atop escarpments each side of the bridge.

The next time I went down this section of Highway One, in daylight, I saw that white stones spelt out Quyet Thang, 'determined to win', in huge letters on a hillside behind the bridge. At the base of the hill was a memorial to war victims, and opposite stood the black remains of a bombed power station.

In 1990, soon after the Government abandoned its fuel monopoly, the four-kilometre stretch of road from here to Thanh Hoa city was lined with *xang dau* (oil and petrol) stands selling fuel from green jerry cans. Many people regarded competition and private enterprise in this communist-run country as good, but how could more than 20 stalls make a living all selling the same product, in the same size container side by side, at the same price? Not for the first time I realised diversification or novelty seemed not to be necessary for attracting customers.

Our first night out of Hanoi was spent at Thanh Hoa, the capital of Thanh Hoa Province. I was so tired I barely noticed the streets we passed through, the food I ate or the room I slept in: 10 tiring days in Hanoi and an interminable five hours on a bone-rattling road had taken its toll. The next morning, I assessed the hotel. It was deplorable: bare concrete floor, dripping pipes, non-functioning basin and an unspeakable toilet. My door was latched with wire, and not a drop of water came from the taps or 'shower'.

Despondent, I lay on the bed—probably on used sheets—and tried to find the reason. Accommodation of this calibre was not uncommon in Asia but not at $22 a night. I had stayed in the equivalent in neighbouring Thailand for $3. Thailand had the second highest growth rate in Asia; Vietnam was one of the ten poorest countries in the world, yet charged far more for far less! Why? The Government was desperate to get foreign currency to improve its economy, so charged one exorbitant rate for foreigners, and one for its own people. Ben had an identical room to mine, for one-fifth the price.

The breakfast room had long tables, green-washed walls, bars on the windows, concrete floors, ceiling fans, fluorescent lights —only one out of three worked—and two groups of Japanese businessmen eating beef noodle soup. One who spoke English said they had come for four days to examine a chromite mine established 25 years ago by the Chinese but no longer operated by them. The Japanese businessman promptly clammed up when told I was a journalist, saying the mine was top secret! He did confirm however that there were numerous Japanese business ventures in Vietnam, and he seemed to think it an injustice that Japan was being pressured by Western countries not to associate with Vietnam because of the Cambodian issue.

Thanh Hoa was heavily bombed during the American–Vietnam War and, according to one amiable official, 95 per cent of the houses were destroyed. While Nhan made arrangements with the People's Committee representatives, I went for a quick drive around the town accompanied by a minor official who made no attempt to stop me photographing an appalling block of three-storey flats. In fact, I think he was proud the State had built these 'international' style apartments; the plans, no doubt, having come from Eastern Europe.

Through a misunderstanding of each other's language, we found ourselves in the home of a Thanh Hoa family—I thought the official was taking me to the house, and he thought he was showing me the bridge beside it. The tiny two-room home was dark, with a low ceiling and black walls. It was difficult to tell whether the floor was hard-trodden earth or concrete. The owner, a jovial man in his 60s, proudly showed me the two sparsely furnished rooms which doubled as eating, sleeping and living rooms. The beds were wooden slats covered with rattan mats (only hotels had mattresses and sheets) and each had a soiled mosquito net coiled on a ceiling hook. The backyard included a squat toilet issuing a pungent smell, a waist-high square concrete water tank from where family members scooped water over themselves to bathe in the open air, and a cooking area under a low woven-palm shelter. As we said farewell I wasn't sure who was more bewildered by the brief tour, the old man or the official.

The People's Committee had arranged for me to meet bee keepers, but I had not expected such a formal affair. At the office of the Bee Raisers' Association we sat along one side of a long white-clothed table opposite the officials. Between us were plates of fruit, cigarettes, upturned glasses and bottles of beer. Nhan asked them to remove the beer, so they brought strong sweet coffee in tiny cups inside a larger bowl of hot water accompanied by a disproportionately long-handled spoon. Over the next hour, a young woman appeared periodically to pour Soviet mineral water, which tasted terrible, and hot drinks, and to serve snacks. These included cakes made with rice flour and eggs, square soya bean and sugar sweets wrapped in plastic, and round Chinese rice-flour cakes with a tantalising mixture of nuts, meat and sugar inside. It was all part of the ritual of entertaining an international guest.

Between sips, the officials told me how a gift of 500 kilograms of paraffin and 4500 kilograms of wire from Oxfam UK in 1983 started a small project to improve honey production in Thanh Hoa. A simple change in hive construction trebled the number of bee keepers and directly improved the living standard of about 9000 families. The province's production increased 12-fold within four years.

'Some families get up to half a million dong a year from bee raising,' said Vice-Director Nguyen Van Van, barely disguising his glee. One Association member swapped teaching for bee farming. 'He has 40 hives and lives in a brick and tile house with enough furniture, a motorcycle, a radio, and watches. And his children are very healthy,' enthused Van.

We went with him down a narrow dirt path to meet another

star bee keeper, Do Huu Nhan. He had retired as director of the local salt farm in 1984 and in four years, with just 39 hives, had become a dong millionaire. His house, on the edge of the city, was in total contrast to the one I had just visited: light, bright and clean, with a verandah overlooking a yard where chickens, vegetables, fruit trees and a fish pond flourished. It was a good example of VAC (the Vietnamese acronym for garden, pond, animal husbandry) which was being encouraged all over the country in order to provide a more balanced diet.

A short distance across town was another aid agency success story. By providing the small Minh Thanh Rubber Co-op with several machines, Quaker Service Australia had helped produce tyres for many of the one million bicycles in this province of three million people. The workshop echoed with the sound of hammers hitting metal pipes. Fan belts spun. I nervously watched as boiling water was poured from a cooker just millimetres from a pair of thonged feet. Amid the suffocating noise, dust, heat and stench of burning rubber, I watched as Le Van Trong squatted on the concrete floor and methodically pulled soft hot rubber inner tubes from a metal mould.

In 1988, 18-year-old Trong was earning 900 dong (30 cents) a day for eight hours work, six days a week. An official explained that after the war, Trong's mother was allocated a plot of land by the Government and she paid professional builders to construct a three-room house. (In 1990, an equivalent house would have cost one million dong.) 'It is a private house so she can sell it or swap it for another house but there is no selling of land,' said the official. When Trong married he would continue living with his mother as he was an only child. 'When the family is large, newly married couples who have been working for the factory for a long time, say 10 years, will be allocated land to build a house, or they can buy one if they have enough money. Alternatively, they can live in small collective apartments—each office or co-operative has resident quarters for its workers who pay for water and electricity but not rent,' he explained.

The cadres here and at Lang Son were more hospitable than those in Hanoi, and devoted most of their day to our visit. (When I later mentioned this to a conscientious Vietnamese friend he was angry. It was an indication of their idleness—they should have better things to do than sit around waiting for 'foreign visitors', he said.) Three times in Thanh Hoa we were offered an extravagant spread of food and drinks, and twice presented with gifts, including a bright red handmade woollen shawl from the rubber co-op. In Hanoi, food was offered only twice, and gifts went in the opposite direction—the Press Centre had to give a surreptitious envelope, usually containing two or three thousand dong, to each person interviewed.

We ate exceedingly well (or extravagantly, as my Vietnamese friend would have said). At the People's Committee we were offered 12 dishes, which was more than eight people could eat. While we consumed with delight vast quantities of soup, chicken, beef and vegetables, washed down with bottles of Vietnamese beer, representative Nguyen Van Lan told me how half the population had been affected by the food shortages three months earlier. 'Instead of the normal 13 kilograms of rice per month, 1.5 million people received only four to five kilograms. We had been hit by a bad typhoon along the coast, crops in the mountains were destroyed by millions of rats, and there was no rain' he said. 'The Government gave us rice for the seriously affected areas but it wasn't enough, so we encouraged people to grow and eat vegetables.' He admitted the May 1988 food shortages resulted in an increase in begging and petty thieving, especially in the city. 'Some people took two or three jobs to earn enough, and others left their villages to live with relatives elsewhere.'

After the People's Committee lunch we took to the road once more. For the next 1400 kilometres, from Thanh Hoa to Ho Chi Minh, Highway One was within 20 kilometres of the coast, which stretched 3260 kilometres southwards from China in a huge yawning curve. Alternately lapped by warm Pacific currents and battered by west-bound typhoons, this stretch possessed some of Asia's most spectacular and unspoilt beaches, although to my disappointment we rarely glimpsed them.

As road maintenance was the responsibility of provincial governments, their condition was an indication of a province's wealth—or lack of. The central provinces—Thanh Hoa, Nghe Tinh and Binh Tri Thien—were the country's poorest. South of Thanh Hoa, the highway had obviously deteriorated since the end of the American–Vietnam War and sections were under repair which further slowed our journey. Reduced to 20 kilometres an hour, we often stopped to let oncoming traffic pass. The van's rocking motion which was generated by the road's corrugated surface was far more pronounced than in a car. Vietnamese virtually never used seat-belts, but to my surprise, and relief, Ben sought the sanctuary of his, saying travel was too 'boom-boom-boom'.

It was rare to see vehicles other than buses and trucks, although an occasional government car (identified by green number-plates) or army vehicle (red plates) appeared over the horizon. Nhan said many taxis and buses in Saigon were private, but not those in the north. Seeing the first private car was as unexpected as meeting Americans in Vietnam despite the embargo. The tiny Saigon-made Mini Moke look-alike was taking a family northward —at considerable speed—and passed us in a flurry of waving arms and horn tooting.

Nhan was keen to point out bomb craters, which were plentiful near bridges. These three- to six-metre wide holes had been turned into fish ponds, or if near houses were used for growing *muop*, raising ducks or for washing (people and clothes). Everywhere people talked about which bridges were destroyed and what proportion of houses in each city were razed, but said they were ready to forget the war and re-establish relationships with America. 'America come back any time, no problem', said a restaurant owner.

In Nga Son district of Thanh Hoa province, there was an air of isolation, almost desolation, which came as a shock after the productive Red River Delta. Hills were planted with eucalypts which struggled to survive against hot winds from Laos and annual typhoons which hit this part of the coast. The soil was sandy and much of it covered in scrub. Only one crop of rice a year grew here, so families chopped and dried cassava, considered to be a poor man's food and traditionally fed to pigs, although during war times many families were forced to use it as a substitute for rice. Even in 1990, there were no signs that economic improvements had reached this part of Vietnam.

Farmers eked out a living growing sweet potato and peanuts, or as the Vietnamese called them, ground-nuts. Thanh Hoa was one of many provinces producing peanuts which since the war had become a fast growing industry, although for the peasants profits were low. I walked across one sandy field to join women harvesting. They talked and pointed to my clothes and several touched my bare arms. Amid embarrassed giggles, they showed me how to uproot the plant, then shake it to dislodge the nuts from the roots. Later the nuts would be washed, boiled and sold in their shells. At first I thought boiled nuts revolting, but soon acquired a taste for them, especially as there was little else available in the way of snacks.

Amid the endless stretch of peanut plots, scrub and thatched cottages, we came upon a line—perhaps two kilometres long—of bright mats displayed beside the road, some draped over fences, others pegged to bamboo frames, all for sale at considerably cheaper prices than in the cities. Made from *coi* plants, a type of reed grown in salt water, these mats were laid on a bed instead of a mattress. Most were woven with a red pattern, and according to

Nhan, newly-wed couples received ones printed with the old Chinese characters for 'Double Happiness'.

In 1988 the central provinces were severely affected by drought. Many fields were not under water, and miles of rice plants were turning the insipid yellow of failure. Broken pumps and a shortage of fuel to pump water added to the problem.

Returning in 1990 it was a delight to see green fields. White-washed houses with red tiled roofs produced a stunning effect against the green fields and I wondered how long before photo-graphers would be here capturing these scenes for postcards. It was also encouraging to see sections of the road widened and resealed.

We stopped for drinks at a Quynh Luu stall where an old woman with blackened teeth sold home-made rice wine in re-cycled Chinese beer bottles. Dang Thi Ninh told me she was 56 and had been making rice wine since childhood. Each day she produced 5 litres which she sold for 1200 dong (25 cents) a bottle or 200 dong (4 cents) a cup. 'You boil the rice, add a "pill" from a special tree which turns it alcoholic, leave it for two days then boil it again and the steam collected is just wine,' she said.

She took us into her adjoining two-room home where an altar was decorated with 14 beer cans and pictures of Mary and Christ. (Nhan later explained that beer cans were *à la mode* in Vietnam, a sign of prosperity. He said the Youth Club in Saigon had a curtain made out of hundreds of beer cans!) Linh showed me her most treasured possession, a piece of blue stone with a picture of Mary which she wore on a red string 'necklace'. At Linh's cafe I noticed a young girl, carried on her mother's hip, had a boil on her head covered with a brown paste; the old woman said it was made of apple leaves and salt and would remain in place for three or four days, 'until she is better'.

In 1988 road works seemed to be continuous from Thanh Hoa, and bouncing around for more than four hours a day became a little tedious. Even bridges had holes. Repair gangs consisted mostly of women, squatting on their haunches and using hammers to break rocks which they then flung onto the road from woven baskets. Others used their hands to push individual rocks into place to create a flat surface. Watching the women, I realised mechanisation would be disastrous for this country; everything was so labour intensive. (In 1990 I stopped to talk with Nguyen Thi Nghia, a road worker, who was loading sharp edge stones into a basket with bare dusty hands. She had worked with the same gang for 12 years. 'I would like an administrative job, working in an office, but this is our duty, it's our job.' She was 30, had two young children and worked 6 a.m. to 6 p.m. for 65 000 dong ($14.50) a month with food and accommodation provided. (A senior university lecturer's salary amounted to 50 000 dong ($11) without food and housing.) Nghia would spend the next four months living in temporary workers' huts with her children and 50 other road builders, while her husband drove Government trucks. They had a house in Vinh but she would only go back there to see him once a month, she said.)

Signposts were rare in Vietnam, but at Dien Chau a rusty hand-painted sign pointed to Do Luong, a highland town halfway between here and the border with Laos. This was one of two roads from central Vietnam leading to the neighbouring capital Vientiane. Like Vietnam, Laos had been ruled by the French, bombed by the Americans, and since 1975 run by a communist government. With a population of almost four million confined mostly to Vientiane and Luang Prabang, the mountains of the north and south were sparse, inhabited mainly by hilltribes. A road from Vinh, further south, provided a direct route through Laos to Thailand, via a winding 240 kilometre long route.

South of Dien Chau, a small temple beside the road provided an interesting and much needed break. It was one of many in the north of the county dedicated to the Viet king, An Duong. The first

An Duong temple is said to have been built in the 3rd century BC at the then capital, Co Loa, 16 kilometres north of Hanoi. In those days there were frequent battles between warlords in what is now Vietnam and China, and Nhan related this particular story while we sat on steps in front of the deserted temple, overlooking the surrounding countryside.

'This kingdom defeated the Chinese kingdom, thanks to a magic bow and arrow given to King An Duong by a turtle god. The Chinese king wanted the secret of the bow and arrow, so he sent his son Prince Trong Thuy to marry An Duong's daughter, My Chau. He married her and succeeded in getting the secret bow and arrow, and returned with it to China. Before leaving, he told his wife if there was war she should drop duck feathers to show him the path she had taken.

'There was war between the two kingdoms. An Duong was defeated, and fled with his daughter. She dropped duck feathers, and her husband followed her and found her father too. The king killed his daughter, then committed suicide. She became a stone and followed the river flow to her native land where villagers placed it in a temple and covered it with a beautiful dress. When Trong Thuy realised he had caused the death of his wife, whom he loved very much, he suicided too.'

The small temple complex had many Chinese characteristics including dragons and Chinese characters on pillars, rafters and along the roof. Inside the dark open-fronted main temple, a dragon-festooned roof was supported by old wooden pillars adorned with Chinese paintings in red, white, blue, yellow, and green. Two ornately-carved wooden chariots sat on either side of the altar, each with a dragon's head at the front. Between them was a well— empty, but dangerously deep. A pair of stone lions at the top of the steps guarded the entrance, and part of a stone wall featured a long inscription in *nom*, the old Vietnamese language similar to Chinese.

Nhan's wife moved around the temple placing lit incense sticks while her husband explained that each Vietnamese village had a pagoda (*chua*) and temple (*dinh*). Pagodas were to worship Buddha on the 1st and 15th of each month, and temples were to worship a god or hero such as a general or a king, usually depicted in pictures or small statues in temples. 'People pray, and they celebrate anniversaries. Lighting incense in temples is one way of worshipping and is a mark of respect, like in churches when you use candles,' he said.

Many hills south of here were devoid of trees, and the starkness was exaggerated by eroded gullies and lifeless soil. Further on, areas had been planted, but the pines were twisted and mal-nourished, and the few eucalypts looked equally pathetic. The area had classic signs of drought—a brown cracked wasteland to the horizon without a blade of grass.

In many ways, Nghe Tinh province, with its capital at Vinh, was the nativity of Vietnam's 'imperial resistance'. This was the birthplace of Ho Chi Minh, and of the 1930 anti-French peasant uprisings which briefly overthrew the French administration and ultimately led to the French withdrawal from Indochina.

Closer to Vinh, houses nestled among trees along the road. Lithe young casuarinas, planted in rows between fields, bowed to the wind. Fields grew more vegetables than rice, and the area became progressively wealthier as we neared the capital.

(In May 1990, I found an amusing, but sad, example of over-enthusiastic construction. Seven kilometres north of the town began a multi-lane super-highway—which almost rivalled Hanoi's Duong Giai Phuong—built to commemorate the 100th anniversary of the birth of Ho Chi Minh who was born at a small village near Vinh. It virtually began in the rice fields but ended abruptly four kilometres later, due to lack of funds.)

In less than 30 years (1947–75), Vinh had been twice reduced to rubble. What French artillery bombardment had left standing, the resistance destroyed rather than allow the city to be retaken. After the peace of 1954, people returned and rebuilt, only to have the city almost completely razed by American bombings between 1964 and 1972, after which it was rebuilt in part with rows of al-most identical, drab-looking four- or five-storey apartment blocks, constructed in concrete with depressing uniformity. Funds and de-signs for the apartments came from what was then the DDR, but the East Germans neglected to impart any of the fine features of their own beautiful Unterlinden Strasse. The front of one apartment block was bedecked with a giant painting of Ho Chi Minh—in a posed cheerfulness made stark by oils. The main street was wide but potholed, and had large arched modern-looking street lamps on both sides, suggesting it considered itself an important town.

Sitting outside the hotel, while Nhan booked us in for one night, I watched an interminable flow of bicycles streaming in both directions through the early night light. Although traffic was con-stant, in 20 minutes only one truck and one motorbike passed. The only sound was of rubber turning on wet bitumen and the occasional creaky bike. My smile generated a response from each cyclist or pillion: broad grins, girlish giggles, nervous nudges and the occasional wave from young men, as they disappeared into darkness.

My room had no shower, so I was taken to one that did. But once the tap was turned on, no amount of straining could persuade it to shut off, and the bathroom, then bedroom, soon flooded. I was taken to a third room, which had no light bulb, so one was taken from the bathroom which was so small that I could only use it with the door shut which meant I was in total darkness. When I then asked for a light bulb for the bathroom, the room attendant shuffled down the corridor in her green plastic sandals and distributed light bulbs to three rooms—Nhan's family's, Ben's and mine. Later I asked for some cold water to drink. She brought—in her fingers—a lump of ice too large to fit in the glass, so she put the ice in a cup and poured hot water from a thermos onto it until it shrunk sufficiently to fit in the glass.

Later I was offered a 'deluxe room'—my fourth in an hour—but neither of the two air conditioners worked properly. Lying on the bed staring at the flaking ceiling, while the bathroom tap dripped incessantly, I realised the core of the problem was lack of incentive. The manager was poorly paid whether there were two or 20 guests in his hotel, whether all or none complained. Light bulbs were there, but no-one had bothered to put them in. As Nhan explained, 'They earn such a little amount, and they don't get paid any extra'. There was also a degree of acceptance—Vietnamese were used to surviving with little, and considered Westerners *ky cuc* (crazy) for complaining when something didn't work. The manager listened politely to my suggestions but said he could do nothing to improve conditions as decisions came from central level. (By 1990 this system had changed considerably. Government hotels were ordered to be profitable and accountable, and many responded by adopting private enterprise practices. Even the Army Guesthouse in Hanoi began taking non-military guests, although still owned by the State.)

At seven the next morning, we set out for Hoang Tru, the small village 11 kilometres west of Vinh where Ho Chi Minh was born on 19 May 1890. Thousands of Vietnamese visited the tiny three-room house of thatched bamboo walls and woven palm leaf ceiling, which was built by villagers in 1959 to recreate the home where Ho spent his first five years. Ho came from humble beginnings, and maintained self-deprivation all his life. Visitors had to stoop to pass through the low doorways. The rooms were poorly-lit and furnished with just a bed of wooden poles with a reed mat on a wooden frame, a hammock of plaited reeds and rope, and an old weaving loom.

Ho Chi Minh used several names during his 79 years. In Paris he called himself Nguyen O Phap (Nguyen Who Hates the French); the alias he liked best was Nguyen Ai Quoc (Nguyen the Patriot); to persuade police in China he was a Chinese born in Vietnam, he started using Ho Chi Minh, which means He Who Enlightens; but the Vietnamese most commonly called him Uncle Ho. He was born Nguyen Sinh Cung. His parents grew up in the same house. His father, Nguyen Sinh Huy, was the son of a concubine. Born into rural poverty and orphaned at the age of four, Huy was adopted by the family of Hoang Thi Loan, whom he later married.

Ho, his older brother and older sister were born in this modest cottage built by his father in Hoang Tru. To shrug off his peasant background, Ho's father studied classical European literature and culture, and rose to become a mandarin and minor official at the Royal Court in Hue. When Ho was five the family moved 350 kilometres south to the Imperial capital. Ho's mother died there when he was 11 and his father, disillusioned by the power of the French rulers, resigned from the Imperial Court in 1901 and returned to Hoang Tru where he continued teaching.

Ho spent his early teens living in the nearby village of Kim Lien with his grandfather who ran a small school. He is said to have begun his revolutionary career at the age of 12 by acting as a courier, running messages between villages. When Ho was 16, father and son went back to Hue where his father continued teaching. Ho Chi Minh began developing his nationalistic sentiments when a student in Hue. Admitted to Quoc Hoc (an elite high school) in 1908, he was later expelled for his involvement in a protest. In 1911, at the age of 21, Ho left Vietnam as a galley hand aboard a French liner and after several years on ships reached Paris where he stayed for six years, mixing in French literary and socialist circles, and learning Marxist–Leninist political philosophy.

During his 30 years in self-imposed exile, Ho Chi Minh wandered the world, working as a gardener in Le Havre, a labourer in Brooklyn, a kitchen-hand in London, a photographic retoucher in Paris, an interpreter in China and a journalist in Moscow. He trekked across mountains on foot, travelled on third-class trains and sought passage on freighters; was extradited from Singapore; escaped from a Hong Kong jail; and was kept in numerous squalid Chinese jails by Chinese nationalist leader Chiang Kai-shek, who, ironically, accused him of being a French spy. 'It was at Kweilin that my teeth began to fall out,' he told a Western friend years later, 'I was skin on bones, and covered with rotten sores. I guess I was pretty sick.'

Ho was an enthusiastic student of French literature, and by his mid-30s he was fluent in French, English, Russian, Mandarin and

Cantonese; he later learned Thai. While learning revolutionary tactics and establishing contacts, he used numerous disguises. In Canton in 1924 he became an interpreter, cigarette seller and journalist, using four different names at one time. The following year, he shaved his head, donned a saffron robe and became a Buddhist monk while mingling among Vietnamese in Thailand. In Hong Kong in June 1929 he used a football match as a cover for a meeting of communist faction leaders who decided to establish the Indochinese Communist Party, which was formalised the following year.

When he finally returned to Vietnam in 1941, it was to the Pac Bo caves in the mountains of northern Vietnam, where he established the Viet Minh and began the armed struggle for independence to which he had aspired for 30 years. While here he wrote his famous poem, later called 'Tho Bac Ho' (Poem of Uncle Ho) which declared, 'I shall build the country with my two hands'. Ho Chi Minh, who loved reading and writing poetry, never married, never kept a diary and rarely contacted his family, and only returned to his birthplace once—on 19 December 1961, eight years before he died.

Driving five kilometres to Kim Lien, one of the poorest villages in the area, I found the house where Ho had lived with his grandfather. It had been rebuilt as a rather dismal tourist attraction, and the bamboo and wood panelled walls were dotted with poor-quality black and white reproduction photos of revolutionaries and old pictures of Hue and other cities, many of them liberated during the French time. Next to the house was a three-room museum displaying shirts Ho wore; poems he wrote; stark black-and-white photographs of revolutionaries imprisoned by the French, with square wooden frames around their necks and wooden shackles on their feet; and the staff given to Ho's father by the king, beside which was his father's famous declaration: 'To be a mandarin is to be a slave among the slaves. So I refuse to be a mandarin.'

By coincidence, I was back in Vinh a few days after 19 May 1990—the 100th anniversary of Ho's birth. In commemoration, two hotels opened that day, and I stayed in the one called Huu Nghi (Friendship) Hotel. The pink and grey concrete and gravel hotel was the tallest building in Vinh. Although tiles were crooked and taps leaked, it had the most comfortable bed I encountered in Vietnam. The bathroom fittings and accessories bore Thai insignias—a sign of the economic times. Thai Prime Minister Chatichai's policy of turning the Indochina battlefield into a market place was working, and Thai products were reaching Vietnam, via Cambodia and Laos.

Before becoming the hotel manager, Hoang Duc Ai had worked for an import–export company which traded Vietnamese-made clothes and household implements for Thai consumer goods, via Vinh's sister city in Laos. The exuberant young Ai, (43 was considered young in Vietnam) who undertook a three-year course in business management, apologised that the hotel wasn't finished, said he knew Westerners expected high standards, and explained he had been trying to repair an old generator since 5 a.m. Ai and his Western-style hotel seemed to epitomise a new era in Vietnam —the emergence (re-emergence in the south) of entrepreneurship, of capitalist practices working in a communist system.

The 18 girls who worked at the hotel were chosen from 300 contenders in a beauty contest, then trained in hotel work. Nguyen Minh Tien, 18, was still at school when she entered the contest, but after working for only a week at the hotel she said she wanted to leave and attend an economics college. However, she was tied to the system which had trained her at the cost of two million dong, the equivalent of 40 months of her salary.

Outside the second hotel which opened the same day, hordes of people were prevented from entering by men with red arm bands—only guests, foreigners and officials were allowed in. Paradoxically, I was told the foyer's life-size statue of a woman holding a lotus represented an ordinary woman welcoming visitors. A foyer shop sold JVC remote control colour televisions, National video players, Sharp video cassette players and a sophisticated amplifying system—none of which had been available in 1988.

On this trip, my host in Vinh was People's Committee representative Dinh Van Cong, who joined us for dinner at the hotel's restaurant. While three or four waitresses fussed around our table, I realised 'ordinary' people who became cadres were uncomfortable with being waited on. I remembered a British friend who first came to Hanoi eight years earlier had told me that cyclos were rare then because in the communist north everyone was supposed to be equal—one did not slave for another to ride.

Cong talked of economic progress in the two years since my first visit. 'The face of the city is changing a lot. We have new roads, buildings, homes, hospitals, schools, and now two hotels. We will make this wider,' he said, indicating the already wide main street outside the restaurant. 'The Poland–Vietnam Friendship Hospital was rebuilt in the past two years. The new bridge will be open in four months. And when the new power line is finished we will have two and a half times more electricity.'

He went on to explain how his own standard of living had

improved. 'I can repair my house and I have a TV and bicycle. Now my daughter goes to school and she can eat what she needs. In the past if she wanted a banana I couldn't buy it because of my salary.' This had risen from 60 000 to 100 000 dong ($21) a month. I noticed he barely ate, and he swapped a Heineken for a Coke. Learning English was now the fashion, he said, adding that his office was paying for him to study three nights a week. Unlike students who liked to practise their English on foreigners, cadres were more self-conscious, and, like Cong, preferred to talk through an interpreter. Although it doubled the length of interviews, some senior officials such as Foreign Minister Nguyen Co Thach, despite being able to speak English well, still used an interpreter as it gave time to compose answers. (Thach's English was such that he often corrected his translator.)

Over a long dinner Cong talked of personal freedoms, at one point saying, 'Vietnamese people are always free'. I felt this was an opportunity to raise a few controversial topics. After a rather heated discussion about freedom, he agreed that he was only free to travel abroad to visit relatives or study if the Government approved. I then asked him, 'What if I gave you a ticket to go to London as a tourist next week?' There were no rules on that, he replied. He would have to consult his superiors.

Recent freedoms had been extended to allow Vietnamese coming back from overseas to stay with relatives—previously they were confined to hotels and were only allowed day-time visits. I asked Cong if I would be free to stay with a Vietnamese family. 'We have not decided on non-relatives, but show us the evidence (letter of invitation) and we will consider it,' he said.

I decided to tackle one more controversial subject before we parted. Newspapers had been exposing corrupt government employees and company directors, so I asked whether the papers would publish a report saying the local People's Committee President was corrupt. Cong said it would be published in the provincial paper, but he wasn't sure about *Nhan Dan*, the Communist Party's national daily. 'The important thing is that the writer has to accept responsibility if it is later found not to be true.' I pushed further: 'What if the report said Vietnam's General-Secretary, Nguyen Van Linh, was involved with the local corrupt People's Committee President?' The response was instant anger: 'Our General-Secretary will never be involved in corruption'.

This was May 1990, and leaving Vinh the next morning, I crossed Vinh's extraordinary floating bridge for the last time, as four months later it was replaced by a high-span steel double-lane construction. The old bridge was a series of barges strung together across the wide river, a treacherous arrangement for a van, as a substantial dip between each section produced a roller-coaster effect which resulted in the front undercarriage scraping piercingly on the metal at each dip. It was more than 800 metres long and single-lane, so north-bound traffic was held at one end while south-bound vehicles crossed.

I remembered how returning from a trip to Hue late one night, we came over the bridge behind an old bus which broke down a third of the way across. Somehow, we managed to manoeuvre past. Assuming we were the last vehicle off, a long line of trucks moved onto the bridge, not knowing they would come face-to-face with a bus blocking their path. I had visions of heavily laden trucks reversing over 600 metres of undulating bridge. Perhaps the first truck pushed the bus back to the other side.

On that first trip with Nhan, a stone roadside post just south of Vinh declared we were 423 kilometres from Danang, Vietnam's third largest city, but the road condition told us we were two days away. Just 60 kilometres west were the mountains of Laos, and beyond that Thailand. Nhan pointed to a road which headed westward to Dong Loc—the most important link road between Highway One and the Ho Chi Minh Trail, or trails, for there were many. This network of tracks and road, which was established during the French resistance and expanded during the American–Vietnam War, wound through sparsely inhabited mountains, sometimes in Vietnam, sometimes in Laos, and ended in Tay Ninh province, northwest of Saigon. The trail was North Vietnam's main route for moving troops and supplies to the south during the American–Vietnam War, but thereafter much fell into disrepair and parts became impassable. The trail was heavily bombed by the Americans, and the Dong Loc link road became famous after 10 volunteer women of the anti-aircraft unit were killed at a ford. Their job had been to stand in the river to guide convoys of trucks passing through, and they had remained steadfast during the bombing attacks.

At Ha Tinh about 50 kilometres south of Vinh, we found soldiers sitting indolently beside a truck waiting for a spare tyre to arrive. I couldn't help thinking how different things were during the war—they would have fixed the tyre, with sticky rice if necessary. Now, they waited for someone else to produce the magic gum. They were young and indifferent, an odd mixture of slovenliness and virility, with hardened expressions and darting eyes. Perhaps they were returning from Cambodia where battle had matured them in a resolute and brawny way. War? So they should be able to fix the tyre, you say. Ah, but this was a regular army fighting guerillas, fighting briefly in someone else's war—not their 30-year battle for independence when they were the guerillas.

Marking the end of town, an arch across the road declared *Dang Cong San Vietnam Muon Nam* (Communist Party of Vietnam Forever). The Communist Party had built roads, a new bridge and a large dam for irrigation. Yet 50 per cent of Vietnamese children still suffered malnutrition (according to the WHO definition), the average diet had 15 per cent less energy (calories) than WHO standards for Asia, and the amount of vitamin A was one-eighth WHO standards. Goitre, caused by a lack of iron in the diet, affected as much as 70 per cent of the population in some areas.

Towns spreading for one kilometre were dotted along the road. Otherwise, houses clustered together in small villages, massed with trees and linked by hard trodden dirt paths. This left fields vast and devoid of buildings, but meant farmers walked considerable distances to their rice plots. Early morning and late afternoon they could be seen walking in single file along raised paths between the fields, their conical hats forming a neat line that rippled and shimmered. (In later years this sight became less common as communes broke up and families began tending their own fields.)

A church spire often protruded above village trees and nearby fields were occasionally dotted with white graves. Bamboo grew in abundance in villages and beside the road and Nhan pointed out its versatility: long poles, which become flexible in summer and hard in winter, were used for house building; smaller ones were for fencing and fishing rods or were cut into strips to weave baskets. Leaves became humus for growing green beans and later bamboo sprouts to be eaten.

I stopped to photograph three boys on a long-horned buffalo, but before I was out of the van, their feet had hit the ground and they were scampering towards us, along with a dozen other children who materialised spontaneously. It was school holidays and skinny-legged youngsters abounded. I was captivated by their innocent curiosity and unhesitating boldness. They were lively and enthusiastic, waving, laughing, poking their fingers at my camera and following me everywhere, although some younger ones stood back timidly when they saw me. Their adorable smiles and infectious laughter belied their hardships. Most were malnourished and poorly educated, lived in sub-standard housing and rarely had access to safe drinking water. They learnt to carry heavy loads at a young age and often carried siblings not much younger than themselves. They were dressed in dirty, worn, torn clothes, the colour of the muddy water in the fields, or wore none at all. They spent a seemingly exorbitant amount of time in or beside ponds, canals and rivers, playing or fishing with rods, baskets and nets.

Boys, sometimes no more than six or eight years old, smoked cigarettes. Youngsters minding buffaloes sat on a bank or on a beast with a stick and comic in one hand and a lead rope in the other. They climbed onto the buffalo by putting their foot on the base of a horn, then springing over its neck while the animal continued eating. Some managed to fling themselves up as if mounting a horse bareback. As an afternoon shower approached, they pulled plastic sheets over themselves and virtually disappeared beneath.

Seeing an open-air cow market north of Ky Anh, we drove down a short track to investigate, followed by dozens of children who skipped mischievously in front of the van or slapped its sides. There were no buildings, no yards, no noisy auctioneers, just an open field where docile brown cows lay or stood idly while buyers quietly perused and negotiated. A more peaceful stock market I had not encountered—anywhere. However, it soon turned into a private prison. While talking to farmers, a crowd formed around us, and as it grew it became a swaying human tide, closing in, almost suffocating us, until it became unbearable. For the first time in Vietnam I felt claustrophobic panic. Clutching my heavy camera bag—perhaps using it as a shield—I burst out of the crowd and made for the van. They were innocently curious and meant no harm, but I envisaged one person tripping and the whole crowd crumbling.

We crossed an arched bridge over a picture postcard estuary with nets raised high in the air, passed kilns with bright red bricks shining in the late afternoon sun, and ran along a straight stretch with sand dunes to east and a dyke on the west, before heading into the hills again. People were few. The only evidence of life was a parked bicycle, piles of wood, smoke, and bright coloured washing strung from the corner of a tiny cottage to a nearby pole.

Before passing through this area in May 1990, I had been told children were so hungry they resorted for the first time to begging from passing traffic, particularly on the Ngang Pass south of Ky Anh. As we approached the summit, seven boys ran barefoot beside our van holding out tattered straw hats, or knelt on the road with the palms of their hands together, the Buddhist gesture of reverence. We stopped and talked with three who said they were doing it for fun as it was school holidays. There was no suggestion of starvation, and they admitted their parents didn't know they were begging.

On that trip, giant electricity towers were being erected to carry power from the new Hoa Binh hydro-electric station to Hue —metallic titans that towered over tiny brick cottages below, so incongruous in this primitive area. Tower after tower, they marched across virgin hills and valleys, cutting an ugly path and highlighting the gap between progress and poverty.

At the beginning of Binh Tri Thien province, Highway One ran along the coast for the first time—and what a spectacular sight it was after hundreds of kilometres of fields and trees: sparkling water and white sand dunes. My spirits were instantly raised, and my body ached for a swim, just like a mouth salivating when sumptuous food is served—then denied. Our flirt with this watery temptation seemed to last only a minute and before I could absorb it, we had moved back to the sandy inland.

Here, field workers, including children, wore woven palm leaf shawls on their backs. Tied at the neck, they hung down to just below their buttocks, to keep off rain and to provide shade. In the north in winter they are also worn for warmth. It was common to see threadbare shirts hanging in slivers on the backs of men walking or cycling. Many children had distended bellies, a sign of severe malnutrition, but Nhan said it was due to worms. His son had worms about every six months, he said—long white parasites contracted from raw vegetables, contaminated water or unwashed hands.

I amused myself studying trucks which all seemed to be old and in need of repairs: one with half the windscreen missing, another with doors that didn't shut, another limping along on flapping tyres. They were seen broken down beside the road, often jacked up with a wheel removed, sometimes with men sleeping fully-dressed lying on mats or hanging in hammocks under the vehicle. When the trucks were working they were a form of public transport. The cabins were always crowded, sometimes with up to a dozen people sitting on each other and the dashboard, the driver presumably supplementing his income on the side.

It was not possible to look at the map and say, 'it's 300 kilometres, therefore it will take so many hours'. To ask how far to the next city was totally irrelevant; asking how many hours was much more productive. Many road signs, although rare, depicted Vietnamese versions of international symbols, such as 'children crossing', 'no entry' and 'approaching corner'. Ben zig-zagged around rough patches, and I questioned which was worse, being shaken up and down, or sideways. Before leaving Hanoi, I was told by an American film producer to wear sunglasses if sitting in the front of the van. He had experienced a broken windscreen, which he said had smashed into small jagged pieces instead of shattering, almost blinding his friend. When Nhan's son wanted to sit in the front, Nhan said, 'No, it's too dangerous'. So what was I doing here? I resolved to wear my sunglasses while travelling, but as dusk approached I felt a little ridiculous and decidedly uncomfortable.

There were no houses in sight, no trees, no ponds, no people cycling, no people fishing, no people anywhere, just wild scrub land and a very strong smell of herbs—sweet and pleasant. In the dark, a stack of wood beside the road, miles from nowhere, added to the air of desolation and I tried to imagine who had put it there and who would remove it. We negotiated a long stretch of deep ruts, then a large pothole forced us onto the verge, and I had visions of getting stuck in the dark of night in a completely deserted area.

In total contrast, we were later treated to a wide road with a reasonably good surface, which wound up a mountain. It was the equivalent of a two- or three-lane highway and must have required considerable rock blasting—certainly the most impress-ive road construction we had seen. The off-side was lined with a barrier of concrete and rock blocks placed a metre apart, and beyond that a steep descent. Ben carefully negotiated the bends, like a blind man feeling his way.

Sleep seemed impossible, but Nhan junior managed. We con-tinued in virtual silence for almost an hour. Even the sight of someone being transported in a hammock hung on a pole between two bicycles—a primitive ambulance—failed to elcit comment from Ben or the trio behind me. Finally, we stopped behind a line of trucks at a road barrier. It was only 35 kilometres from Dong Hoi, our destination, but it was going to take another two hours to get there.

It was almost pitch black but beyond the barrier, a ferry was crossing a little bay—maybe it was a river, I couldn't be sure. I didn't know what we were meant to do here but there were vehicles and people everywhere, although no-one was doing much. There was an eerie air as if we had come uninvited into a time warp. The trucks loomed out of the darkness like tired cumbrous giants; men huddled in small groups, their cigarette ends glowing intermittently; tiny lights in fish cages bobbed up and down in the water beside the wharf, delicate and distracting. A single naked light bulb shone above the door of a hut. It was some time before I realised we had arrived at the Gianh River ferry crossing.

The blackness made it impossible to gauge the river's width, and the opposite bank was distinguishable only by the blur of cafe lamps and the headlights of north-bound trucks waiting on the other side for the ferry. Children and young women wandered among the vehicles clutching dirty kettles of tea and unwashed plastic mugs, trays of sliced water melon or baskets with hard boiled eggs insulated in woollen jumpers. One 15-year-old girl said she had been working at the crossing for five years and on average sold 50 eggs a day, earning 25 cents a day. Others sold boiled peanuts, measured in rusted condensed milk tins and dropped into the buyer's lap.

While trying to acquire a liking for soggy tasteless nuts, I playfully picked up Nhan's son and hoisted him onto my shoulder. It was our first physical contact and I was surprised, and pleased, that he responded approvingly, although it was not repeated later during the trip. I had been thinking of my young nephew, and missing body contact. Here, it was not possible for me to hug or even touch a man, as I would with friends elsewhere. I had noticed that Nhan and Ben often walked off with an arm around the shoulder of a man they had just met. This kind of interaction between men had caused many American servicemen to refer to the Vietnamese men as 'a bunch of faggots' without accepting that it was normal behaviour here.

The ferry arrived and unloaded its cargo of old trucks which hauled themselves noisily up the steep ramp and back onto land. Three equally decrepit south-bound trucks gingerly negotiated the ramp and ventured onto the ferry, which drew away with half a load, leaving us watching its parting stern in disbelief. We later learnt we 'missed' the ferry because we had not greased the palm which turned the wheel, so we were made to wait for the next ferry as a 'punishment'.

Coming off the ferry we were greeted by three merry youths, led by one playing a guitar—at 10.30 p.m. on a black night. We proceeded to Dong Hoi, tired and silent, only Ben fully alert. It took seven and a half hours for the 180-kilometre trip from Vinh, and I had never counted distance posts so meticulously as during that last 35 kilometres.

Sunrise from the balcony of the hotel room was refreshing, and renewed my flagging enthusiasm after the previous day. The beach could be heard, as small waves flopped onto the sand in quick succession, and smelt—that invigorating mixture of salt and

seaweed which tantalises the nostrils. The coolness of pre-dawn soon evaporated and by the time I reached the riverside market at 6.30 a.m. a hat was a necessity.

Near where the Nhat Le River met the ocean, sellers and buyers met early each morning to bargain and banter. Women rowed their produce down the river in long blunt-nosed wooden boats, to the sandy bank where it was unloaded and carried in cane baskets to the market. A nearby 'store' ostentatiously exhibited on its rough-cut wooden shelves its entire stock: cans of condensed milk imported from Thailand, packets of biscuits, baby soap, one-kilogram bags of MSG, Saigon beer, handbags and peanuts.

I returned to the hotel's vast, almost deserted dining room where the president of the Dong Hoi People's Committee and his deputy were having breakfast with my entourage. The permanently stained table cloth was littered with the remains of fried eggs, toast and coffee. Paradoxically, the Vietnamese guests had ordered a Western breakfast, while I opted for their more traditional bowl of *chao ga* (chicken and rice porridge) and green tea. Before the American–Vietnam War, Dong Hoi was a small and very beautiful town, according to the president, Nguyen Xuan Cham. 'It was the first town in North Vietnam to be bombed and was completely razed. Nine per cent of the population were killed—my family lost five children,' he said. Dong Hoi had been rebuilt, like Vinh, in concrete, partly with funds from socialist sister countries. 'The Soviet Union built a 14 000 kilowatt electricity station and Cuba built the hospital,' he said with convincing admiration.

Sand encroachment was a major problem along much of the coast. Large areas of farmland were buried under sand drifts which each year edged their way further inland. Cham took us in a Russian-made army-style jeep to a fishing hamlet two kilo- metres inland, where sand covered the backyards and piled up around the doorsteps of small white homes. Even the cemetery was covered in sand. 'Every year when the typhoons come the rice fields are covered with sand, and the seawater enters the reser- voir,' he said. The United Nations' World Food Program (known to the Vietnamese as PAM, from its French initials) initiated a major tree-planting program aimed at holding back the sand, reducing crop damage and providing firewood, and by mid-1988 more than 600 000 casuarinas had been planted along the coast. 'PAM gave 450 kilograms of wheat flour per hectare which we swapped for rice to give to workers as payment for breeding and planting trees. Each worker gets 2.5 kilograms of rice for planting,' Cham said.

We were later driven for half an hour on a dirt road to the Bo Trach Hospital. This was one of the roads leading to the Ho Chi Minh Trail, and Nhan revealed that he had travelled it several times during the war as an army official. He was full of surprises and seemed to have been all over the country. The area was poor- looking, almost barren, and grew mainly scrub and manioc (cassava). What rice fields existed lacked the neat orderly appear- ance of those further north. But as usual the people were more welcoming than their surroundings, and the hospital director, Dr Ho Van Bang, was happy to give us a guided tour of his humble but important establishment which consisted of beds half-filled with women and children.

For lunch—with district cadres and senior hospital staff—food was spread over a long narrow table, and there seemed to be no shortage, although to me it was largely unpalatable. The others ate dried roast chicken, tasteless slices of rare-cooked beef, chicken soup (a whole chicken boiled in a large pot), pieces of pork wrapped in thin rice paper which I found too overpowering, and squid with a pork stuffing. I was looking forward to the fresh bean shoots with spring onions, until I found they were adulter- ated with fish paste.

Every meal since Hanoi had been 80 per cent meat: chicken, fish, beef or pork, so I vowed to order three plates of vegetables for dinner that night to put some balance back into my diet. A normal Vietnamese meal consisted of 80 per cent rice, with a few pieces of meat and vegetables, often in a soup. All the way down

Highway One I felt I was being used as an excuse to have extravagant meals. Although large spreads were part of traditional Vietnamese hospitality, driving back to Dong Hoi, I found it difficult not to think of the people who barely made a living scratching in the sandy soil.

Returning to Dong Hoi in 1990, I hardly recognised the town, such was the immense building program underway. Houses, cafes, public buildings, roads were all under construction, as if the whole town was being built or rebuilt. The reason was a sudden injection of government and private money into Dong Hoi when it became capital of the new province Quang Binh. The previous year, Binh Tri Thien reverted to its pre-war boundaries and once again became three provinces, with Dong Hoi, Dong Ha and Hue as capitals.

Many former residents of Dong Hoi returned and brought with them money to build new homes. Dinh Thi Le, 35, came back to run a roadside restaurant for a company which was building two more restaurants. She cooked *nem* (spring rolls) and fried frogs' legs for us then talked while we ate them, watched with curiosity by her eight-year-old son. She had been cooking for 16 years and had worked in a hotel in Hue before returning. Now she lived in a hostel with five other staff, but hoped to have a house when her husband returned from Iraq where he was working as a driver. She would see him in two years. 'For Vietnamese that's normal,' she said, but admitted she missed him. 'Many construction workers from Dong Hoi go to Iraq, and it's good for relations between countries,' she said. 'But now we need them here. Thirty buildings are under construction and soon there will be 50. The Government is building a large tourist hotel, an import–export office and a local office of the Ministry of Finance.' Lunch over, she led me to the 'toilet' which consisted of a roof, four walls and a square slab of concrete with nothing except a small hole in one corner. Outside was a barrel of water and a plastic bowl to slosh the concrete. On another occasion when I requested a toilet at a cafe, I was taken behind a partition to the back corner of the cooking area, and handed an aluminium bowl.

Heading south from Dong Hoi on my first trip down Highway One, we progressed 65 kilometres in two hours. About 90 kilometres from Dong Hoi we reached the most important landmark in the Vietnamese wars against the French and Americans—the 17th parallel, which divided North from South Vietnam. When France surrendered its 93-year dominance, its legacy had been to divide the country in two. This marked the end of one war and the beginning of the next. Under the Geneva Agreement, signed in July 1954, the north became the Democratic Republic of Vietnam under Ho Chi Minh's government, and the south was given over to Ngo Dinh Diem, until nationwide elections were held. America's involvement began not in 1965 when the first troops arrived, but less than three months after the Geneva Agreement was signed, when the US Navy began ferrying anti-communist refugees from north to south, and provided $100 million to Diem's Government —the first in a long line of payments which propped up South Vietnam's numerous governments for more than 20 years. Three months later the US offered to train South Vietnam's army. With US support, Diem denounced the Geneva Agreement and refused to hold elections. Vietnam remained divided at the 17th parallel until the fall of Saigon in April 1975.

The vast river flats of the old Demilitarised Zone (DMZ) were peaceful rice fields with workers cutting and carting paddy. An old single-lane Bailey bridge crossed the old divide, 94 kilometres north of Hue and 1600 kilometres from Cape Camau, the southern-most tip of Vietnam. I wondered how long before tourists —perhaps returning veterans—would stand in the middle of the bridge, in the middle of the DMZ, with one foot in the north and one in the south, to have their photos taken. Where soldiers once guarded the bridge, 15-year-old Lien earned 40 cents a day selling cigarettes, sweets and bananas from a tiny table, two kilometres from the nearest village. Since she was 13 she had been walking to the bridge each day to sit alone and wait for passing traffic.

Coming around a corner just south of the 17th parallel, we were confronted by an abandoned military tank sitting beside the road, its gun, rather dramatically, pointing towards us. Four more tanks lay rusting in fields further south, one with children playing on it.

Two years later, the tanks had been removed—presumably relegated to a scrap furnace somewhere in Japan, along with the piles of scrap metal that appeared at intervals along the road.

I stopped to talk with 20-year-old Mai Hoang Long who said he had collected about 5000 tonnes of scrap metal in five years. His pile included mortar shells, broken guns, bicycle parts, railway iron from the French era, parts of an American truck, window frames and pieces from a dismantled bridge. Men who collected war debris from fields and forests often came across unexploded shells, and Long knew of five who had been killed. But ncw less war scrap was being uncovered and Long hadn't taken his usual hire truck to Danang the previous week because he didn't have enough to make a load. There hadn't been a price rise for more than two years—despite high inflation—and Government import–export companies had bought more than they could handle, he said. 'Danang and Ho Chi Minh are full of scrap metal because there are not enough ships to export it.'

The most dramatic difference after crossing into what had been South Vietnam, was the road—wide, smooth and fast. In places we were able to reach 60 and sometimes even 80 kilometres an hour. The other difference was the appearance of war cemeteries—orderly and clean, each with a tall concrete pylon topped with the Vietnamese yellow star. (The only one I saw south of Hanoi was half covered by sand.)

A tall skeletal building beside the railway line and a derelict church were stark reminders that this part of South Vietnam was heavily bombed by the Americans attempting to eradicate the North Vietnamese and Viet Cong. Some bombed buildings had been turned into 'houses' or had new houses attached to them. Fences and additions to houses were often made with rusted sheets of metal.

It was not unusual to see Lao-registered vehicles, or products from Thailand smuggled through Laos via Highway Nine and minor roads linking the two countries. At the next town of Dong Ha, women in the market sold Thai shampoo, Chinese flasks and Japanese stereos.

From 1973 until the end of the war, Dong Ha was the capital of the Provisional Revolutionary Government (PRG), the communist's self-proclaimed government in opposition in South Vietnam. Most of the PRG Cabinet remained in the jungle where they set up temporary 'offices', while the only two women ministers, Nguyen Thi Binh (Foreign Affairs) and Dr Duong Quynh Hoa (Health) remained at the PRG headquarters to receive ambassadors and other foreign guests. (Mrs Nguyen Thi Dinh, Vice Commander-in-Chief of the Viet Cong army, had ministerial status but was not a minister.)

South of Dong Ha we came to the small town of Quang Tri, which had been the site of a massive communist offensive in 1972. Four times in four months the town was lost and retaken. The US had bombed the area unrelentingly, destroying Quang Tri and killing thousands of civilians as they fled south along Highway One which was dubbed the 'highway of terror'. West, along Highway Nine, was Khe Sanh which had been an isolated minor US base used to arm and train highland tribes. In January 1968 it was a bloody battleground which saw 10 000 communists—yet only

500 American marines—die. During the two-month battle, the US had pounded the area with bombs, some days dropping 1000 tonnes of explosives. Thick highland jungle was reduced to a blackened desolate expanse which 15 years later was being reforested.

Highway One moved away from the coast, closer to the foothills of the Truong Son range where eucalypts had been planted. Occasionally people attempted to wave us down and hitch a ride. As vehicles were rare any willing to take paying passengers became public transport. A truck trundled by; young men in army greens sitting on the roof, arms around each other. Groups of boys sat on the road, or played soccer in the dry rice fields. There seemed to be more dogs here, and in better health. A woman on crutches—possibly the victim of an unexploded shell—was the third amputee I had seen in an hour, yet I hadn't seen a single amputee during my two weeks in the north.

Approaching Hue at dusk was a delight—picturesque and tranquil, with green paddy fields in the foreground, green-grey foothills in the distance and the hazy mountains beyond. The city had an unhurried, peaceful air, despite the movement of people and vehicles. At 7 p.m. it was growing dark as we weaved our way through foot traffic, hawkers and cyclos, and over the bridge to the Huong Giang Hotel beside the river.

Travel weary and in need of a shower, I disappeared upstairs, then later arrived in the dining room to find Nhan, his family and Ben enjoying a sumptuous meal. I had expected to join them, as we had always eaten together, so I felt offended when Nhan suggested I sit alone. They finished eating then drove off, leaving me confused and humiliated. Rejection is hurtful, especially in a foreign land by the guardian who you rely on for everything from telling you where the toilet is to getting an interview with the president. Assuming I'd done something to upset him, I ate in gloom, then abandoning all caution, I hailed a passing cyclo and set out to explore the city alone. At that stage *doi moi*, or openness, did not extend to journalists taking cyclo rides around strange cities without their guide, especially in Hue where the local authorities were known to be conservative. The next morning not a word was said about the previous night, nor me taking a cyclo.

Hue and Danang:
culture and commerce

*If there is a fire in the forest, should we wait for
someone else to come?*
Vo Van Tien, government official, defending Vietnam's
involvement in Cambodia

The old city of Hue, with its magnificent Imperial Palace, sturdy
colonial buildings and romantic Perfume River, was once the
jewel in Vietnam's crown. By the time I first visited, the palace
had become a shadow of its former glory, the colonial buildings
were soiled and the river hinted of pollution, yet still the city
evoked images of a past glory. Scratch the surface and beneath
the use, abuse and decay, the old city could still be revealed.

Its endearing feature was the Perfume River (Song Huong)
which began amid pale blue mountains south of Hue where the
fragrant shrub *thach xuong bo* proliferated; it then flowed slowly
and majestically through the city, and into the Bien Dong (Eastern
Sea). Because of its romantic aura, it was for centuries the
essence of poems and novels—and the city itself.

Wooden boats crammed together along the river bank as if
huddling for protection, their flimsy domed bamboo covers gilded
by the dawn light. A lone fisherman, his nets in neat piles, headed
upstream to an unknown destination. A narrow open boat was
rowed mid-stream with its sole occupant squatting at the rear,
expertly cutting the water with a short paddle—left, right, left, right
—in quick, rhythmic strokes.

From the Huong Giang Hotel rooftop I watched this tranquil
scene but not without a tinge of sadness for what had been. To
the West, Truong Son, the rugged mountains once known as the
Annamite Cordillera, were silhouetted as tiers of decreasing blue.
Behind the palace's crumbling walls, glimpses of temple tops
and fading golden roofs suggested a wealth of architectural and
cultural delights once lay within. Between the treetops, the city

emerged as a mixture of concrete, tile and rusted iron. And in the foreground the beautiful Perfume slipped by.

The east bank, which was once the old French administrative quarter, was flanked by a long riverside park, once beautiful, but now dishevelled, and Le Loi Street which featured colonial buildings and more recent additions including the square concrete, architecturally incongruent Teacher's College.

Opposite, a long promenade dotted with old *phuong* (flamboyant) trees ended at the Dong Ba market: a vast collection of tightly packed squat huts sprawling haphazardly around a covered bazaar and cascading down wide steps to the river's edge. Here, produce and passengers were unloaded from narrow boats which plied the Perfume. Young men humped and heaved heavy loads, the early light turning their faces a soft orange.

I wandered over to the market for a closer look. Inside, amid the labyrinth of stalls, shoppers, pedlars and beggars, local and imported products changed hands in an immense melting pot of colour, sound and smell, a sea of necessity and small-scale luxury. Vendors displayed French brandy and colourful liqueurs, pure white lilies on long stems and delicate blood red roses, bright tiers of succulent yellow mangos and dark green shiny limes, small bags of dried chillis and barrels of powdery spices, pathetic piles of pale pink offal and steaming bowls of cooked noodles.

Pharmaceutical stands offered a multi-coloured collection of tiny tablets in plastic bags, contoured contraceptive packets, and little white plastic bottles of drops and nasal sprays. The tablets had no names, the contraceptives no boxes, the sprays no instructions. The ailing had a choice of paracetamol and antibiotics smuggled from Thailand, rheumatism and stomach ache cures from Bulgaria, and fansidar for malaria, microgynon-30 for contraception and vitamin B complex for good health from elsewhere.

Youngsters seemed to assume all Caucasians were Russian, and often called out to me *lien xo* ('Russian'), although adults sometimes asked foreigners if they were American. While I was in the market the inevitable Pied Piper effect developed, mothers clutching podgy babies, young girls with matted hair and old men in dirty shirts, all staring. My companion told the gathering I was *lien xo* and the crowd dispersed! It was a barometer of public opinion towards the large Soviet presence which filled the vacuum left by the Americans.

The rambling, elongated market ended where a wide canal joined the Perfume, and here, amid the cacophony and pervasive smell of rotting food, women balanced baskets of beans on long poles and barefoot young boys scurried down slippery steps with bags of rice slumped across their shoulders to where barges waited in line along the canal. Further downstream, yellow-green willows drooped over the riverbank, lazily trailing long twisted tentacles in the hurrying current. Sampans, with neat domed homes, lined the bank, some with washing flapping in the breeze. A speeding two-wheel Honda broke the tranquillity.

Hue was a sleepy town trying to be a bustling commercial city without surrendering her long-treasured grace. It was the third-largest university city in the country and a centre of tourism, light industry and culture. During the first half of the century, Hue was home to prominent prosaic figures and a hot-bed of political and religious unrest, from anti-French peasant uprisings to Buddhist protest. Its rich past began in 1601 when Hue became the capital of central Vietnam. Exactly 201 years later, Nguyen Anh established the imperial capital in Hue, and proclaimed himself emperor with the title Gia Long. He had attained power with the help of a French priest, Pigneau de Béhaine, who had sheltered the would-be emperor on an island in the Gulf of Thailand, before he returned to quash the famous Tay Son uprising. Although the priest did not represent the French Government, his action was a prelude to French intervention in Vietnam in the 1880s. After Gai Long, 12 emperors ruled from Hue during a colourful but turbulent era which saw the French and Japanese come and go as colonial rulers. The imperial era ended when Vietnam's last emperor, Bao Dai, abdicated in 1945 during a small ceremony where he handed over the emperor's sceptre and seal to representatives of Ho Chi Minh's Provincial Revolutionary Government.

Hue's royal palace, which took Gia Long 27 years to build (1804–1833), was partly styled on China's imperial palaces and temples, including Beijing's famed Forbidden City and Tienanmen. Chinese influence was equally strong in administration and custom: for example, the emperor surrounded himself with mandarins, called himself 'Son of Heaven', wore imperial yellow silk, and lived in a city forbidden to all except the imperial family. Court proceedings were as mystical and exotic as the best fairytales.

Encircled by an inner and outer moat, the palace compound covers 525 hectares and houses several palaces including the Thai Hoa and Long An palaces (Vietnam's largest existing wooden structures), and Ho Quyen arena where the royals watched fights between elephants and tigers. Within the compound is the much smaller Imperial City (606 × 622 metres), and within that the Forbidden City.

I found the moats around the complex choked with a thick carpet of green lotus leaves and weed. Bananas grew wild, roofs rusted and verandahs sagged. People pedalled or pushed laden bicycles across small arched bridges that once linked the two different worlds of the mandarins and the peasants, the imperial and the commercial, the old and new. Dusty back lanes weaved past former residences of traders and artisans who had served the Imperial Palace. Taking a cyclo through here was more like a horse-and-buggy ride down a quiet leafy country lane in England, even though the city's main street and central market were only one block away.

Inside the palace compound, beyond the towering red brick walls with the four massive gates of Noon, Peace, Humanity and Virtue, is the Imperial City. Until 1945, any commoner who set foot inside here without imperial consent faced execution. Now tourists, local and foreign, wandered around the old palaces and gardens, as emperors once did. Nhan and his family came with me and saw the palaces for the first time.

Entering the Imperial City was like descending the ages to absorb a very special era of Asian history. It is a magical, enticing collection of ponds and pavilions, moats and canals, stone bridges and graceful roofs. Nature and wars had damaged the great inner enclosure but several buildings still stood as masterly remnants of the Nguyen Dynasty. The guardian of the Imperial City was the beautiful three-tiered Noon Gate, the pavilion of which offered panoramic views of the palaces and royal grounds. I sat there, on wide stone steps, and imagined the pomp and ceremony of the past: rows of bare-foot soldiers in traditional dome-shaped hats with brilliant brass spikes, mandarins in colourful embroidered silk gowns and curly-toe shoes, and elephants carrying brightly decorated howdah, all bowing before the emperor in his splendid robes. This era had passed forever. Now the ponds were virtually empty and moss filled the cracks of the decaying buildings. The sight was still grand, but sad.

On the far side once stood the emperor's residence, destroyed in 1946 by the Viet Minh who in order to spite the returning French sacked many public buildings and factories before retreating to the jungles. I found only a large brass water tank in a field of vegetables, part of a bullet-pitted stone wall and some worn steps leading to what had been a splendid courtyard but was now covered in grass. Where the emperor once slept, cows now grazed.

Behind the magnificent Palace of Supreme Harmony— undamaged but in need of repair—I found the two mandarin palaces. Damaged in the 1968 Tet (New Year) offensive (the stone verandah of one was pocked with bullet holes), they had since been beautifully restored with UNESCO funds and featured bright coloured paintings of animals on the ceiling, walls and pillars.

After Bao Dai's abdication in 1945 the palace remained empty, except for a month when tragically it hosted the longest and fiercest battle of the 1968 Tet offensive. Just after midnight on 31 January, on the first day of the new year celebrations, traditional firecrackers could not be distinguished from gunfire as Viet Cong and North Vietnamese forces attacked 36 of South Vietnam's 44 provincial capitals. The offensive failed as most towns quickly reverted to Government control although it is arguable that the Tet offensive was a turning-point in the war in that it persuaded the US to begin withdrawing troops. In Hue however the communists remained entrenched in the palace complex for 24 days, despite constant attacks from American, South Korean and South Viet- namese forces who bombed the ancient royal palaces. By the late 1980s, most of the damage had been repaired, although splin- tered doors, bullet-grazed metal and smashed porticoes were still evident.

Five kilometres upstream, where the only sounds were of birds and passing sampans, a series of sweeping steps reached the imposing seven-tiered octagonal Phuoc Duyen Tower. It stood guard over the Thien Mu (Heavenly Lady) Pagoda, where in 1601 Emperor Nguyen Hoang built Hue's first pagoda and established the capital. According to Monk Thich Hai Trang, who had lived there for 11 years, when King Nguyen Hoang spent a night on the hill the Heavenly Lady appeared and told him he must burn incense then walk along the river carrying it and where the incense finished burning should be the site of the palace com- pound. And it was.

Trang hurried off to join colleagues for a communal lunch of

noodle soup, so we retreated to the dim interior of the temple. The government official accompanying us slipped off his shoes to reveal missing heels in his socks. Kneeling, he bowed awkwardly three times, struck a gong thrice, then lit several incense sticks. I guessed it was more for show than homage to Buddha.

Thien Mu Pagoda made international news in 1963 when its chief monk, Thich Quang Duc, ignited himself in central Saigon during a Buddhist protest march. His dramatic self-immolation drew world attention to Catholic President Diem's unsympathetic treatment of Buddhists. The monk's act was later emulated by more than 30 monks and nuns. After lunch, Trang showed me the old Austin in which Quang Duc was driven through Saigon, leading the rally. It was housed in a garage at the pagoda and on its windscreen was displayed the graphic photo of the revered monk sitting cross-legged on the road with a fireball rising from his erect body.

On the east bank of the Perfume River, Hue's old French buildings epitomised the wealth of the colonial powers. They were now crumbling and sagging, with broken shutters, collapsing roofs, dilapidated outhouses and chickens scratching in once beautiful gardens.

The Chinese quarter was a curious blend of East and West, a tightly-packed collection of single- and double-storey terraces with curling dragons, stuccoed arches and porticoed balconies. Young boys played in the courtyard of the old Chinese Hai Nam Temple, then jocosely jostled each other to be included in my photo. The temple had been deserted since 1975, and exquisite ceiling paintings, depicting courtiers in the countryside and emperors surrounded by their subjects and servants, were fading and flaking.

Nearby, a large white building intrigued me. It had graceful arches and pillars which appeared to be a cross between a Catholic church and a Moslem temple. According to Nguyen Van Phuong who lived there, it had been used during the French period as the headquarters of Hijiri, an obscure Islamic sect from India. Phuong, his wife and three children had lived there since 1983 when it was taken over as staff accommodation by the electricity supply company for whom he worked. 'The Government allocated it on condition that when necessary the State could repossess it, for example, if they wanted it for historical purposes. One condition of living here is that we do repairs including the roof and floors,' he said.

Later I discussed living conditions with Nguyen Dinh Ngo, the Vice-President of the People's Committee, when we met him at his office in the former French Governor's residence beside the Perfume River. He was concerned that living standards had changed little since 1975. 'As one of the leaders responsible for this province I am not happy. We now have three times more running water than in 1975, but still only half Hue has water and electricity. Equipment and infrastructure is still very rudimentary and housing is a problem. We have better health care and education and more material goods,' he said optimistically, but when prompted he said these 'material goods' included such basics as mosquito nets.

From the Vice-President's first-floor balcony, it was easy to imagine the masterly French governor standing there half a century ago overseeing the activities of his city. The French and American eras had passed, but Ngo's province endured the legacy. 'We had to remove millions of unexploded shells, grenades and bullets, and in doing so, three to four thousand people were injured or killed. Dead people were buried everywhere, so we have to remove many remains before building houses and schools, and we have more than 10 000 seriously disabled by the war.

'The most significant change since liberation is that we manage our country without being dominated by others. We want co-operation with all countries, but re-establishing relations with America is what we want most.' He acknowledged, however, that some people may not want the Americans back. 'Everyone has 10 fingers, some are long, some short. It is reality that some families who had members killed will not be so willing to forget,' said Ngo, through Nhan's translation.

He took us to meet Le Thi Bich Van, a 44-year-old mother of three who ran a scrap metal yard—and there was nothing sexist about that, she said while loading old tank chains with her ten (male) workers. Eight years earlier she had given up selling meat in the market, and put her gold savings into setting up a scrap yard which she regarded as her greatest achievement, although she admitted it was not very profitable. Her main complaint was the number of middlemen through which exported scrap metal passed. 'I sell to local companies and they sell to the province and the province sells to foreign trade companies in Vietnam, and they sell to the Japanese.'

A former student of Hue took me to a backstreet restaurant he had frequented during his courting days—not to relive the past, but to introduce me to *lau* (island). On the table, a steam boat with a central funnel (an island) to hold burning coal, was part-filled with simmering stock in which paper-thin slices of beef were fleetingly cooked by diners. Removed with chopsticks, the beef was wrapped in sheets of dry rice paper with thin slices of green banana and several varieties of mint leaves. The mini-roll was then dipped in a bowl of fish sauce to which crushed peanuts and chilli had been added. Hue's specialty, and my favourite!

Walking back to the hotel through virtually deserted streets, the Voice of Vietnam suddenly began blasting unintelligibly from a loudspeaker atop a pole. Many families do not own a radio and rely on street broadcasts which emanate from Hanoi three times a day, providing music, sport, news and comment.

At night Hue was an odd mixture of romance and consumerism, liberty and conformity, hope and despair. Children played in the streets; music and laughter wafted from homes and cafes; men linked arms; and patients waited for an acupuncturist. A cyclo driver took me along a street lit by tiny flickering candles then down two blackened streets, and for the second time I experienced deep apprehension. A single rat scuttled for cover, and a group of young men cast errie bouncing shadows as they moved down a half-lit street. Thankfully we emerged on to the main street where men and music met in coffee shops with green light bulbs, where loudspeakers blared boisterously and traffic hustled.

Footpaths were almost as crowded as during the day, with people ambling, sellers touting and mechanics repairing. Cassette music mixed unsympathetically with gibbering television sounds. Hawkers lined the road with little collapsible tables laden with cigarettes, nuts and sweets, each table lit with a tiny central lamp. The streets were much livelier than in Hanoi, and there seemed to be more motorbikes, some transporting families of four or five, all happily balancing on the seat, petrol tank and foot rests. Crowds of people, bright fluorescent lights and loudspeakers denoted a lively and well-attended lotto game. The music from a disco, brightly lit with red, yellow and green lights, wafted across the river. Outside, hundreds of bicycles were stacked in neat rows while the younger generation danced inside under neon lights to loud 'modern' music.

A large billboard at the Trang Tien Bridge featured a socialist-style advertisement: a mother with one hand held high in the air and the other holding a baby, beneath which the Government declared: *doi moi de tien len*, 'renovation is the way forward'. On the bridge, the homeless prepared for another miserable night. Young men and mothers with babies and young children lay on dirty rattan mats with their worldly possessions tucked beside them in soiled bags held together with scraps of string.

Along the western bank, teenage girls clustered in giggling bunches. Occasionally one or two approached a man to ask for his custom. Service and price negotiated, he would be taken further down river where prostitutes waited in houseboats. Later, a satisfied customer would disappear into the night, and teenage touts and boat owners received their cut of the takings.

Bangkok is famous for its bar girls, Amsterdam for its window ladies and Las Vegas for its hotel hostesses. Hue had boatgirls who operated along the Perfume River in hired sampans, a woven reed mat the only furniture. For extra dong, the boat could be moved mid-stream, or to a secluded location. Hue's boatgirls probably offered the most unusual and most romantic venue for the world's oldest profession.

One of Hue's favourite sons, poet To Huu, depicted the despairing life of a boatgirl in his famous poem 'Tieng Hat Song Huong' (Song of the Perfume River), which became the basis of Dang

Nhat Minh's controversial film *Co Gai Tren Song* (Girl on the River) in which a boatgirl escaped her immoral life and later married a former southern soldier.

> My life is spent in the lonely sampan;
> When will I reach the landing place
> And escape my immoral life?
> Oh heaven, will my poor body cease
> To be battered and twisted all night long?

Like all good romantic tales, it ends on a happy note, when she is told:

> Tomorrow, from the depth of your heart to the palms of your
> hands
> You shall be filled with the sweet essence of jasmine
> . . . all the merk of foul memories
> Shall dissolve with the shadows of this night.

Hue had long been synonymous with literature, and poetry was its life force. The Vietnamese delighted in verse, from sentimental love tales to rousing war songs, and the city's grace and romance inspired many celebrated writers. During the 1930s and 40s it was a vigorous city bursting with literary energy and simmering dissent. Writers and scholars would stroll along the river bank or sit long hours in teahouses, sharing literary criticism or political comment, generating a fervour not seen elsewhere in Vietnam before or since. They might swap underground newspapers— perhaps containing articles by exiled nationalist Ho Chi Minh—and at night gather on a sampan for a clandestine meeting of the banned Communist Party.

The germinating ground of intellectuals was Quoc Hoc, the elite high school established on the east bank. Many of Vietnam's famed passed beneath its elaborate arched gateway, including Ho Chi Minh, the north's Prime Minister Pham Van Dong, the south's President Ngo Dinh Diem, military commander General Vo Nguyen Giap, and poet To Huu.

When I visited Quoc Hoc in 1990, former secondary teacher Dang Xuan Truong had been the director for 13 years. 'During the French time this college was the largest in Vietnam and was the college to educate mandarins and students of the royal family. Only after finishing here would pupils be sent to Saigon or Hanoi to continue their education,' he said. All lessons were taught in French until the 1945 August Revolution. After the Revolution the school no longer had just elite students, Truong said, and a proportion of places was set aside for top students from other parts of the province.

Famous for its alumni who became leaders, the college regarded political studies as an important part of the curriculum. 'In the 10th grade we teach the Constitution of Vietnam, in the 11th they do philosophy and economic science and in the 12th we teach the way to build socialism,' said Truong. Textbook revisers were not able to keep pace with social, economic and political changes created by *doi moi*, he said. 'The regular subjects like maths, physics and chemistry are not changing much, but the social sciences are. In the past we taught only about the State and collective sector, but now we mention the private sector too. Previously, the central level gave us a plan which we had to follow, but now we have to work out our own plan,' he said walking us around the stately buildings.

Hue was also famed for its traditional weddings, and on a visit to the city in 1989 my guide and I were spontaneously invited to take part in Tong Phuoc Kim Giao's marriage to Than Trong Long. The daylong celebration began with a tea ceremony hosted by the bride's family to welcome the family of the groom. About 40 family members—women dressed in beautiful formal *ao dais* and men in suits—crammed into a long room to eat a variety of cakes including the traditional sweet orange *qua hong* made with agar-agar.

While guests sipped tea across a courtyard Giao and Long knelt before an elaborately carved altar. Upon it were placed red and blue dragon-patterned bowls of fruit, candles, flowers, numerous pictures of Buddha and a large bronze urn. Family members had placed on the altar traditional offerings including betel nuts and leaves, and tins of tea for happiness. With palms together, the bridal couple bowed three times to Buddha and four times to their ancestors. During the absorbing 15-minute dedication, two red wooden bowls materialised bearing two rings and two bracelets of gold—bridal gifts from the groom's family.

Two hours later the family moved to the Song Hoang Hotel where about 100 guests had already assembled for a banquet which began with eight hors d'oeuvres including fermented pork, fried bread, and soup of tapioca, egg and crab, with labelless bottles of local beer.

The couple planned to settle in Tokyo, where Long had lived since winning a scholarship there in 1970. 'Long has chosen another country to live in,' announced an uncle who lived in the US, 'but his mind and heart will always be in the old country.'

We toasted the old country with sweet, unpalatable Bulgarian vermouth.

A marriage produces children, and in Buddhism the life–death cycle is a continuum—for each new soul, another departs. Seven of Hue's emperors are buried in elaborate tombs in or around the city. On the outskirts, amid the rolling pine-clad hills south of suburbia, we arrived at the tomb of Tu Duc, the fourth king of the Nguyen dynasty who used his mausoleum (built between 1864–67) as a second imperial palace. The grounds were extensive and all consuming and it was easy to become lost—physically and spiritually—in the myriad of pebbled paths and gracious gardens. I climbed stone steps and discovered statues of elephants, horses and mandarins on an open terrace surrounded by trees. Four huge copper doors opened onto a courtyard, bare except for the emperor's mammoth circular tomb which was once guarded by blue-robed mandarins and red-uniformed royal soldiers. Atop another set of sweeping steps children were selling faded post-cards in front of a museum displaying imperial furniture. Below was a small elegant pond-side pavilion where the emperor had spent many leisurely hours, drinking, loving and writing poetry.

Leaving Hue was like farewelling a beloved grandparent—old, worldly and wise, with just a hint of devilment. Fifty years ago it would have taken a wood-burning train three days to reach Saigon from Hue, but it would take us four days by van to cover the 800 kilometres.

It felt good to be back on the road, to be going places. It was mid-afternoon and the stench from a market drifted across the road and filled our nostrils with the sweet sickly smell of over-ripe fruit. Women crammed into a battered blue bus, some clutching bags of bananas, others sucking on ice cream sticks, while the driver cursed me for taking photos. Younger women sported stylish haircuts, a smattering of make-up and jewellery, and short-sleeve blouses, while their elders, with long hair clasped at the neck, covered their arms, at least to the elbow. Older women seemed never to wear cosmetics and rarely ornaments except for perhaps a ring or jade bangle.

The highway ran along the thin coastal strip between mountain ranges and the South China Sea, yet we only glimpsed water occasionally. As elsewhere, rice was the predominant crop. Although the region was poor and sparsely populated, it lacked the desperate look of the previous provinces.

Four men in shorts and floppy cloth hats used their bare feet to turn a primitive, but effective, water wheel. Perched on a bamboo

frame they peddled relentlessly to pump water from a canal to the rice fields. Near here, I saw one of my saddest victims of the American–Vietnam War, a teenage boy with a distended chest and hunchback which twisted his body into an S-shape. Sad, not because of the grotesqueness of the injuries, but the eyes that were trying to smile, trying to ask the Westerner for understanding. Behind the happy-go-lucky facade lay years of emotional torment, but with a cheeky wave, he jumped on a concrete wall and without prompting posed for a photo. His dirty loose shorts, oversized peak cap and bright blue plastic sandals represented a combination of Vietnamese peasantry, leftover Americana and recent consumerism.

From Hue to Danang, Highway One climbed over two ranges. Between them lay a long sandy palm-fringed beach with haughty blue mountains rising majestically from a lagoon. Bulky wooden boats lolled in the sun until just before dusk when young men rowed them across the lagoon, standing tall and paddling with a foot wrapped around an oar. Having travelled this section several times, and watched the lagoon change from brilliant blue to soft pink as the day faded, I considered this my favourite region in Vietnam.

The centre of activity was Lang Co village which sprawled along both sides of the highway filling the narrow neck of land between lagoon and beach. Thatched roof homes and cafes nestled just off the road amid trees. The cafe owners would rise at about 5.30 a.m. to light tiny fires beneath pots, and prepare to display their merchandise—beer, cigarettes and biscuits. The first customers, usually truck drivers bound for Hue, would sit at wooden tables drinking strong black coffee or steaming bowls of *pho bo* (beef noodle soup).

In 1990 I spoke to Nguyen Thi Hai Loan who had, with hired help and 50 000 dong ($15), built a cafe after the closure of the State-run restaurant where she had worked. 'It didn't make much profit partly because it was badly run,' she explained. Closure of non-viable State enterprises became widespread in 1989–90 after the Government ordered them to operate on a profitable basis. Spurred by the new push towards private enterprise, Loan and several of the other 24 retrenched women opened roadside cafes; hers was built with metal sheets salvaged from a former US helicopter base. 'We are free to run them as we like as long as we give the State 70 000 ($22) a month in tax.' This was double the monthly wage of her husband who had been a policeman for six years. 'We will have to wait till we earn more to have a second child' —a comment I heard frequently in Vietnam.

Leaving the long line of roadside cafes, we climbed Hai Van (sea and mountain) Pass, the highest point on Highway One. From part-way up the pass, the beachside village of Long Co appeared to be engulfed in a blanket of palms laced with white sand. The spire of a church protruded above the tree tops, reaching for the sky. As we ascended, the coastline emerged as a series of rugged headlands and sandy coves; boats dwindled into small black dots and dashes on a blue-grey background of water. It was an impressive sight, hardly imaginable in a country usually perceived as infinite sprawling tropical green.

The air was wild and invigorating, and I wanted to ramble over the hills covered with thick scrub and cut by deep gullies, or to clamber along the rocky coastline. I wanted to feel free and un-cluttered. The locals regarded the hills as uninhabitable and useless except as a source for meagre supplies of firewood which were sold beside the road. Fresh mountain streams cascaded down rocks and under the road. Enterprising roadside sellers had established small stalls beside the streams where truck drivers stopped for natural refreshments. Landslips and large areas of burnt scrubland suggested human interference, but there was no sign of civilisation. As dusk fell, we wound our way up the pass, negotiating hairpin bends and avoiding fallen rocks. The sea below gradually took on the appearance of a city coming to life at night, as one by one fishing boats turned on their lights.

The summit, 79 kilometres from Hue, marked the northern boundary of Quangnam–Danang province, and offered a spectacular view of the sprawling metropolis of Danang city and its huge harbour. The city extended from the mountain base to the sea, covering the flat coastal plain. The harbour created a smooth curverous indent in the coastline. From 1965–73, when Danang was one of the largest US military base in South Vietnam, this was home to thousands of American servicemen. Remnants of an old French fortress stand aloof at the top of the pass to remind travellers that the French had ruled here before the Americans set up coastal bases. The tiny red bricks of the main tower were fretting but the concrete bunkers remained solid, although overgrown with scrub.

The road winding down the pass was strewn with large stones, the debris from broken down trucks and buses. Nhan explained that in lieu of brakes, drivers used rocks as wedges under the rear wheels of their vehicles and then drove away leaving the road scattered with boulders which subsequent traffic had to avoid.

From halfway down the mountain's southern side I could see far below a picturesque bay which I was told was home to about 70 inmates of a leprosy centre. (In 1989 French and Singaporian developers talked of replacing it with a Western-style holiday resort. The wide sandy beach and sheltered bay appealed to foreign investors who were looking for a secluded tourist site only a few kilometres from Danang.)

We left the mountain and travelled along more familiar flat ground where we were greeted by the wonderful smell of fresh cut paddy in the early evening air. Around the harbour, waves lapped the deserted beach which once was crowded with American marines bathing in the tropical sun. The first American combat troops in South Vietnam splashed onto this beach from amphibious landing craft on 8 March 1965, and later established an air base with the largest runway in Southeast Asia. Virtually nothing remained to testify that Red Beach had once been the second largest 'American city' in Vietnam. With one-fifth of the US forces based here, Danang was transformed from a relatively sleepy town of cyclists and fishermen to a bustling city swamped by thousands of soldiers, helicopters and military vehicles, and became known as the 'City of Soldiers'.

Coming into Danang at night was not the best way to see this city: it appeared to be totally haphazard. The buildings blended into a confused mass; cyclists moved as one, and pedestrians were indistinguishable from one another, but streets were better lit and more energetic than those in Hanoi.

In the early morning light of the next day, Danang emerged as large, modern and urban, with wide streets and high-rise buildings under construction (three to four storeys was considered high). Shops looked brighter and slightly more Western than those in Hanoi, and they offered much more variety. (This became more apparent the further south we moved, due, no doubt, to lingering American influences and capitalist tendencies.) I was surprised to see for the first time in Vietnam crispy baguettes—a legacy of the French era? (Before my next trip to Hanoi in 1990, I asked a Western friend what I could bring as a gift from Bangkok. Her answer was fresh bread, which was widely available in the south but still not in the north.)

Frivolity was in the air, giving the impression that every day was a holiday. Danang was an unfussed city. *Khong sao* (no problem) it seemed to say, sit awhile and have a drink. Few people hurried. Fruit and flower sellers employed quick deliberate movements which came with years of repetition, but they were not hurrying. Men lingered in coffee shops as if the world would go on forever without them. There was no official siesta, but for all intents and purposes there might as well have been.

Like Vietnam's other main cities—Hanoi, Haiphong, Hue and Ho Chi Minh—Danang was dissected by a river, the Song Han, which ran into the harbour. At dawn, I watched two small rusted ferries slip across the river with practised ease, stopping for a few minutes on each bank before returning to repeat the act, like slow, rhythmical dancers—step, pause, step, pause, always circling each other but never meeting. At each stop passengers streamed on or off in virtual silence—like the ferries, the people had been doing this routine for a long time. The early morning sun splashed a tinge of rustic orange on the old waterfront buildings, and from the opposite bank they looked more European than Vietnamese—many were, in fact, built during the French period.

One Sunday afternoon on my 1989 trip to Danang, I borrowed a friend's bicycle and explored the south side of the harbour where women were spreading fish on bamboo mats in the sun, and barebacked men were laying watery white squid on drying frames.

I took a bumpy, sand-covered road which ran parallel with the beach. Between the road and the beach lived fishing families, and narrow sandy paths weaved like a maze between houses, some with high fences protecting privacy, others with front doors opening onto paths. An old woman sat in the shade crocheting, a young mother rocked her baby in a hammock, and a family enjoyed a late lunch at a table in their front yard—all watching me as if I was an alien.

Within a few minutes of entering this labyrinth, 20 to 30 youngsters began pursuing me down the narrow lanes until it became almost suffocating. I was becoming hot, sweaty and irritated, and sand in my shoes didn't help. I was beginning to wonder how I could get out when a family invited me inside for a much needed drink of water. But this was no escape—half the neighbourhood followed me, cramming into the two-room house until I was almost crushed. I couldn't believe so many people could fill such a confined space. The internment and the smell of human closeness was overpowering. No-one spoke a word of English—except the universal 'hello' which the kids echoed a thousand times amid much laughter—but we managed to communicate, and, as was always the case in Vietnam, everyone giggled when they discovered I was 30 and not married, a rarity for women here.

During this visit I was lodged on the third floor of the Hai Chau Hotel opposite the city's cathedral, and the dawn light on the old sandstone steeple with rows of pale blue mountains in the background was spectacular. French built, it was known as Con Ga (Cock) Cathedral in honour of a cockswain atop its spire. On the first morning, my curiosity aroused, I joined the throngs gathering for a dawn confirmation. More than 100 people milled around, nuns looking demure in white cotton habits, smart young boys with white shirts and neat haircuts, anxious mothers in beautiful *ao dai* with bodices elegantly embroidered with dragons and pheasants. The girls, round-faced and youthful in simple white gowns and silky black hair seemed to epitomise all that was innocent and virginal. As they shuffled past me into the cathedral several hid their faces and giggled with the innocence of pending puberty.

They filed inside, and filled the front pews with the precision of those well rehearsed, then sat rigid and attentive before three bishops who wore stunning ankle length blue robes. The cathedral was packed, so I opted for a side door crammed with proud parents who almost climbed over each other to witness their offspring being blessed. I wriggled through to the front to watch the bishops offer each child a pat on the head and a fatherly word. Several local photographers were recording the event for posterity—and for several hundred dong, no doubt. One was delighted to see I was using a Pentax, and excitedly showed me his battered 1960s model. 'How much?' (it was a standard question here). I doubted he would believe I paid 64 pounds for it in a London sale ten years earlier, so I said 'four hundred dollars', which was closer to its present market price. 'This two hundred,' he said triumphantly waving his in the air with one hand.

Next morning I set off at 5.30 a.m. to take photos. As doors opened, the city began to stir, but a homeless woman remained curled up on the footpath, her bundle of possessions at her bare feet and a short blade knife in her right hand—limp yet ready. Youths in flimsy shorts shuffled rather than jogged along the waterfront, shaking and flapping arms as they went. An unseen radio jabbered faintly through an open door. Two dogs growled at each other as they foraged in a pile of refuse. A gap-toothed crone cleaned string beans in a metal basin beside her front door. An emaciated pony clip-clopped past, head down, ears back.

Where the river meets the harbour, fish was brought to a stinking market on old wooden banana-shaped boats which nosed and bumped as they crammed along the bank. Huge dripping baskets of wet slithering fish were hauled ashore to be haggled over by dozens of buyers—all women—milling in the muddy arena. In a conglomeration of pointy hats, they bantered and bargained their way around the sellers, waving woven bags and smoking fat cheroots, their bare feet squelching through black mud.

I bought a warmed bread roll crammed with pâté, onions, tomatoes and mint leaves, topped with chilli sauce, and watched a crazed beggar—deranged or drug-induced, I wasn't sure—as he wandered among baskets and umbrellas clutching a cloth, cupped in the shape of a bowl. Most people ignored him, but his unshaven appearance evoked giggles from teenage girls who saw me watching him. This was not a beggar living off the generosity of foreigners, for there were few here—he didn't even approach me—but a genuine has-been. Perhaps when not shuffling and eddying around the market he went to the street where the homeless slept. This short street near the ferry wharf was a collection of pots and piled rags by day and dark hunched bodies at night.

Returning to the vast restaurant area of the Hai Chau Hotel for breakfast, I found tables littered with used cups, glasses and teapots, as dozens of men gathered for pre-work drinks. Coffee and companionship blended in a male dominated ritual. While women tended their homes, men sipped coffee, strong and black or thick and creamy. They talked as freshly ground coffee dripped through individual aluminium filters into thick, squat glasses, many of them part-filled with condensed milk which was then stirred through the coffee to make a sweet syrupy drink.

I stayed at the Hai Chau for two weeks in 1989 before it was classed as a tourist hotel, after which the price of a room went from 13 000 dong ($4) to $23. (Thereafter, foreigners were not permitted to pay in dong.) Almost every day I was approached by young men wanting to practise English. A surprising number were, or said they were, in their mid-30s and not married. They would approach with stern expressions, 'coos me mam, may I sit with you awhile?', or perhaps, 'can I have a short talk with you?' Invariably, the first question concerned age, the second marital status. 'I not get married yet 'cos not enough money', seemed to be a standard response. Then they would proceed to tell me how many of their father's sisters, or mother's sister's children, were in America or Australia, and how they would like to go there one day, and could I help them.

I always found translated menus to be amusing, and one night I ate at a restaurant offering 'vapourised sea fish with shredded meat', 'braised duck with eight assorted', 'seaslug soup with three varieties' and 'fish tripe with chicken cream crabs'. After consuming the latter—the contents of which were as indecipherable as the menu—I returned to the Hai Chau just before midnight. I was invited to join a large rowdy group of men who had obviously been feasting and drinking for several hours. As tables were customarily not cleared until diners left the restaurant, the table was strewn with unsightly remnants of a banquet: food scraps, frothy glasses, bottles and stacks of grimy plates.

I joined in a popular Vietnamese way of drinking beer which was to fill glasses then tap them together at a certain height to indicate whether a third, half or all was to be quaffed by everyone at once. Although repeated sessions of this were guaranteed to induce quick inebriation, this group appeared disproportionately drunk for the number of empty bottles on the table, until I had cause to look under the table where dozens more were piled up haphazardly on the floor, that repository of all things rejected. When finally we all shuffled out, the relieved waitresses, who had been waiting to clear the debris, moved in. I glanced back and the sight of the table with piles of food above and empties below has remained fixed in my memory.

Meeting cadres in each province became predictable and a little tiring, especially as everything had to be translated. Meetings generally followed a protocol repeated from north to south, with little variation. One memorable exception on my first visit in 1988 was Vo Van Tien, Vice-Director of the Danang Forestry Services who, after a lengthy interview on reafforestation, was coaxed into a debate on Cambodia.

Typically using metaphors, he explained why Vietnamese troops went into, and remained in, Cambodia. 'If a neighbour who was in trouble asked you for help, would you help him?' he asked, knowing the answer would be 'yes'. 'And if that neighbour had been really badly injured and needed a long time to recover, would you stay with him during that time?'

Like many Vietnamese, Tien asked what would have happened had Vietnam not gone into Cambodia and stopped the murderous Khmer Rouge who had been responsible for the deaths of possibly one million Cambodians from 1975–79. Should Vietnam have sat back and waited while other countries decided how to stop the bloodbath, he asked? 'If there is a fire in the forest, should we wait for someone else to come, then argue who should be first to put it out?'

It became abundantly clear during my first two weeks in Vietnam that the West and Vietnam spoke a different language when it came to propaganda. There are two versions to every story, one portrayed by the West (usually through the media), and one by the Vietnamese Government. As Tien pointed out, Westerners talked of the 'Vietnam War' and the 'fall of Saigon'; Vietnamese called it the 'American War' and the 'liberation of Saigon'. We said the Vietnamese 'invaded' Cambodia; they said they 'liberated' the country from the Khmer Rouge.

Tien said Vietnam, although extremely poor itself, offered help to Cambodia. The West on the other hand said his Government 'Vietnamised' its neighbour and installed a 'puppet regime'. The Vietnamese referred to their Cambodian involvement as *nhiem vu quoc te*, their international task, yet the West punished Vietnam by imposing an embargo which stagnated the economies of both countries and left probably 70 million people in a state of poverty for more than a decade.

Apart from his interest in Cambodia, Tien ran the Forestry Service which started a major tree planting program immediately after the American–Vietnam War ceased. 'Dioxin affected all the western half of the province and the south. Before, there were large, beautiful trees but now only scrub and climbing plants. Some dead trees are still standing along the Tra My River south of here—they look like big black poles,' he said. 'When I was small there were *filao* (casuarina) trees all along the coast, but the

Americans and their puppets (the South Vietnamese) cut, bombed and bulldozed all the trees south of Danang so they could have a clear view to and from the sea, and they didn't like the forests because we could take cover there.'

I recalled reafforestation expert Professor Vo Quy telling me, in his tiny upstairs office at the University of Hanoi, that as much forest had been lost since 1975 through logging and slash-and-burn practices, as was destroyed during the war. However, while Western countries talked endlessly and loudly of the need to regenerate diminishing forests worldwide, Vietnam had been quietly planting forests and mangrove swamps, preventing erosion and logging, and rebuilding waterways. Conservationists also succeeded in generating the world's first tropical forest, northwest of Ho Chi Minh. According to the World Wide Fund for Nature, Vietnam had one of the best re-greening programs in the world, despite the fact it was one of the poorest and most densely populated countries.

Reviving Danang's water system had not been as successful. From a pile of dust-covered papers in his office, Water Supply Director Ho But removed plans drawn up in 1970 by the Australian Department of Housing and Construction to replace Danang's then antiquated water system. The American–Vietnam and Cambodian wars delayed the project, and now the city had to contend with a desperate shortage of water and a system which should have been replaced decades ago.

Only 20–25 per cent of houses in Vietnam's third largest city had running water. 'And the water is not always purified because the pipes are too old—they date from the French time—and we use electricity to purify the water but the supply is not always stable,' But said. Those without their own supply of water took from public wells in the street, or paid a neighbour for shared use. 'Even water from wells is not safe which is causing health problems—we have epidemics of diarrhoea and in the past, cholera.' He laughed when I asked him whether the director received preferential treatment. 'For several years after liberation I didn't have water and had to get it from the street wells,' he said. 'Most of the time now I only get water at home from 1 a.m. to 5 a.m. so we have to get up early and store it in large jars. For washing, we take water from a garden well which is used by several families, but in summer it dries up during the day and we can only get water at night.'

The city had not grown significantly in area but had become considerably more densely populated. As But said, 'I have one house and when my children get married I will build a small house behind it. We have great difficulties with housing. Some families of five people live in only nine square metres. Although I'm a director, my family of five live in 26 square metres.'

People rather unconvincingly offered to find remains of US servicemen who had been missing in action (MIAs), either soldiers who failed to return from sorties or airmen shot down during bombing raids or reconnaissance missions. Remains had been found in mountains around Hiep Duc and Tra My south of Danang, and a Western diplomat later said it was plausible that people knew where the graves were but didn't want to disclose them because of possible real or imaginary repercussions, although they might reveal sites if they could leave the country.

For years the US declared it would not restore diplomatic relations with Vietnam until all Vietnamese troops were withdrawn from Cambodia and the MIA issue was solved. In an unprecedented top-level move, President Reagan's special adviser General John Vessey met Foreign Minister Nguyen Co Thach in July 1988 after which the two countries agreed on a joint search for MIAs. By November 1990 the remains of 174 Americans had been returned to the US, but a year later the State Department claimed that there were still 1656 MIAs in Vietnam. Some people believed that a handful of MIAs were still being held as prisoners; others said some MIAs had stayed on after the war, married Vietnamese women and integrated into the local community. Vietnam had thousands of MIAs of its own—their deaths were not reported and their bodies not returned to next of kin. The human cost of the war to Vietnam was staggering: between 1965 and 1973 in South Vietnam alone the war killed 1.4 million civilians compared to 58 000 American servicemen, left 300 000 invalids, one million widows, 800 000 orphans and more than three million jobless.

Many American, and to a lesser extent South Korean and Australian, servicemen married local girls or had casual affairs, and the result is possibly 20 000 children of mixed blood, with at least 1000 of them in Danang. Now in their late teens and early 20s, these Amerasians are caught between two worlds, unsure of whether they belong in Vietnam or the US where most of their fathers have since married and have brought up a family of teenagers.

Children of mixed parents are nothing new in Vietnam. During the colonial days many Frenchmen took Vietnamese wives, and in the mid-1920s there were an estimated 40 000 *metis* or people of mixed blood. These Annamite–French were referred to by the derogatory term *dau ga dit vit* (head chicken, tail duck). Amerasians are called *con lai* (children of mixed blood) or *my lai* (American mixed blood). A particularly insulting phrase is to say they are mixed with dog's blood. 'Dog' in Vietnamese is used as a curse.

Danang had shrugged off its wartime image, but was still repairing, replacing and recovering. Where once US naval vessels had tied up at the wharves, now cargo ships waited to load agricultural products, timber and handicrafts—the region's main exports—and to unload fertilisers, building materials and machinery—the most valued imports, from mainly socialist countries. Danang is the gateway to neighbouring land-locked Laos which is linked by mountainous Highway Nine. Ships from Japan, Taiwan, Hong Kong and Singapore also frequent the port bringing with them consumer goods and equipment for Laos and Vietnam and taking away timber and seafood products. The former American-built military airport, now used for domestic flights, was being up-graded to international standard in anticipation of an increase in tourists, businessmen and air cargo.

By 1989, the standard photo of former president Ho Chi Minh, seen in all buildings in Vietnam, had been replaced in my Danang hotel by a stylised painting of an American singer. As a gesture of goodwill, the local authorities had closed the Museum of American Crimes (ironically, the former American Consulate), and would not allow even journalists to see the evidence of brutality. Since the end of the war the museum had displayed graphic pictures of Americans killing Vietnamese civilians, burning houses and using chemical warfare, and featured rows of large glass jars preserving new-born babies with gross deformities, the result of exposure to dioxin (Agent Orange) which was sprayed over vast areas of South Vietnam by the US and South Vietnam Air Force during the war. (The museum made no mention of atrocities committed by the North Vietnamese or the Viet Cong against the Vietnamese people.)

Most foreign visitors had been subjected to a routine propaganda tour of the museum. Instead local authorities now ushered businessmen around the province's many potential developments, from glass and carpet factories to sand and granite deposits. Quangnam–Danang province was famous for silk which was now being exported to France, Italy, Thailand, Singapore, Japan and Hong Kong, and for handwoven woollen carpets which were going to mainly socialist countries.

According to Ngo Van Tran, Director of the Foreign Economic Relations Department, more lucrative resources were offshore—

sea products and fuels. By late 1990 more than 120 foreign fishing boats were working Vietnamese waters, most from Thailand, Taiwan and Hong Kong, along with nine European, Canadian and Indian oil companies (including BP, Shell and Total) attempting to tap deposits off Haiphong, Danang and Vung Tau. 'The most difficult problem with all developments is that we lack capital and foreign markets. We have agricultural products we cannot export—paper, ground nuts (peanuts), sand, cassava, cashews, soyabeans and green bean.' Tran admitted the economy suffered from inappropriate decisions. 'Because we won the war, we thought we could do anything successfully, so we have made many mistakes in economic management. And we closed the doors for too long.' This kind of self-criticism was part of *doi moi*, and no doubt he would have criticised nothing more than what had been ideologically sanctioned by higher authorities.

While Tran happily talked within the 'official' confines, others who went outside those limits were not prepared to be named. One middle-ranking cadre was surprisingly vocal in his condemnation of Vietnam's involvement in Cambodia and the current leadership, but panicked when he thought he was going to be identified. 'When we are attacked, there are many ways to defend ourselves without taking up arms. The Khmer Rouge attacked across the border, and we responded by entering the whole country, but I think we could have avoided the Cambodian war,' he said. 'Many Westerners think the Vietnamese are warring people and in some ways that is true—we have had more than 1000 years of fighting, and in my time we've never had peace. When you have a fighting mind you don't have a peaceful approach. Our old leaders are better at leading in fighting, not in peace time. Peace is a time for intellectuals, for people with the mind, not the hands.' He fell silent and I guess he had said more than his indoctrination allowed. Instead of pursuing the conversation I went with him and several friends to a coffee shop where we talked about how he could not afford to replace his dilapidated bicycle with a much dreamed-of Simson motorbike from East Germany.

A few blocks away, beside the Han River, I found the former US Press Centre which had become a fish factory. Opposite, an elegant if unpretentious building housed a remarkable collection of statues from an ancient empire. The four-room museum, built by the French Institute for Far East Studies in 1936 as a series of open pavilions, housed remains from the Cham kingdom—Asia's equivalent of the Roman Empire—which extended over what is now southern Vietnam, eastern Cambodia and southern Laos from the 2nd to the 15th centuries AD. These were not the best examples of Cham art; the finest were carried off by French archaeologists to be later displayed in their country's museums or in private collections.

Wandering amid well preserved and well presented sandstone statues, busts, friezes and altars, I was taken back 1200 years to when Cham craftsmen carved masterpieces. In front of me was an altar depicting the wedding of Prince Rama to Princess Sita in which more than 60 delicate characters were masterfully crammed into four scenes. Craftsmen also left their mark in elaborate statues of elephants, lions, deer and cows. Some human statues had stunningly realistic faces; others had strangely distorted features, such as flat noses, thick lips, bulging eyes and heavy eyebrows. The Chams took aspects of Buddhism, Hinduism and Islam and combined them, as could be seen in several small Buddha statues.

Many pieces in the museum and in Paris came from My Son, a prized archaeological site 68 kilometres southwest of Danang. This was the Cham's only holy land, from the 4th to 12th centuries AD, during which time about 100 temples were built in a beautiful valley surrounded by rocky mountains. It was here that the kings came to worship their gods and erect temples. Although less grandiose and less diverse than Cambodia's magnificent Angkor Wat and the vast temples of Pagan in Burma, it represented a much longer culture, covering seven centuries. My Son also holds a mystery that archaeologists only guess at: how do the bricks of the towers and temples hold together? A popular theory is that the Chams used a kind of botanical oil common in the central provinces. The first monuments were built in the 4th century AD, although none of these remain. Only 20 of the more than 70 built between the 7th and 13th centuries survived weather and wars—many were damaged or destroyed during the French and American–Vietnam wars. Most remaining temples, once dazzlingly adorned with laminated gold, had been reduced to ruins, although the provincial government regarded My Son as potentially a major tourist attraction, and attempts were being made to restore the temples with the help of Polish archaeologists.

South to Saigon

I realised that all my Western concepts and training were useless in an Eastern environment.
Western doctor returning after 15 years

The rugged blue hills south of Danang are referred to by Westerners as the Marble Mountains as three contain valuable deposits, but to the Vietnamese they are the Ngu Hanh, the five Element Mountains, so named for they represent the elements earth, water, fire, metal and wood. According to legend, the five limestone peaks were the remains of a cracked egg shell from which a turtle spirit emerged.

Thuy (Water) Mountain was famous for the Trang Thiem Pagoda, built more than 200 years ago by King Tia Long. I climbed part-way up the mountain, then feeling like Alice in Wonderland, I followed a fairytale path which led through several ancient stone arches to the entrance of a vast inky cavern guarded by a gargantuan Buddha statue, said to have been carved from rock by King Long's children.

Dankish steps descended in almost total darkness to the bowels of the mountain from where impregnating odours filled the air and I detected an unpleasant amalgam of bat smells and stale incense. Halfway down, before my eyes adjusted to the darkness, I was confronted by two grotesque statues, one on each side of the steps guarding the inner sanctum. These were the personal protectors of Huyen Khong grotto. Once inside I found myself in an area that could have accommodated a seven-storey office block. The floor of the cave was damp hard-trodden earth and issued a distinct odour and atmosphere. Thirty metres above, harsh shafts of light pierced through cracks in the ceiling, casting ghostly images from dangling vines and roots protruding from the ground above. I was told that during the American–Vietnam War, the cave was used by the Viet Cong and North Vietnamese Army as a first aid station, and was bombed, resulting in the ceiling cracks. In this enormous cavern were two temples, several shrines and a number of Buddha statues. It was an eerie yet captivating place,

where silent worshippers moved like floating figures through the smoky air. High above one temple grew stalactites which with some imagination depicted a frog pouncing on a bird and half of an old man's screwed up face. (Other visitors said they saw the leg of a horse and the tail of a fish.) I was led to a tiny niche in the cave wall and in the darkness told to feel two rounded water-worn stalagmites, said to represent breasts. One was wet, the other dry, because according to the legend, when the king touched one it stopped producing milk.

Emerging from the cave, we climbed on up the mountain, following a narrow path which wove between boulders and unidentified bushes. The air was cool and fresh. At the pinnacle, a rock formed a natural archway over the trail and we lingered there in the shade for a while, taking photos and talking to two girls selling battered cans of soft drink which presumably they carried up the mountain each day, then down again if unsold. A middle-aged beggar in what Westerners would call rags approached me and after I gave him some dong he returned to sit on his rock with the subtle manoeuverings of a territorial cat. Below, a wide sandy beach stretched southwards like a pure white ribbon slightly curved by the wind.

Heading down the ocean side of the mountain, we stopped at a temple where women in white robes faced a draped Buddha. Kneeling they bowed their brows towards the floor, and a young brown-robed monk reverently struck a gong. While I stood quietly taking photos, several women caught my eye and smiled like sheepish schoolgirls caught out of class. Outside, a nun appeared from apparently nowhere and presented me with a mug of water. I returned the favour by taking her photo but, as with many older people, her smile disappeared and her pose became stiff, military-like, with clenched fists beside thighs.

I had seen the spectacular beach from the mountain and now, after climbing up and down, I was longing for a swim, and was further tempted when I saw three girls bathing fully dressed, as was the norm here. They splashed and frolicked, then emerged with shirts and trousers clinging to their bodies. Without bathers or a change of clothes I was forced to forego my frolic.

An abandoned hull lay half buried beneath sand. Further along the beach, bicycles were propped up against a 'basket boat' or traditional *thung*. One and a half metres in diameter, these vessels are made from tightly woven bamboo covered in a thick water-proof resin and are the Vietnamese equivalent of a fisherman's dinghy. Paddled in a seesaw motion, these round boats seemed to defy physics but somehow they move forward with surprising speed.

Just south of here in 1535, a trader, Antonio Da Faria, sailed into a sheltered harbour, raised the Portuguese flag and established the first permanent European settlement in what is now Vietnam. Earlier, a Japanese named Fuji Maru had built a small village here, but it was not until Da Faria arrived that the settlement known as Faifo became the main trading center for the southern half of Vietnam, serving Chinese, Japanese, Dutch, Italian, French and English merchants. It was here too that the Catholic missionaries established Vietnam's first church. The Portuguese hoped Faifo would become a major enclave like Macau on the coast of China, but alas, the arrival of the Chinese in the 17th century transformed it into a Chinese rather than a Portuguese center.

Faifo has since been renamed Hoi An, but remained much as

it was in the 17th century, with narrow streets, wooden houses, quaint bridges, and strong Portuguese and Chinese influences: bulbous lanterns, decorated doors, ornate carvings and dark interiors. It had ignored in a sleepy way the advancing years, and remained as a living museum of a past era. Men met at corner cafes to prattle and rattle as traders would have done, and worshippers burned incense as their forbears had. In dim corners, panels with exquisitely inlaid mother-of-pearl characters told poetic stories in Chinese characters. At the riverside wharf, small freighters and fishing boats bobbed and bumped. Lithe shirtless bodies lumbered Indonesian cement from the waterside to warehouses, and children guarded red chillies drying on the footpath.

The 6000 Chinese who lived in Hoi An were descendants of five small groups who sailed here from southeast China in the 1600s. Each of the five groups retained its identity and had its own pagoda. The Phuc Kien pagoda, maintained by descendants of those who are believed to have come from Fukieu province in 1697, was the largest and best preserved. Inside, visitors entered a mystical, mythical world which could have been in Kowloon or Canton. Incense filled its dim niches and small rooms. On one wall, a painting depicted a man on horseback riding into battle in 17th century China. Two colourful statues on the main altar represented the mythological characters of Thien Ly Nhan (meaning eye) who was believed to 'see 10 000 miles', and Thien Ly Nhi (ear) who was supposedly able to 'hear 10 000 miles'. A stiff graceless statue of Thien Hua, heaven's daughter who was responsible for helping people in danger, stared over the world from her resting place behind the main altar.

We took a dirt road to a nearby beach, past vast prawn farms where caretakers lived in small straw huts between ponds where noisy little pumps worked continuously to aerate the water. A dozen primitive cafes stretched along the beach. Young women huddled under tarpaulins to avoid the sun, and tittered when I photographed them. Something had been prodding the back of my mind, and there, with the giggling girls, I realised what it was: the forthrightness of the Vietnamese. They wouldn't catch your eye then divert their gaze, but instead looked you right in the eye without flinching.

Just off the coast, on two small islands, a select group of men, nicknamed the gold diggers, gathered birds' nests from high cliffs, crevasses and caves. These were not ordinary nests, but those of salangane swallows, which built their nests with an inordinate amount of saliva, regarded by the Chinese and Vietnamese as a life-giving force. Nest collecting was a rare skill, often passed from father to son, and sometimes boys as young as six and seven were shown how to scale high cliffs for these precious nests which would be processed in Danang then exported to Hong Kong, Singapore, Japan, Thailand, the Philippines, or to satisfy the desires of wealthy diners in Ho Chi Minh. Extracts from the nests would be used in tablets or medicinal syrups to cure a range of ailments, notably heart and lung complaints.

Back on Highway One, we came across a funeral procession where a brightly decorated altar and coffin were being carried by pole bearers dressed in white. As Nhan explained, 'Traditionally, Buddhists buried their dead and Chams were burned, but now many Buddhists also cremate their deceased because it is easier to look after the ashes in the home or pagoda. In the Mekong Delta they usually burn because the land is too valuable to bury. For a Buddhist funeral, monks come to the home to pray for a happy life in the next world, the family puts rice, fruit and flowers on the altar for the deceased in the next life, and incense is burned in a bowl beside a picture of the deceased.' After one or two days, the altar and coffin, which is painted red and decorated with flowers, are carried by up to 20 people from the family home to the cemetery or the crematorium, where people wail and burn joss sticks. The spouse and children wear long white robes and other mourners wear dark colours.

Half the highway seemed to be taken up by a continuous row of recently harvested rice spread out to dry in the hot sun. It was constantly swept with long handled soft brooms or stirred by women with wooden rakes—or occasionally with their bare feet—and driven over by bicycles and trucks. Some of the women were tossing it in shallow baskets to separate the chaff which was then carried away by the breeze. After being treated thus for one to two days it would be scooped into huge baskets or bags and taken away for storage.

As a Westerner used to modern trucks with soft seats and air-conditioned cabs, I was a little taken aback when I first saw a laden Vietnamese log truck. The cabin was non-existent and the log extended through to the front of the truck, so the driver and passenger sat shoulder to shoulder with a gigantic fallen tree which dwarfed them. Like huge missiles on wheels, these trucks took valuable hardwoods from the mountains bordering Laos to local and ultimately international markets.

Local buses were short and squat, disproportionately high with snub noses, and looked dangerously unbalanced when piled high with goods. Pigs in cylindrical cane baskets shaded with eucalypt branches travelled on roofs, and some protested with furious squealing when the bus stopped and the rooftop cargo was rearranged.

One such bus—which looked as if it ought to be in a museum but was nevertheless crammed with people and stacked high with goods—hit a dog as it hurtled through bustling Tam Ky town. When the dog emitted its deathly howl, people momentarily froze and a toddler burst into tears. It left me with an inner chill, and the silence in the van suggested my fellow travellers were also thinking of the brown dog with pointy ears, but after a brief reflection, Nhan's son resumed his animated chatter.

South of here, the landscape turned to sand dunes where even casuarinas struggled to survive. Houses and fields were derelict, the former made of corrugated iron held together with rocks and wire, some nothing more than twisted rusted iron scrap jumbled beside the road. I spoke into my tape recorder: 'very very very poor', and the poverty really tore at me this time. These people had nothing but their corrugated iron huts, not even a sprout of vegetation—the environment offered nothing but a wasteland. The inhabitants were as destitute as their landscape. I couldn't imagine what sort of lives they led.

Vietnam seemed not to have prominent slum areas like the Black Hole of Calcutta, or Hong Kong's Walled City, or Bangkok's Klong Toey. Here almost everyone appeared to live in poverty which was spread throughout the country rather than concentrated in particular areas. The Red River and Mekong Deltas were wealthier than the northern and central provinces, but only marginally. I had the impression that around 90 per cent of the population made up the (poor) middle class, 5 per cent were in dire poverty, and 5 per cent represented the wealthy, although when I visited in 1992 the wealthier were more obvious, especially in Ho Chi Minh.

Opposite this pathetic collection of corrugated homes, was the former American air base of Chu Lai which once stretched along the coast for about 10 kilometres and served as the most important US base after Bien Hoa, near Saigon. Now a wasteland of exposed sand dunes, it was a lifeless reminder of a past era. Generally, the Vietnamese try to forget the war, but how could these people forget when they have tar-covered mounds separating them from their beloved sea?

The mountains to the west were pale and inviting. Yet I wondered what secret horrors they still retained from 20 years ago when they were bombed, stripped of vegetation and scarred for decades. The once magnificent forests of Tra My, Kham Duc and Tan An were now reduced to black stumps protruding from useless savana grasslands—no longer home to man, or beast. Staring at the blue-grey distance, it again struck me that war is not just wicked, but unforgivably monstrous.

As if the others in the van sensed my thoughts, we continued in silence to the next province, Nghia Binh, where the town of Chau O—renamed Binh Son but defiantly clinging to its old identity—straddled a wide river. Houses on stilts lined the banks and wooden boats lulled patiently. Three brown-clothed monks with wide-brimmed hats cycled towards Danang.

At 11.30 a.m., the road was crowded with school children bicycling home after morning lessons—all in white shirts, with identical brown satchels either balanced on handlebars or clutched to sides. It was close to the hottest part of the day, and several shirts clung to sweaty backs, as bicycles weaved and wobbled with childish enthusiam. The children appeared so carefree, educated but unspoilt. I would have liked to have known them, to be part of their jokes.

The girls rode in twos or threes, upright with long hair trailing behind. It was then that I realised virtually all school-age girls had long hair, most middle-aged women wore their hair short, but it was rare to see old women without their long hair bunned. At what point they made the transition I was not sure, for there seemed to be no women in the intermediate stages.

When we made a comfort stop beside a small river where ducks squawked and splashed in shallow water, I was again reminded why Vietnamese women opted for baggy trousers which could be pulled up rather than down. Although the fields are deserted at midday, there are always eyes willing to spot a bare bum.

An aged man hauled a fishing net through a pond, and a lone woman ambled along a dirt track carrying a basket on each shoulder. Rice paper dried on woven frames, and manioc chips dried on the road—it would later be used in cooking, or crushed into a powder to make noodles or cakes. Beautiful long-legged white cranes strutted and pecked in the fields with the authority of those who belong. A signpost suggested we were 1014 kilometres from Lang Son, but the landscape suggested another country. Here, the fields were flat and fecund, the houses were made of thatch rather than clay, and the dress more modern.

Now well past the old north–south divide, I reflected on the extremes of what had been two countries between 1954 and 1975. In mountainous Lang Son peasants scratched earth's skin to make a living and hid inner thoughts with smiles. Here, a land of flat green fields and wide brown rivers, laughter came easily. In the north, tradition was revered and expressed in house, dress and dance. In southern cities, tradition had been lost to a melting pot of modernity, liberalism and Westernism, and the dance was more likely to be disco than folk. Here, a bride in white dress may be driven to church in an old Chevy, but north of Hanoi she would wear traditional dress of heavy cloth and bright embroidery and probably walked.

On my first trip to Vietnam I moved south down Highway One, but on the second visit I spent two weeks in Ho Chi Minh then a delightful two weeks in Danang before reaching Hanoi, and having moved south to north the most noticeable difference between the two for me were the smiles. In the south and centre, a smile was always returned, but in the north smiles were much slower in coming, and sometimes I received stony bewilderment, a puzzled look that seemed to say, 'Is she crazy, why is she smiling at me?' In the centre and south children flocked around and were a delight, but in the north they were more hesitant, presumably because during the war Westerners were regarded as the enemy by those in the north, and possibly because Government control was tighter and it was still not acceptable to associate with foreigners.

About 130 kilometres south of Danang and just north of Quang Ngai (the next major town) a dirt road led off Highway One towards the small fishing village of Song My where American soldiers killed more than 500 civilians in a four-hour rampage that became known as the My Lai Massacre. It happened on 16 March 1968.

The Americans, believing the village was harbouring a Viet Cong battalion and spoiling for a fight, shot or stabbed almost everything that moved, and then set fire to homes. But the enemy was not there. No Viet Cong was seen and not a shot was fired at the Americans, yet they continued their rampage. Elderly people and children were not spared. Many women were raped, sodomised, scalped, disembowelled and had their hands cut off. Bodies were strewn around the village; many were found heaped in ditches, some still alive buried under the dead.

Although 504 civilians and no enemy were killed, US reports said 28 civilians had been accidently killed in crossfire and 128 Viet Cong eradicated. My Lai was hailed as a great success; the commander of US forces in Vietnam, General William Westmoreland, sent congratulatory telegrams to Charlie and Bravo companies; a helicopter pilot was awarded for bravery against hostile forces. (Ironically, the hostile forces were American soldiers trying to kill civilians. The pilot had placed his aircraft between the soldiers and civilians, aimed his guns at the Americans and threatened to shoot them if they shot the civilians.)

It was 18 months before the truth of My Lai reached the American public. Consequently, 12 officers were charged with covering up a war crime, but all charges were later dropped. There was said to be sufficient evidence to charge 18 soldiers with murder, attempted murder, rape and sexual assault, but none were convicted. The entire blame for the My Lai Massacre was shifted to William Calley, the leader of Charlie Company's 1st platoon, who was charged with murdering 109 civilians. Found guilty of murdering 22 civilians, he was given a life sentence with hard labour which was reduced to 20 years, then 10 years, and in 1975 he was released on parole without spending a day in jail due to the personal intervention of President Richard Nixon.

After much detouring and backtracking, we found our hotel in Quang Ngai, a double- and triple-storey town with a wide main street. At $10 a night, the hotel was the cheapest I stayed at on this trip. The standard was quite reasonable, with a double bed, 'Made-In-China' sheets and a mosquito net. However, once I had turned off the light it would not come on again, and just as I was about to squat under the tap, the water ceased running.

We had been eating extremely well although our gastronomic excesses were certainly not an indication of how the locals ate with an average of 13 kilograms of rice per person per month. Some meals cost the five of us as much as 14 000 dong. Although only $4.50 to us, it was a third of a factory worker's monthly wage.

We usually had breakfast on the street, but lunch and dinner at a tourist hotel or restaurant, where I paid for all of us, and Nhan and his family ate well. In Quang Ngai, Nhan's wife and son declined dinner, so Nhan took Ben and I to a street cafe for the first time. After my considerable experience with Asian 'restaurants', eating in a small dark room with a dirt floor, using chewed chopsticks, and having dogs lingering around the tables made me immediately apprehensive, but so as not to offend I turned a blind eye to my surroundings and ate. The result was diarrhoea within hours. (Guides were told not to take foreigners to such places, and one later told me that when a foreigner insisted on trying locally brewed unbottled beer, the guide poured canned Heineken into his glass then brought it to the table.)

Breakfast at a small open-air cafe the next morning was only marginally more hygienic. It attracted more flies than I had ever seen, and they sat all over my bread and honey roll, the coffee, the table, the noodles—everything. While Nhan and his family ate, I entertained myself taking photos of pool players at an open-fronted shop next door. Half a dozen young men tapped balls around a small battered table, and when two posed on the edge of the table for their photo to be taken, I was reminded of a 1960s cigarette ad.

Out in the fields, 825 kilometres from Ho Chi Minh, the harvest was being gathered by women draped in protective scarves and men with bare backs. Their shoulder and back muscles were extraordinary, yet they were so skinny, like poles of muscle. Older women were seen in the markets and to a lesser extent along the roads, but old men were scarce. 'They die earlier than women because they work harder than women,' said Nhan with a twinkle in his eye that suggested he had been down this path before with a women's 'libber'. 'Some play cards and drink at home or in the cafes, while the women work,' he added, and I wasn't sure whether he was teasing or appeasing.

Country life here was as colourful as anywhere in Asia: a bride rode pillion on a Honda with her white veil streaming behind; trucks top-heavy with sugar cane sagged and swayed precariously as they cornered; cafes hid beneath bright drooping bougainvillea; neatly planted casuarinas and eucalyptus encircled orange orchards; cows wore hand-woven straw muzzles to prevent them eating rice plants; hand painted road signs warned of road works; and people on old Dodge buses slept, sitting any which way.

The flat coastal strip south of Quang Ngai made this a more productive area, and here, amid the neat rice patches of Mo Duc district, we passed the small thatched house where former Prime Minister Pham Van Dong was born in 1906. Coming from an educated family, young Dong was sent to Hue's elite Quoc Hoc high school where he became involved in the student movement. In 1930 he joined Ho Chi Minh and colleagues in Hong Kong to form the clandestine Indochina Communist Party. (After Le Duc Tho died in 1990, Dong was the only surviving member of the original stalwarts). Arrested by the French in the 1930s, he was sent to the notorious Poulo Condon island prison until the end of World War II when all prisoners were released. His close friend Ho Chi Minh appointed him Foreign Minister in the post-French government, and he later became Prime Minister. The elder statesman, regarded by many Vietnamese as the most popular leader after Ho, spent his latter years as an adviser to the Party's Central Committee.

After leaving Dong's district we came across many bridges in need of repair and negotiating some was nerve-racking, although generally the road was in reasonable condition, allowing us to do 90 kilometres per hour in sections.

When I returned in mid-1990, a bridge replacement program was in full swing, and detours around construction sites became a little tedious. However, wide modern bridges still alternated with rickety single-lane Bailey-bridges left after the war. At regular intervals the road was dissected by new culverts carrying water between the fields, and it was necessary to almost stop to pass over them. House building had also taken on a vigorous momentum, with many towns sporting new single- and double-storey brick homes and shops. The other notable change was the emergence of recycled Coke and Fanta bottles selling oil and petrol from small wooden tables beside the road, indicative of the new privatisation policy.

During my April 1990 trip, roadworks often halted our progress. At one stop, while lumbering black machines rolled back and forth over steaming tar, I wandered over to a tile factory where hardened women were softening clay with water and moulding it into rough slabs which were slipped under a hand-operated press. Like labourers on any production site, they were bored with the repetitive process, and welcomed me as a diversion. We laughed and joked as best we could with sign language, and when I re-emerged, the van and my colleagues were on the other side of the freshly-sealed bridge. By the time I reached them, my shoes were covered in soft sticky tar. I wrapped them in newspaper and left them on the floor, not sure whether I would ever wear them again.

A large state-owned salt farm near Sa Huynh consisted of neat rectangular ponds and the occasional pile of white raw salt. The vast salt flats extended into the distance, broken only by scurrying black blotches as dozens of workers busied themselves raking and bagging the precious sun-dried salt. Thin white bags stood stiffly beside the road.

Highway One rejoined the coast briefly at Sa Huynh. Driving past, I filled my nostrils with fresh salt air which seemed to give instant energy. After bouncing down a dusty road for days, it seemed like paradise. Peaceful and cool. Twice in 1990 I stayed at the Sa Huynh 'guest house' which was classed as a resort but was no more than a truckies' stopover, and I nominated it the most appalling hotel in the most romantic setting. After recovering from an electric shock which threw me against the bathroom wall, I sat on the beach till midnight listening to the waves and watching prawn boats working off the coast, their lights blinking from afar. Nowhere in Vietnam did I find a seat so cool, quiet and fresh. Just after dawn, a mist rolled in off the sea to engulf the 'resort' and surrounding hills. The sea disappeared, but the memory lingered.

South of Sa Huynh the highway, railway and telephone lines intersected several times as we zigzagged through flatlands and hills covered in thick scrub and huge boulders. Riding the hills made a pleasant change from the flatness, and summits offered sweeping views. This area was most prominent for its acres of reed which was cut when a metre high, then laid along the road to dry before being bundled and later used for roofing, baskets and sleeping mats.

Children splashed in several huge ponds covered in white lotus—the most versatile of plants. Seeds from the heads of the lotus would be collected and eaten raw, cooked in soup or used in medicine; the sweet roots were eaten fresh or cooked; and the stems (bitter but good for health) would be chopped up for soup pots or added to tea. I was once warned earnestly not to eat the green coating of the seed as it caused infertility.

When travelling with Nhan, we would hit the road early each morning, rarely stopping except for lunch and pre-arranged visits. It may have been his way of operating, or perhaps he was under instructions not to stop, or he may simply have wanted to get back to his beloved Saigon as quickly as the road permitted.

When I retraced this route in early 1990, each time with a different Government guide, we still left early morning and drove hard all day and half the night, but broke the journey with many unscheduled stops. The fact we were allowed spontaneous interviews was partly a reflection of the 'loosening-up' which followed the 6th Party Congress, although after mid-April, just before the 15th anniversary of the 'fall of Saigon', the door began to close again, which meant, like several other journalists, I was not allowed to visit certain areas in central Vietnam.

One of those unscheduled stops early in 1990 was at Hoai Nhon where I disappeared into the labyrinthine market to take photos. A crowd soon formed around me, and before long I could barely move. I was again hemmed in, with the claustrophobic smell of hard work and uncleaned teeth, stale clothes and yesterday's garlic. They touched me, my clothes, my bag, and chattered vigorously as if analysing each freckle, each stitch, each button. Someone threw a handful of gravel to disperse the crowd. The result was a furious argument between a couple of women. Vietnamese women may be regarded as reticent—what is more demure than a long-haired beauty in an *ao dai*?—but in the market they could fight like alley cats. Only a few nights before, I had witnessed a smartly-dressed woman in her early 30s—one of Danang's trendies—arguing with a cyclo driver. The poor man had lost the argument before he uttered a word.

Twice in early 1990 I returned to Hoai Nhon, known as Bong Son during the war. The first time was with a remarkable Vietnamese woman, Dang Thi Thanh, when she was returning home after major reconstructive cranio-facial surgery in Australia. Remarkable, because she survived perhaps the worst napalm injuries of the war (a more severe injury would have been fatal); remarkable also for her personality.

For 17 years, from the age of nine, she had lived with a hideous facial disfiguration—not unlike that of the 'elephant man'—which caused extreme emotional as well as physical torment. The heat of a 1972 napalm attack 'melted' the skin and flesh of her lower face onto her neck and chest, welding her chin to her chest and left shoulder, where it remained until 1989 when surgeons literally cut her from ear to ear and separated chin from chest. For the first time since she was a child, Thanh could lift her head and eat normally— and smile. After three major operations and eight months of treatment she returned to Vietnam with a new face and new personality.

As a friend of Thanh's I was asked by the medical team to accompany her from Bangkok to her village west of Hoai Nhon.

During that six-day trip, Bangkok–Saigon–Danang–Hoai Nhon, we developed a special bond which negated language and cultural barriers. Again, I was reminded in the most intimate ways that we were women first and nationality came a distant second. I will never forget how, through eyes, not words, she challenged me to react to the hideous groin scar left after the surgeons removed a flap to create a new chin; I then realised that the two small black hairs on her chin were probably pubic hairs.

When Thanh arrived at her mud-and-thatch village at the end of a meandering dirt track, she was greeted by the entire population which laid down tools and abandoned classrooms to see the 'new' Thanh. Her village had not changed, but she had. She had been partly Westernised, a process not easily reversed. And in those first few hours, seeing the poverty again for the first time in eight months, she was confused and wretched, and sought emotional support, but it was my shoulder she cried on, not her mother's.

That day in Thanh's hamlet I learned a lot about relationships and life in a remote rural village. Crowds swarmed into her yard and, like over-enthusiastic football spectators, pushed down the fence. Here, everything was public property—the fence, the yard, even other people's children belonged to everyone. Thanh's mother had not greeted her with any sign of emotion, not even a welcoming hug, which was later explained as a typical reserved response in the presence of a foreigner. While Thanh cried openly in front of the villagers—which was definitely not typical in Vietnam—her mother and sisters remained indoors, embarrassed that they had not prepared a meal for the foreigner. After much debate, Thanh, the interpreter and I were taken by the village chiefs to the local 'restaurant'. After further procrastination they announced there was no food. Only eggs and bananas could be found, so we were served greasy fried eggs—or were they 'omelettes'?—and green bananas with lukewarm tea. It was one of the least gourmet meals I had eaten, but it was the most memorable.

I returned to Thanh's village two weeks later with a film crew making a documentary on facial disfiguration. She admitted it had not been easy readjusting to life in rural Vietnam and said she realised she could not flaunt her Western clothes without creating resentment, which obviously disappointed her as she was proud of her new acquisitions.

While bouncing towards Quy Nhon, our next destination, with Nhan and his family asleep in the back, I noted some of the practical aspects of travelling by road in Vietnam. By now I was used to the bumpy roads, constant horn tooting, sudden stops, jerky swerves and exhaust fumes, and found travel no problem, especially south of the 17th parallel where the highway had improved considerably and was similar to other Asian roads except for the streams of people and bicycles.

Westerners could only stay in certain hotels, and local authorities were notified in advance of a foreigner's visit, but lack of phones meant they couldn't be notified of a delay or changed schedule, so several times we had to drive well into the night to reach our destination, passing other hotels en route. Before I left Hanoi, I had to submit to the Press Department a list of places I wanted to visit and people to interview, and if I decided en route to add another interview to my itinerary, it had to be cleared by the Press Department in Hanoi. This required several telexes and several days' delay, which was not possible on this trip. (During a visit to Hue in May 1989, the local authorities had not received permission from Hanoi to grant my requested interviews—the vital telex had not been sent—so my one-day stay had to be extended to four days. On the other hand, the Lang Son authorities did not receive a telex from Hanoi on my first visit, yet instantly arranged a program.)

As we bounced southwards I realised one of the many reasons I enjoyed being here was the instant friendliness and hospitality of the people. Nowhere were we left standing. Drinks were always served before talking began. Body language—especially touching within sexes—was much more prevalent than I had encountered elsewhere. It seemed natural to put a hand on the arm of someone I had known only for half an hour, or to hold hands with another woman.

As my reflections deepened, I began to feel very emotional, without knowing if it was because I was so far from my own family, physically and socially, or because I felt a real affinity with the people here. Perhaps it was because we were driving through beautiful countryside at dusk and that softened the senses. This was my first visit to Vietnam, and I resolved to return many times. I had similar sentiments when I had been in Yugoslavia, and also towards the older Chinese people when I had lived in Hong Kong. They seemed to hold a mystery that was unfathomable, a secret locked from all except those diligent and dedicated enough to attempt to understand what lay behind the facade.

Remembering my conversation with the Danang forestry official about Cambodia, I realised just how saddened I was by what had happened to Cambodia in the past 20 years. It was a country little understood by the outside world, and here I was, close to it, circling all around it—literally and philosophically—but not yet able to touch its soil, or talk to its long-suffering people.

Driving through the south of Nghia Binh province, I was reminded that during the American–Vietnam War, the US II Corps established several important bases west of here, notably at An Khe, Happy Valley, Pleiku, Plei Me and Hawthorne. These hills, many covered in thick forest, were also home to Viet Cong guerillas. After flying over the area on his first day in Vietnam in 1965, First Cavalry helicopter pilot Robert Mason commented, 'It looked like a great place to have a guerilla war, if you were going to be the guerilla.' In the next 12 months Mason flew more than 1000 combat missions around the mountains and valleys of these central provinces, between the coast and Cambodia, dropping men and supplies, collecting the wounded and the dead, and ferrying intelligence officers and commanders. His exploits in these parts later became the basis of the autobiography, *Chicken-hawk*, which I had read on a beach in Thailand but had not comprehended until coming here.

His descriptions of the provincial capital Quy Nhon and his mis-adventures with the city's bar girls were amusing but irreconcilable with the city 23 years later. I found Quy Nhon, 300 kilometres south of Danang and 300 kilometres north of Nha Trang, an odd mixture of modernity and quaintness, a country town trying to be a seaside resort and a bustling small-scale metropolis. Aged jacaranda trees shaded streets, and bright red and pink bougainvillea crept around shops, houses and fences, livening up what would otherwise be a poor shabby city. The other redeeming feature of this potpourri town was a palm-dotted sandy beach—very alluring on a hot day, except it was also dotted with human excreta, left by fishermen who lived in boats on the beach and had nowhere else to relieve themselves. A few metres from me, one dropped his trousers, relieved himself, stood up and walked away without a sideways glance.

Men hung in hammocks strung between palm trees, a group of card players sat on the sand in a tight circle, and a young boy with a tray slung from his neck hawked cigarettes. Something about that boy is still with me—perhaps the eyes searching me, trying to understand this fair-skinned freckly foreigner; or the sadness in his eyes when I walked away without buying. At the beach-side hotel, I complained of a smell which persisted until I realised the offending material had stuck to my shoes after I had inadvertently wandered into the public defecation department on the beach.

The hotel's 'bathroom' was disgusting and unuseable. With the van as my dressing-room, I somehow managed to spruce myself up, look and feel fresh, and be alert enough to ask intelligent questions at my first interview in Quy Nhon.

Party President Truong Dinh Trac talked of converting Quy Nhon and its beautiful white beach into a tourist attraction. 'We have made it known to businessmen that they can build hotels and we will be glad to co-operate, but so far no-one has responded,' he said with the kind of fatalism I had noticed among many cadres. They seemed to think all they had to do was make an announcement and their desires would materialise, and when nothing happened their attitude was 'so-be-it, we tried'. 'We have asked private Vietnamese and foreign investors, including Japanese, to set up hotels,' he said. 'They have to submit construction details to the Construction Commission for approval, guarantee comfort and safety for guests, and pay taxes.'

Trac was also hoping to attract foreign investors to establish small industries in this relatively poor province of 2.3 million people. The Soviets were considering a textile and shoemaking factory; East Germany was interested in developing coconut fibre to make mats; Czechoslovakia may be interested in a hydro-electric power project; and a delegation from Poland expressed interest in restoring Cham monuments. 'UNDP [the United Nations Development Program] started a shrimp breeding project in 1987, and we have a well developed shrimp export industry. A Japanese company has begun construction of a ship repair factory, and another Japanese firm has started to examine sand for glass making.'

Inflation was a big problem, he said. He had to be coaxed, however, into saying how much it had affected his personal life. Embarrassed by what he obviously regarded as trivia, he grudgingly revealed he had to pay 300–350 dong for a bowl of noodles which a year before cost only 200 dong, his daily newspaper went from 20 to 50 dong, and beer doubled from 600 to 1200 dong, but his wages increased only marginally—how much, he wasn't going to say.

Quy Nhon had been the temporary base of Australian doctor John O'Donnell who worked at the Holy Family Hospital until the North Vietnamese advanced southwards in April 1975. He and his wife—a nurse at the hospital—were evacuated, but had to leave behind the boy they had unofficially adopted. In 1990, O'Donnell came back and attempted to find the boy, now 19. 'Arriving in Quy Nhon, I had an overpowering sense of, "come back to the place whence you came and know it for the first time". It was as if all the things I'd been thinking of in the past 15 years were crystallised in five minutes. I can't tell you what an intense emotional sense it was to drive through the hospital gates. Halfway through my reception, the Director went out and came back with my old office sign saying Bac Si J O'Donnell. It was very, very emotional. I was in tears. It was my breaking ground, the point of realisation that all my Western concepts and training were useless in an Eastern environment unless I modified.

'I was determined not to leave till I'd made an effort to find the kid's family, but the doctors warned that too many wars and too many years had passed. We found an old nun I'd known before. She remembered everything and said she knew where my old interpreter lived in Ho Chi Minh. There was an enormous sense of discovery when I met the nun, I really felt it was only a matter of time before I'd find the family. I had terribly mixed emotions. In Ho Chi Minh I went looking for the interpreter. We went over the outer suburbs, left, right, down lanes, and it was getting dark and quite scary. Finally, there was the doorway, 472–5. I showed them my album, and a man said "Quy Nhon". He said, "wait here". I sat there for 20 minutes surrounded by 50 people. Then a girl came out and said my interpreter had used this address for the past 15 years but no-one knew where she was. I had a terrible sense of having found and lost all in one. I realised how futile it was to look any further. Like the doctors said in Quy Nhon—too many wars and too many years.'

While many other Asian countries cluttered their streets and roads with giant billboards advertising the alleged benefits of cigarettes or powdered milk, Vietnam's landscape remained relatively free of such visual pollution, although by 1991, advertisments were omnipresent in Ho Chi Minh. Occasionally, Government placards promoted *doi moi*, encouraged food production or warned of road accidents. One depicted, in a highly-stylised way, an accident in which two bodies, a wheel, a headlight and blood lay on the road. Another declared, 'Children are precious and we must protect them'.

Road signs indicating destinations were rare so it was not always easy to find the way out of a town. However, distance posts were plentiful, and I was marvelling at this, until I saw one that suggested Nha Trang was 200 kilometres further on. Then, six kilometres closer to Nha Trang, another said Nha Trang 206 kilometres. I guessed those two posts had been inadvertently swapped until two kilometres further on another said Nha Trang 206 kilometres!

About an hour south of Quy Nhon, and 650 kilometres from Ho Chi Minh, Highway One wound over the Ca Pass which formed the border between Nghia Binh and Phu Khanh provinces. During the American–Vietnam War, the pass was a stronghold of South Korean forces who were entrusted with preventing this vital part of Highway One falling into Viet Cong hands. South Korea, having been supported by America during the Korean War, sent more troops to Vietnam than any other country except America. Its White Horse division of 10 000 to 12 000 men was stationed in Binh Dinh (renamed Nghia Binh) and Phu Khan provinces.

In 1966 a BBC film crew spent almost three months with the South Koreans, known as the Tigers, and 24 years later Australian-born cameraman Butch Calderwood returned to former Tiger territory, near Quy Nhon, to make a documentary. 'Eleven weeks with the Tigers gave us a great insight. They were pleasant to be with but I wouldn't like to be on the other side of them—they were pretty tough. They were also very disciplined. I have film of them going along a trail, suddenly a hand goes up and they all disappeared. You can stop that frame and not see anyone. With the Americans you could smell their aftershave before you saw them,' he said. 'The Tiger's base camp had a gigantic helipad, and tents everywhere. The western suburbs of Quy Nhon were all tents. Quy Nhon wasn't much of a place, and we only went into town three or four times, to have a drink, then fled back. It was really a Dodge City, and it's the same today. The Tigers were responsible for the region around Quy Nhon, and this enormous area was completely safe. It included Phucat—but not An Khe where the Americans had a base—and a town called Go Boi, famous for its *nuoc mam* (fish sauce). One day the *nuoc mam* factory was hit—and what a terrible smell!'

One of Calderwood's most memorable films for the BBC was on pig farming. 'USAID [US Assistance for International Development] decided to improve the quality of pig farming—the Korean major used to say "Vietnamese pigs number 10" [number 1 being the best]. Just outside Quy Nhon, USAID designed and built new pig pens to Milwaukee standards. When they came back they found the pigs were in the Vietnamese houses and the Vietnamese were in the pig pens which had concrete floors and walls and nice roofs. Another USAID project was to ship out from the US, aluminium sheeting rejected by Coca Cola or beer canners because the colours were not right. So you would be driving along and among the thatched roofs was this wonderful house made out of Nestlé or Pabst beer sheeting.'

The Koreans operated a market, on top of a hill near the Ca

Pass, known as Tiger Market. 'Women and children from the other side came for treatment and, sometimes, wounded men came. The Koreans would give them food from their combat rations—then fire on them later in the day. The war stopped for a couple of hours each morning for the market.'

When I passed through in 1988, nothing remained of the market, but Xuan Dai Bay presented another aspect of this surprisingly diverse country. On this remote central coast was a rugged serenity not seen elsewhere. A series of small sandy shores, separated by rocky outcrops jutting into the ocean like short fat fingers clutching at nothingness, and the South China Sea gently pounding the coast, casually tossing 'white horses' into the air with unrestricted gaiety. The area was devoid of life—not even a village could be seen—yet a small cluster of fishing boats lurched and pitched like flimsy toys just off the beach. Further down the coast were long sandy beaches, palm, pine and banana trees, interspersed with mud and thatch cottages.

The landscape was very different from elsewhere—no flat endless fields of rice, just uncultivated hills with little except palm trees, prickly pear and scrub, broken only by an occasional vegetable garden or crop of manioc, sweetcorn or sugar cane—both depressed and depressing. Everywhere the trucks, buses and pick-ups were old—Desoto, Hino, Honda, Izuki—and many lay beside the road waiting for spares or repairs, often with drivers and passengers sitting in the shade of their vehicle. Three four-wheel-drive Toyota Landcruisers, identified as aid vehicles by their 'PAM' or 'Unicef' stickers, were the first we had seen outside Danang, and I wondered what projects their occupants were working on. One of the frustrations of this trip was not being able to stop and ask—it would have taken two months to reach Saigon had we stopped each time I wanted to. Poverty was everywhere: dirty, tatty clothes, scruffy looking children, some with hair tinged ginger, evidence of malnutrition. Brick and tile homes were rare; windows consisted of small branches in vertical rows across a hole in a wall, like the grilles of a prison. People sat on or beside the road as if it was an extension of their homes.

My comment on the harsh living conditions prompted Nhan to relate a Vietnamese saying: 'for a rich man, a cut on the finger is the equivalent of a cut in the throat for a poor man'. The threshold of endurance among the Vietnamese was considerably higher than in the West—they had a seemingly infinite capacity for work and an abnormal ability to endure physical and emotional pain with comparatively little complaint. More fatalistic than Westerners, they seemed to believe suffering was their destiny. Although they were amazingly resilient in the face of war and poverty, a surprising number seemed to go down with non-specific ailments. 'He's sick' or 'She not feel well' was so common I began to wonder if half the nation was struck with a mystery illness.

Further south, galvanised iron replaced thatch on the roofs of some homes, and those made of brick or concrete were painted with bright coloured patterns, triangles and squares—blue, green, purple, yellow, red, orange—which made a cheery contrast to the monotone of mud and thatch. It grew dark, so the travelling circus in the blue van stopped at a cluster of roadside cafes for a meal. Before the doors were even open a group of children descended on us. Their initial target was the driver, but Ben ignored them and wandered off to give the cafes a quick inspection, before opting for one with teenagers playing cards outside and several men eating inside.

The cafe he chose was larger and cleaner than its neighbours. It was run by an energetic 40-year-old grandmother, Le Thi Thom, who had been a farmer before setting up her private cafe, which consisted of a rectangular building with a wide open front, palm-leaf walls and brick floor. From the thatch roof, supported by eight sturdy wooden pillars, hung two kerosene lamps. Devoid of decoration other than necessities, it attracted the custom of mainly truck drivers.

Initially Thom was reluctant to talk and I could not be sure whether this was because she was busy or my translator was a Government official, but she eventually did while her daughters prepared the food. She said she decided to open a cafe after the Government issued its new policy encouraging private enterprise at the end of 1986. 'We saw more buses and trucks and more restaurants on the road, and decided it was time to open,' she said. The People's Committee took two months to approve her application, then she was allocated a plot of land. The family built the cafe in one month, and opened in September the following year. Of her nine children, aged between 4 and 24 years, three helped run the cafe from early morning until almost midnight, while her husband and the other children continued to farm their small plot two kilometres away. 'At night, I sleep here with some of the children and my husband goes back to the farm,' she said.

Under the palm roof, she served 70 to 100 people a day, taking an estimated 30 000 to 50 000 dong ($7.50 to $12.50) a day, which easily covered the Government's monthly tax of 50 000 dong, but she didn't know, or wouldn't say, how much profit the family was making.

By travelling after dusk we missed the scenery, but night-time activity was just as interesting. In most countries watching the highway ahead was often a recipe for boredom, but in Vietnam it was a kaleidoscope of activity. The road, like footpaths in Vietnamese cities, was used for drying, chopping, washing, storing, playing and sitting, as well as walking, cycling and driving. Apart from bicycles, traffic was rare, so each time we dispersed a group of people from the road it was like breaking up a private party, the equivalent of bursting into a living room and telling everyone to leave. The road dwellers reluctantly moved off what they truly believed was their territory to let vehicular traffic pass; anything faster than a bicycle was regarded as a 'speeding' vehicle.

Travel was slower and more nerve-racking, partly because people didn't see us coming from behind and they often wandered across the road without looking. Some trucks overtook where they shouldn't, and twice we came across four headlights staring at us, sending a chill down my spine. As in the north, a frightening number of trucks had only one headlight, and those that had two kept them on high beam while approaching us.

Coming upon a brightly lit road block in the dark was a little awesome, but the officers with stern looks and wearing the 'CSGT' (Canh Sat Giao Thong) uniforms of transport police didn't stop us—they were more interested in trucks they suspected of carrying blackmarket coffee from the nearby highlands, high quality timber or possibly opium from Laos.

The highlands to the west towards the Cambodian border, are home to 30 or more tribal groups, including the famous Montagnards, a group of tough independent hilltribes who subsistence-farm the rugged high plateau. They regard themselves as a separate race, and resent the Vietnamese, especially the new settlers brought recently from the overcrowded coastal areas to live in Land Development Centers (LDCs). During the American–Vietnam War, they formed impressive self-defense units and carried out highly efficient attacks against the Viet Cong who used the rough sparsely inhabited highlands to launch hit-and-run attacks against Government and American troops.

We arrived in Nha Trang, the capital of Phu Khanh province, after six hours and 300 kilometres, with great relief. The road into the city was lined both sides with small cafes displaying a delightful variety of lights including red bulbs, fluorescent lights, kerosene lamps and tiny flickering candles. Houses were tucked behind bamboo and banana trees and an occasional burgeoning bougainvillea bush. The city was still alive at 10.30 p.m., whereas Hanoi would have been asleep. Bicycles buzzed past; even cyclo drivers pedalled fast. Young women looking smart in bright clothes and a splash of make-up rode behind young men on motorbikes, sitting astride, not side-saddle as in the north. The gaiety and relative wealth was refreshing after the drabness of poverty further north. Outside the railway station, about 100 people milled around, many sleeping or attempting to sleep on ground mats, with their small bundles of possessions beside them. Some were waiting for a train; the rest were an ad hoc collection of traders, food sellers and the homeless. Along the waterfront, dozens of tents were pitched by schoolchildren on a camping excursion.

We had dinner, then checked into the Government-run hotel which seemed to take for ever, even for a veteran like Nhan. As we were being shown to our rooms, a friendly but broad and possibly intoxicated, 'G'day' boomed across the dark courtyard. It was the first Western voice I had heard in seven days and, at almost midnight, in the depths of Vietnam and 1370 kilometres from Hanoi, it was as unexpected as an elephant at a ballet. The voice belonged to Australian fish importer Michael Byrne who lived in the hotel while supervising operations at the local processing factory for Perth-based Independent Seafoods, one of the first Western companies in Vietnam. 'Barter is the best way to do trade here,' he said the next morning. 'Most companies make the mistake of trying to sell their products here, but the Vietnamese can't afford to buy. So we look for products to exchange. We take out $1 million of seafood, chillis, black pepper, tapioca or prawn crackers and supply them with $1 million of goods such as cool stores, processing equipment and consumer items like milk powder and plastics.' (Impressed by this barter system, Vietnamese authorities subsequently referred to the Australian company as a model trader.)

Byrne worked alongside the local Vietnamese processors in the Nha Trang factory, and his hands-on approach had earned respect from the Vietnamese. 'Greg Poland [Independent's Managing Director] came to the factory and taught them how to fillet and prepare fish and pack it properly. Understanding the Vietnamese is essential to doing business here,' said Byrne who had made an effort to eat, speak and think Vietnamese. 'Before the war, the Government insisted on quantity, and fishermen forgot about quality because there was no financial benefit. Five years ago, 80 per cent of their fish for export was spoiled before it hit the beach, now that's down to 65 per cent.'

Other people told me how local fishermen sold their catch

offshore to Thai trawlers in exchange for consumer goods, then returned to port empty or with only part of their catch. As one Westerner said: 'There are Thai boats sitting out there full of beer, whisky, cigarettes and televisions. A lot of seafood never reaches Vietnam, it is caught off the coast and sold out there on the black market.' During a long evening, mixed with frankness and twinges of bitterness, the same Westerner also gave his explanation for the country's economic difficulties: 'The problem is these people have such grand ideas—they want the biggest and best of everything. Take for example the Cau Thang Long bridge in Hanoi which is a great white elephant going nowhere. It was started by the Chinese in 1972, abandoned in 1978 then finished by the Russians. And the Chinese steel mill in Thai Nguyen north of Hanoi, build 20 years ago, it still hasn't reached its capacity. After the 6th Party Congress, 100 projects that had already started were dropped because they just weren't needed.'

Nha Trang's huge bay, protected by Hon Tre island and edged with a magnificent curving sandy beach, was the city's main asset. Calm and sheltered, it was ideal for swimming and water sports, and offered the same potential for development as Thailand's famous Pattaya Beach did 30 years ago. People gathered on the beach early in the morning to sit, paddle and bathe, leaving their bicycles propped upright in the sand. Everyone, male and female, swam in shorts or trousers and a shirt. I was told they lacked swimwear not because they couldn't afford it, but because they were 'shy and afraid of showing their bodies in public'. As Byrne said, it was only a matter of time before the palm-lined beach, dotted with bicycles at dawn, would be sporting striped beach chairs and umbrellas as well. Like their northern neighbours, local cadres here wanted to develop tourism which would bring much-needed foreign currency. They were upgrading the city's two tourist hotels, and had talked with France's Club Med about building a Western-style holiday resort on the picturesque bay.

Although their homes were generally clean, the Vietnamese showed little understanding of environmental pollution and what was expected by Western standards. Rotting garbage, flies on food and scavenging dogs were accepted as the norm. Some cadres admitted they had to clean up the hotels, beaches and cities. Others saw nothing wrong and expected tourists to come anyway, which was partly true as Vietnam had been effectively closed tthe West since American troops left, consequently it was among the few countries in the region that remained unaffected by tourism. Small numbers of Soviet holidaymakers came but were not as fussy as Westerners.

At the People's Committee, Vice-President Nguyen Tuong Thuat talked of his plan to attract tourists and investors. 'We are ready to receive foreign investors to build hotels. We have land, enough electricity and enough manpower—not well trained but we are prepared to train them. We want to produce high quality products. And we don't want to import consumer goods, we want to import equipment and machinery to produce the consumer goods ourselves. We open the door to any foreigner, even overseas Vietnamese who come back—they will have no restrictions and no discrimination—even the countries who fought against us. We are ready to forget the past; in fact we have forgotten the past. What is more important is friendship and co-operation.'

Nearby was the Pasteur Institute which, after the founding institute in Paris is the oldest of the 40 worldwide Pasteur Institutes. It dates back to 1893 when Alexander Yersin, a 27-year-old student of the renowned French scientist Louis Pasteur, landed at Nha Trang, decided it was an ideal place to research rabies, and built a small hut for the purpose. Yersin later went on to Hong Kong and is credited with discovering that rats carry the bacteria that causes plague.

Nha Trang's Pasteur Institute was the only one worldwide to have a woman director—the affable Prof Nguyen Thi The Tram whom I met in her expansive upstairs office overlooking the bay. A native of Nha Trang, she did part of her medical training in East Germany during the American–Vietnam War and was appointed to the Institute at the war's end. Much of her work involved administering health surveys and research projects, although she was still a doctor at heart. 'When one is healthy one forgets us. But when one falls sick, we are to be blamed,' she said. 'Our main concern is for the children,' she said. 'We are responsible for five provinces covering 1000 kilometres with 8.7 million people, and each village must have at least one mobile vaccination unit.' A mobile unit was not a vehicle on four wheels, but a group of three to five people who visited hamlets on foot or by bicycle, carrying with them all they needed. 'Our aim is to vaccinate 80 per cent of children under five against the six preventable childhood diseases but it is dificult to get to the children in the mountains.' Many of the 250 000 children under 12 months suffered Vitamin A deficiency, malnutrition, whooping cough and malaria.

Nhan took me to the Oceanographic Institute to meet Vice-Director Nguyen Huu Phung. The Institute is Vietnam's marine watchdog: monitoring pollution, silting and erosion, assessing typhoon patterns and damage to delicate coral beds. 'We study meteorological conditions—winds, fogs, rain, sunlight, typhoons, water flow, waves—for the petroleum and gas exploration services, and we monitor water pollution along the coast. At the mouth of the Saigon River the quantity of fish has diminished, and the sea at Vung Tau has been polluted by waters coming from the factories of Ho Chi Minh, so we have proposed chemical and biological control measures.' The Institute had also asked the Government to pass legislation banning the exploitation of coral. 'There is no law yet, but the Government is sympathetic to our proposal,' he said with considerable optimism. (A couple of years later in June 1990, the National Assembly did pass a maritime law which included the protection of coral reefs.)

The Institute's museum, which looked more like a warehouse, contained an impressive collection of dried, stuffed, frozen and otherwise preserved specimens. Phung pointed to the awesome shell of a 146-kilogram giant clam, and the snout of a six-metre long sawfish on another wall. The exhibition included 400 species of coral—twisted and distorted but strangely beautiful—a collection of shells and crabs from the Spratly Islands, and thousands of sea creatures preserved in jars. The preserving solutions were of transparent orange or murky opaque brown and, when back lit, they cast a strange light between the rows of shelved specimens.

As we crossed the courtyard in the midday sun, Phung explained that he had trained as a biologist in the Soviet Union in the late 1950s, and had been with the Institute all his working life. He showed us the narrow shelves of the Institute's library, crammed with more than 20 000 books, many dating from the last century. This was said to be one of the most comprehensive collections of marine books in the world, but unfortunately, most books were covered with dust and many were disintegrating. 'We have no means to preserve them. Each year about 200 people from Southeast Asia and the Soviet Union come and use them but they don't repair them and they don't give us money to preserve them.'

At the northern side of the city, a wide concrete bridge, gently shaken by the rumble of trucks and buses, crossed the Cai River which emptied into a sheltered harbour crowded with rows of tightly packed fishing boats. The uniformity of their raw grey wooden hulls created a monotony broken only by the painted bright red stripes of the bows. Beyond them, lining the river, grey wooden houses stood on stilts over the muddy bank, like giant crabs poised to run.

A young boy standing in shorts and thongs appeared from beneath the bridge floating in a basket boat which he paddled with a short-handled oar. Realising he was being photographed, he grinned and waved wildly, tilting the boat perilously. Within

moments, he was joined by a friend in another basket boat and together they skimmed the surface in tight eddies, occasionally bumping into each other, all the while grinning up at me. On top of a hill beside the river stood the Po Nagar temples, among the most important collection of ruins from the Cham Empire which had flourished here from the 10th to 14th centuries. The empire began to disintegrate after 1471 when the Viets progressively pushed southwards into Cham territory. In the 17th century King Nguyen Hoang's southward drive ended at present-day Phu Khanh Province. His children, however, continued with the southward drive and went on to conquer the Chams and Khmers in the Mekong Delta, giving the Viets for the first time complete control of Vietnam. By the 1700s little of the great Cham Empire remained. Most Chams had married and assimilated into Vietnamese life, although about 25 000 remain as a separate race, many of them in this region.

At the temple entrance, a gaunt woman with a furrowed face and shaven head begged from those who took the long steps to the summit. With her spine shortened into an osteopathic stoop, she held out a fraying conical hat, in blind hope. As the only foreigner visiting the temple complex, I became an instant Pied Piper, and within minutes more than 20 children appeared from nowhere. They followed at a respectful distance, loitering under the trees and on the rocks scattered around the grounds. On Nhan's advice I ensured before giving them any money that I had enough for all, but I was totally unprepared for the instant frenzy that developed as soon as the notes appeared. Thirty or 40 children grabbed, snatched and clawed at me, some practically climbing up my body. Overawed, I retreated with weak knees, and it was only Nhan's intervention that finally drove them off. I have encountered many beggars and many poor children, but the intensity of those few moments was extraordinary, and I realised how easy it is to be intimidated by a group of seemingly amiable children turned by poverty into clutching desperadoes.

Pretending not to notice, was a soldier with a rifle and silly grin whose job it was to guard the temple and keep children under control. Like most in Vietnam, he was a young conscript who would not win 'the smartest dressed man' award. He lolled in the shade on a rocky bank from where he overlooked the city as well as the temple. Below him, at the foot of the hill, the Cai River curved and widened before reaching the bay. Upstream, a handful of long wooden boats rested on a long fecund island thick with bamboo, banana and palm trees.

The three temples, dedicated to Princess Vana, her husband and her adopted father, probably dated from the seventh century. I slipped off my shoes and entered the main temple which housed a four-metre high stone statue said to be 1000 years old and to weigh seven tonnes. It was wrapped in gold coloured cloth and adorned with dozens of bead necklaces.

Sitting on a shaded rock, Nhan told me of the temple's origin: 'Long ago on the top of this mountain called Dai An there was a husband and wife, both old and poor, who grew water melons. But their water melons had been stolen at night, so the husband tried to catch the robber. One night he saw a young lady about 19 years old taking water melons under the moonlight and caught her, but she seemed nice, not like a robber, so he brought her home and the couple adopted her as their daughter. She was a Cham, and grew up to be very good and very beautiful. One day it rained very heavily and there were floods and everything was destroyed. The young lady took three blocks of stone and built a dam to stop the floods. In return, the people built a small temple in gratitude. Then one day she disappeared. Later, the Bac Hai prince heard about this beauty and fell in love with her without seeing her. After waiting many days and nights, finally he caught her. She told him her name was Thien (meaning god) Vana. He asked for her hand and and she went with him as his wife. They had two children—a boy named Tri (which means spirit) and a girl Qui (princess). Both were beautiful. One day Vana returned to the Dai An mountain, but the old couple had died. She repaired the house in respect for her dead parents, and since the people were backward she educated them in farming, making clothes and ceremonial formalities. The people's lives improved day by day, and the region became prosperous. One day when the sky was bright with no clouds, a big bird flew down and she stepped on to its back and flew away. The people were so grateful to her they built this temple in 817 AD and every year on the day she flew away they hold a big ceremony here.'

That night, in a small, slightly gloomy room at our hotel, the People's Committee hosted a dinner party in my honour. It was an excuse for the local cadres to enjoy a night out and indulge in gastronomic delights only dreamed of at home—and they revelled in it. We were waited on by a young man obviously trained by someone who had worked under a Western hotelier—except they forgot to advise him against serving lemon juice in a glass with double red lipstick imprints.

The meal included fish bladder soup, a Chinese and Vietnamese delicacy which I could have done without. It was explained to me that the bladder, which is filled with air when the fish dives deep, is only found in certain fish during the two weeks they migrate from the ocean to mountain rivers to breed. Before me, sat a delicate blue and white bowl with an unattractive warm glutinous soup which wobbled when touched. With the facade of a confident experimenter—but secret loathing—I let the bladder slide down my throat. The result was a slightly slimy sensation which was just bearable. I left the cadres to enjoy their final drinks—reminiscent of allowing mischievous schoolboys to continue with a forbidden party—and went to what I had been told was a cultural show near the hotel. High wire gates outside the concert hall were barred and reinforced by several security guards. On the street side, more than 100 young people, many with tight jeans and smart hair cuts, pushed against the gate and called to the guards to let them in. Several slipped through when the gate was opened a fraction for me.

Inside a pop concert was in full swing with center stage given over to an energetic Ngoc They Thanh Nam, who, at age 18, had become a national celebrity. Sporting a shiny contour-hugging jumpsuit covered with silver glitter and topped with sparkling gold embroidery and wide belt, she belted out pop songs, 1970s-style. The band, Dang Cong San Vietnam Quang Vinh Muon Nam (Long Live the Vietnamese Communist Party), consisted of three electric guitarists—two male, one female—a drummer and keyboard player. They all sparkled in gold glittering trousers topped with white shirts.

After two nights in Nha Trang, our travelling circus hit the road again. We intended to cover the 432 kilometres to Ho Chi Minh in one day. With the sun barely up, we stopped about 10 kilometres south of Nha Trang at the lone grave of Pasteur's protégé Alexander Yersin. On top of a small hill where woolly sheep with long tails grazed amid prickly scrub, the grave was marked by a large flat stone and a small white temple surrounded by trees. Early in the morning, long before the ground dew lifted, I could hear buffalo bells and birds.

South of Nha Trang was Cam Ranh Bay and its controversial Soviet military base, not seen from the road and in 1988 strictly out of bounds to foreigners. Developed by the Americans during the war, the huge base became a Soviet foothold after liberation, giving the Soviets a major presence in the Pacific, and worrying Western and ASEAN countries which warned this would destabilise the region. Vietnamese authorities refused repeated Soviet requests for permanent rights to the base. (In 1990, as the US prepared to reduce its bases in the Philippines, Moscow began scaling down its Cam Ranh Bay operations, and later Hanoi announced the facilities would be open to foreign commercial vessels.)

Cam Ranh Bay marked the beginning of Thuan Hai, the last province of the central region. A poor area, devoid of major rivers, it survived mainly on coffee and cashew nut growing, timber and fishing. The natural forests included teak and other rare timbers used for furniture. Fifty and sixty years ago, hunting expeditions, organised for French colonists or wealthy foreign visitors, stalked native tiger, giant seladang, muntjac deer and wild buffalo in the forests and plains to the west. During the American–Vietnam War, when vast areas were sprayed with defoliation agents such as Agent Orange, herds of mutjacs, wild cattle, elephants, wild pigs and a number of monkey species were wiped out or migrated into Cambodia. Many forests that survived chemical spraying have since been progressively depleted by loggers, so the tigers and elephants have gone.

Heading inland from Phan Rang, a slow winding road led up into the hills of Lam Dong Province to the capital Dalat. Once the exclusive domain of Montagnard hilltribes, it became in the 1920s a hunting base and favoured destination of Cochin-China's French aristocrats and wealthy mandarins who spent leisurely cool summers here. At an altitude of 1500 metres, where temperatures averaged 16°C, Dalat was a refreshing escape from Saigon's oppressive heat. The French established a convent and seminary, a prestigious girls' school, another Pasteur Institute and several hunting lodges. Emperor Bao Dai maintained a summer palace overlooking the Xuan Huong Lake, and at times administered

South Vietnam from here. Later, the Americans built a military airfield, an armed forces training college and a nuclear reactor.

By the late 1980s, Dalat had fallen into disrepair and lacked the romance and class of its heyday. Even the once grand Lang Biang Palace Hotel was dilapidated. By 1990, Dalat's magnificent springs, waterfalls, lakes and cool pine forests were once again attracting foreign tourists and Ho Chi Minh's wealthier holiday-makers. According to a director of Saigon Tourist, Bao Dai's palace and the villa of Tran Thien Khien (South Vietnam's former Defence Minister) had been restored by the provincial tourist company, and authorities were negotiating a joint venture with a foreign company to restore the old Palace Hotel.

South of Phan Rang, Highway One headed inland, rejoining the coast near Ca Na. Most of this stretch was poor, arid, rocky, scrubby, useless country where people made a living scraping together bits of wood for sale beside the road. Drivers were just as dangerous as everywhere in Vietnam. A fully laden bus approached us sideways as it skidded around a corner. A more sombre atmosphere engulfed our van, and I was left with the feeling that we could have been wiped out if the bus had kept coming. Apart from flying, the only real danger for travellers in Vietnam was the road and its users. Outside Ho Chi Minh, the chances of foreigners being mugged, shot or otherwise injured were remote.

Wanting to stop for a drink, Ben drove through the next town slowly, calling out to each cafe, before halting at one selling coconuts. With four or five expert strokes of a long sharp knife, the owner's teenage daughter slashed the top off four large green-husk coconuts. With the tip of the knife, she cut a tiny hole large enough for a plastic straw to be inserted. Fresh coconut juice, although not chilled, was tasty, refreshing, and more importantly, totally sterile and therefore completely safe to drink, although the presumably recycled straw negated that. (Coconut juice was often injected into veins to replace lost blood volume during jungle warfare.) By comparison, the brightly coloured locally made soft drinks—orange, lime, pepsi—were sweet and sickly. They were made with water of dubious purity and sold in recycled bottles, equally questionable. In towns, the alternative was to drink cans of imported Coke or 7UP, sold at much higher prices and rarely chilled. I sipped the lukewarm coconut juice and realised I was sitting on what had once been the fuselage of a US jet.

A lunch stop at Phan Ri Cua presented our only mechanical problem in almost 1700 kilometres—a flat tyre. While Ben tended to the replacement, I headed for a cafe hoping to find a toilet—not always an easy task in a town. First, I had to replenish my supply of toilet paper which took considerable effort and was only achieved after I drew a diagram and a young girl was sent to another shop. The 'toilet' was an almost pitch black featureless concrete room with a tiny hole in one corner and a water scoop outside. While I sat drinking outside, the usual crowd gathered around: children with sweat beads on their noses, youths with stubbly chins, lethargic old men puffing on strong-smelling local cigarettes. A woman in a colourful floral top eased herself to the front of the gathering, and in broken English told me her sister had gone to the US as a boat refugee, and she was waiting to join her. From a vinyl bag which appeared to be the repository of all things valuable, she pulled some yellowed papers from the American Government's Orderly Departure Program, which allowed Vietnamese people to emigrate to the US. 'ODP say I go America,' she said emphatically, spreading them reverently on the table before me. 'But not know when. They say OK to go, but still I wait.' I couldn't read the papers, but '1986' was clear and she said this was when ODP approved her emigration application, although there was no indication of when she would emigrate.

I felt compassion for her, seemingly isolated in that small country town, surrounded by lifeless fields, half a month's salary by bus from ODP officers in Ho Chi Minh. She wrote her name and address in a large halting hand in my notebook. I closed the pad and continued on my way to Ho Chi Minh. Once in the southern capital I forgot about the woman, and looking at the writing now gives me twinges of guilt because I made no attempt to help.

By mid-afternoon the road was a constant stream of carts with huge wheels pulled by bullocks or buffaloes and piled high with paddy, straw or bamboo poles. Large jute sacks stuffed to bursting point with charcoal were sold along the road. Huge baskets of live hens were being loaded onto the back of an army truck which carried a menacingly long missile, a reminder that even military vehicles are used as commercial transporters, as drivers attempt to bolster their meagre incomes.

The provincial capital of Phan Thiet was a small sea port famous for producing *nuoc mam cau*, or fish sauce. Tiny seawater fish and an equal amount of salt are packed tightly into wooden barrels, bound and left for three to six months, after which time the barrel would contain a pungent liquid, the taste depending on the type of fish used.

The comparative wealth of Dong Nai, the last province before Ho Chi Minh, was obvious by the standard of houses and crops which included cane, corn, cashews and rubber, with tea and coffee further north. This was the second most industrialised of the southern provinces and was well endowed with natural resources including South Vietnam's second largest river, timber in the north of the province and oil exploration and refining centred around Vung Tau in the south. And Bien Hoa (known to Westerners as once the largest US air base in South Vietnam), boasted of having the south's largest paper production center and a hydro-electric power station which harnessed the Tri An River.

Motorbikes and tractors were more noticeable here, and wood was carried not on the backs of people, but on bikes or trailers pulled by those funny little machines with long handle-bars seen all over China. The emission of fumes from some trucks was so thick, it obscured vision for six to seven metres. As we entered the Catholic belt, about 70 kilometres from Ho Chi Minh, churches became more common. Many appeared after 1954 when about one million Catholics moved from communist north to the south, boosting support for the Diem Government.

Approaching Ho Chi Minh, the villages merged into suburbia and the highway became more congested. Late on a Saturday afternoon it was a drifting, almost noiseless movement of animals, vehicles and people going about their business in a world apart from each other. Like a segment of a movie played over and over in the mind, slender young girls walked tall and elegant, their jet black hair set against their white or pale coloured calf-length traditional *ao dai*.

Americanism became more obvious. I watched a litle girl in a pink dress—the first I had seen—riding behind her father on a Honda, her tiny arms wrapped tightly around his waist. I wondered where the youth on the back of a crowded pick-up acquired his 'USA' baseball cap (worn back-to-front) and eagle-embossed T-shirt; and what past exploits a faded cream Chevrolet had been used for.

As we entered the outskirts of Ho Chi Minh, I realised this trip had been much quicker and easier than I envisaged. I had expected worse roads in the south, hassles with getting interviews, and more mechanical breakdowns. As it turned out, we had to change one tyre and had no delays at all. Once I got into the swing of it, I felt I could have kept going indefinitely. I had even become used to being a curiosity. The only lingering irritation was the incessant horn tooting which still made me cringe.

Streets were crowded with motorbikes which far outnumbered bicycles and cars. Sleeves were shorter and jeans tighter than in the north. A skirt and permed ginger hair on a motorbike seemed odd after 1850 kilometres of black trousers and bicycles. There were traffic lights and pedestrian crossings, although neither seemed to work (they did by 1991). Women passengers on motorbikes held bright umbrellas to shade themselves and their drivers; others sported brightly coloured elbow-length gloves to protect their arms from the sun.

The comparative affluence and Westernisation here was obvious—in clothes, houses and means of transport—and made a refreshing change after days of depressing poverty or near poverty, but I was totally unprepared for the explosion of sight and sound as we entered old Saigon, 11 hours after leaving the tranquillity of Nha Trang.

Motorised cyclos roared past, a Ford transit van belched black smoke as its driver changed gears, thousands of bicycles, motor-bikes and cyclos crisscrossed in a bustle not seen elsewhere in Vietnam. Between the constant tooting to get through the traffic and Nhan's son screaming (on top of which I had diarrhoea and a full bladder), I was sure I was going to be a nervous wreck by the time we reached the hotel.

We tooted our way through the crowds; passed a white twin-towered mosque; over a bridge straddling a murky black river with shanty houses on stilts along its edge; caught a glimpse of the former palace at the opposite end of a park where soldiers were training to use rifles; rounded the splendid twin-spired cathedral where a woman slept in the doorway; passed the post office which looked more like a railway station with its clock tower, arches, green shutters and white painted art deco trims; headed down Dong Khoi Street, lined by tall trees with white painted bases and shops selling antiques and mother-of-pearl inlaid lacquer ware; and there at last, the Cuu Long Hotel. Ah! the Cuu Long, with its clean spacious rooms and *two* thick bath towels!

Ho Chi Minh: Saigon reborn

This is my country, why should I leave?
Woman who had the opportunity to emigrate to the US

When the French arrived at a small trading post 90 kilometres from the mouth of the Saigon River in 1859, they swiftly captured the wooden fort and ensconced themselves in Cochin China, establishing Saigon as the capital of their newly conquered southern lands.

By the 1920s Saigon was a thriving French city, 'the Pearl of the Orient', with beautiful villas, wide tree-lined boulevards and neat parks. It was a gay city, with open-air cafes, tea parties in shaded gardens and glittering balls—as Somerset Maugham wrote, 'a blithe and smiling place'.

Sixteen thousand French ruled 15 million Annamese and lived as well or better here than they would in Paris. Surrounded by Parisian trimmings, from champagne and shimmering evening gowns to fashionable jewellery shops, they 'engaged' local workers in factories, farms and plantations, and as a result shipped thousands of tonnes of rice, rubber, salt, tobacco, alcohol and opium to the homeland and elsewhere. The sweep of the Saigon River was transformed into bustling docklands, and the metropolis spread westwards to the twin city of Cholon, sprouting factories, trading houses and opium dens. The French built a magnificent City Hall, the Gia Long Palace, Governor's residence, Duc Ba (First Lady) Cathedral (nicknamed Notre Dame), and on Rue Catinat which linked the cathedral to the docks, they erected an imposing gothic National Assembly and beside that the stately Continental Hotel.

During the late 1960s and early 1970s, the 'Paris of the East' took on aspects of an American city, with hundreds of restaurants, bars and discos to entertain servicemen, many of whom were stationed at nearby Tan Son Nhat base. Rue Catinat, the street that represented all that was Saigon, was renamed Tu Do (meaning liberty), and French cafes became girlie-bars and strip-joints, juke-boxes replaced string quartets and broad Chevrolets purred beneath tamarind trees where the French had once parked their fine horse-drawn carriages. There was a war going on—with the inevitable blackmarketeering, prostitution and poverty—but Saigon was a vibrant city, unsuppressible, like a rebellious teen-age girl out to have a good time. The gaiety, self-indulgence and corruption all came to an end on 30 April 1975 when the North Vietnamese and Viet Cong entered the city. Tank 843 triumphantly crashed through the gates of the Presidential Palace and the last US helicopter lifted like a giant eagle from the roof of the American Embassy. It marked the end of more than 30 years of civil war and armed struggle for independence, first against the French, then the Americans.

In the last hectic days, helicopters worked frantically day and night to evacuate American citizens but left behind thousands of distraught Vietnamese who had worked for the US or South Vietnamese Governments or American businesses. Some later escaped by boat, others were taken to re-education camps, but the majority resigned themselves to a new life under a communist regime, ruled from Hanoi. Thirteen years later, they all had a story to tell.

When I first visited the southern capital, renamed Ho Chi Minh City, in August 1988, it was an unimpressive blend of dusty French graciousness, lost American dreams, and present-day forlorness; an architectural mishmash of tumbling colonial terraces and Soviet-style concrete blocks; of quiet shady verandahs and dingy squalid lanes. Here could be found barefoot beggars, disco dancers and opium addicts, and amid the festering debris, colonial culinary influences.

Everywhere was ingenuity born out of necessity—or was it a latent capitalist streak? This agitated but inexplicably sad metropolis struck me as a mixture of poverty and emerging small scale affluence, with splashes of leftover Americana; a city contrasted with streaks of happiness and tinges of fear. People wanted to live a half decent life but were not sure when to start smiling, or for how long, worried that if they earned too much or spent more than others they might be regarded as bourgeois capitalists. It was 13 years after socialism officially replaced capitalism. The old urge was still there, suppressed but seething and straining to be unleashed.

People here called the city Saigon, not Ho Chi Minh, and they talked of events before or after '75, not before or after 'liberation'. They were more entrepreneurial and less pro-Government, but still very much Vietnamese. As one woman who had the opportunity to emigrate to the US, said to me, 'This is my country, why should I leave?'

Tu Do Street, renamed Dong Khoi (General Uprising) after 1975, was still the main thoroughfare, now lined with antique and handicraft shops. Freighters of Soviet, Czech or Cuban origin sat boldly along the Saigon River, floodlit and flags flapping. Some anchored just outside the Majestic Hotel (renamed the Cuu Long, meaning nine dragons) which retained touches of Frenchness. Cars were comparatively few, mopeds and motorbikes numerous and bicycles abundant. The American Embassy had been taken over by the State Oil Company, but Maxime's still served crème caramel in the French tradition.

The first four people I met in Ho Chi Minh were all supporters of the former regime. The cyclo driver said he had been a 26-year-old captain in the South Vietnamese army, and talked of events 'after '75' with disdain. 'Now I cannot get job. Only cyclo. Very poor.'

At a restaurant (which I later realised was Brodard's), I was invited to share a table with a middle-aged man dining with a former girlfriend of 20 years ago who was now divorced and was, somewhat reluctantly, reliving the past years after they had gone their separate ways. In his haste to seat me, he dropped his glasses which smashed on the floor. What a waste, I thought, all for the sake of wanting the company of a foreigner. He had drunk too much and now talked too much—more than he probably should have for his girlfriend was worried the secret police had followed me. She may have been right, for this was 1988 when foreigners were few and people still reticent about talking with Westerners. Besides, the man reading a newspaper on the steps of the restaurant was the same man I spotted earlier outside my hotel and looked conspicuously like a 'tail'. The couple were both 'very rich' before 1975 and were now poor, they said. 'After 1975, we had to give everything to the communists,' she lamented. 'Everything they didn't take, I had to sell, bit by bit, to get money to live. Even my piano.'

Around the corner, I stopped to talk with a 17-year-old girl who made a living selling cigarettes from a tiny table on the pavement. She said her father had been in a re-education camp since 1975 because he was a military commander in the former regime. She talked of being brought up in a convent, said she had no brothers or sisters and didn't know where her mother was.

Between sales, she was learning English from a former French–English teacher who squatted beside her, under the dim lights, with an exercise book open. Now in her 40s, the teacher had worked for the Americans. She told me that her husband went to the US in 1980, leaving her with four children and no income. In 1982 she sold her jewellery and attempted to escape, but the boat was picked up by coast guards who she said took her wedding ring. She and her daughter, now eight, spent a month in jail. She had no identity papers, lived on a shop floor and earned money teaching French and English privately. She said none of her children attended school, as she could not afford the school fees or uniforms. She came to my hotel the following evening bearing a letter telling of her plight and asking for $20 to 'feed and clothe my children.'

I soon learnt that many people told stories of grief and hardship to impress or gain the confidence of foreigners. The cyclo driver, the drunk and the teacher were probably telling the truth, but I later learnt that the cigarette seller's father was not in a re-education camp, but was a carpenter in suburban Saigon where he lived with the girl's mother, brother and sister. The fabrication, which she maintained for the two and a half years I knew her, was part of her survival kit. She assumed (correctly) that foreigners would find both her and the story about her father interesting, therefore take pity on her and support her with a gift here or dinner there.

Before dawn the next day, I watched Chinese women (or Vietnamese of Chinese origin) congregate on the sidewalk beside the Saigon River for their morning exercises. The atmosphere was solemn, the sky heavy with mist, and the Saigon River a steely grey mass which moved silently southwards. The aged exercisers stretched, nodded, jigged, bent and twisted, then waved flabby arms in slow arches. Men in flimsy shorts streaked past, and boys played badminton on the street. A cyclo full of ice covered by a dirty brown cloth slid past with steam rising from it. The streets were mildly busy, silent except for the occasional motorbike, but lacked the magical lure of a Hanoi dawn. But, then again, it was never in Ho Chi Minh's nature to emulate its northern rival.

Dong Khoi Street turned its back to the river then road up the tree-lined incline of Saigon Hill to where the faithful were massing around Notre Dame cathedral (Nha Tho Duc Ba to the Vietnamese) for the 6:30 service. Twin towered and red bricked, it was an imposing building with ornate round windows, a triple-arched front and a small green garden. The devout turned out in their thousands to attend mass, with sombre faces and shuffling steps, and at 5.30 a.m., 6.30 a.m., 7.30 a.m., 9.30 a.m., 4 p.m. and 5 p.m., the pews of the century-old cathedral were packed with grandmothers, couples, teenagers and toddlers, enclosed beneath

the massive gothic ceiling. The central statue of Christ on the cross was lit by an arched neon light, an incongruous sight in this colonial treasure. Lifeless fans hung on long cords from the inner arches, so several women fanned themselves. The congregation included elderly Chinese women, men in gaudy 1960s ties and Amerasian teenagers. Although there were no skirts, there were splashes of make-up and earrings. Several blue cloth-covered collection buckets were passed around, but not all made offertories. The tone of the Lord's Prayer was the same as in any other language, and the chanting ended with 'Amen', there being no equivalent word in Vietnamese. Across town at the Baptist Church the scene was in dramatic contrast: the minister, in white shirt and tie, addressed a congregation of only 12 in a cavernous hall. Yet at another Catholic church, people crammed into aisles and doorways, and those who couldn't fit in the church remained outside sitting on bicycles and motorbikes under shady trees following the service on loudspeakers. 'More people are coming now than before '75—more young people. Most of the congregation are between 18 and 30,' said a tall priest, elegantly attired in lengthy black. 'Before '75, the church had schools, hospitals and orphanages and got money from the government to run them. But the church supported the old government, so after '75 we lost those privileges.'

In a small room at the rear of the church I was introduced to two middle-aged priests in open-neck shirts. They talked of Catholicism before and after 1975. One asked not to be named. The other was Father Chan Tin, a prominent anti-communist, anti-government figure during the American days who became politically active again in the late 1980s. Churches didn't close their doors after the fall of the southern regime, but many priests were detained and sent to re-education camps, he said. Slowly, Catholics were being given more freedom. Some seminaries had re-opened and local authorities were more willing to grant permission for religious events, but the situation was not as good as before '75, he said. Gradually, the second priest revealed that he spent 13 years in a re-education camp. 'After liberation, I decided to stay with our Christians. I was in Saigon one month, then I was called for re-education. They said all the chaplains should be re-educated, and I thought it was a good idea to study the new policy, then come back and serve our Christians. I was told it would be for one month, but I had to stay 13 years.' As a

military chaplain with the rank of major, he was sent initially to an old military camp near Bien Hoa with 2000 other chaplains and high-ranking officers. 'At first I went willingly because I wanted to know the new policy, but as soon as I saw the camp I knew it was a mistake. We slept on mats on the dirt floor with about 100 men per room. They said we used to give commands, and now it was time to do things for ourselves. Every day, in groups of 300 to 400 we had political classes run by political propaganda cadres from Hanoi or Ho Chi Minh. I changed camps 11 times, some in the north, some in the south. No-one knew where I was—my father didn't know whether I was alive. At the end of 1979 the Government allowed us to write to our families, and my father said he had been searching for me for four years.' In February 1988 the chaplain was released along with more than 2000 other re-education inmates. The Government then claimed that only 156 men detained since 1975 still remained in re-education camps. (In June 1992 the Government announced that it had, on 30 April that year, released the last of the estimated 100 000 former South Vietnamese soldiers, civilian officials and associates who had been taken to re-education camps in 1975. An unknown number of political prisoners arrested after 1975 remained.)

I returned to Brodard's Restaurant for breakfast. The drunk of the previous evening had said he would join me but I ate alone. Perhaps the thought of the 'tail' was too much. At this hour, Brodard's was a coffee shop rather than a restaurant, filled with— surprise, surprise—mostly young men, drinking tea, coffee, iced coffee, beer and liqueurs (yes, for breakfast!) but not eating. Some were smart in casual dress and used Dunhill cigarette lighters. A young family came in: mum with sunglasses, tight jeans, make-up and high heels, her young son with a plastic automatic rifle—such a contrast to the north that I wondered if I was in the same country. The family ordered eggs and French bread. I opted for *pho ga*—probably the only customer to order Vietnamese food. The waiter—tall with the shadow of a moustache—returned, saying they didn't have any chicken noodle soup, but instead presented me with two chicken legs in a stew. I couldn't face this for breakfast so I reordered, much to his amusement.

Contemplating the city from behind glass, I realised there was an air of mild despondency with just a glimmer of hope; an underlying resolve to fight, to beat 'the system' when the time was right. These were people who had stayed to face communism because they chose to, or lacked means to leave. Now they were nurturing the next generation—not all of whom were gun-carrying. But what did they hope for their children? 'Peace and prosperity,' replied one. 'One day, a non-communist system', said another.

Leaving Brodard's, I turned left down the short street leading to Nguyen Hue Street, and passed the old Royal Hotel that the BBC cameraman Butch Calderwood had talked of with such affection: 'It was one of those old cast concrete buildings which always echoed, run by a Frenchman, Jean Ottvaj, who had been there from the 1930s, so in 1966 he was maybe 80. We'd go off to the war for the day, come back, have a gin and tonic at the bar, and the shoeshine boys would come and do our shoes while we drank. Then the old Frenchman would come and say, "dinner is served". We'd slip our shoes off and go in socks to the dining room. You'd be having dessert and suddenly find your boots being put on under the table. It was such a gentle, glamorous place—neat and clean.' I found a photocopy shop where Calderwood and colleagues had once sat on high stools.

It was Sunday morning and my guide Nhan was home with his family, so I toured the city with an eager young cyclo driver. I was so unused to traffic lights in Vietnam that when we stopped I started to get out, assuming we had reached the address I'd given him. The city was famed for its tamarind trees which in June displayed small cream coloured flowers, and beautiful 30-metre-tall leafy dipterocarpus said to be 100 years old, yet there were few birds.

Early in the morning just off Dong Khoi Street, women sold fish from the pavement. In a side alley, harbouring years of accumulated waste, a pockfaced Chinese man in pink and white shorts stirred simmering soup over a wood fire. A boy who looked about 10 but could have been 14, carried on his back a younger boy with two grotesquely deformed eyes who held out a pitiful hand. This was the city were everyone survived which ever way they could. Barefoot teenagers with hollow smiles and a limited repertoire of English hawked old stamps and coins from identical albums (evidently supplied by an old man who had 30 children working for him). Shops along Dong Khoi Street offered old clocks and watches, jade jewellery, Chinese porcelain bowls, silk paintings, Chinese lithographs, dolls dressed in *ao dai* and 'nacred' statues.

Few shops were open, but there were plenty of roadside sellers offering everything from cigarettes to plastic sandals. Fruit displays were more creative, colourful and orderly than those I'd seen elsewhere in Vietnam. Some sellers had chalked signs advertising prices—100 dong for peanuts, 400 dong for rambutans—which were not evident in the north. I watched as one mobile vendor peddled his cart down the street with a wood fire burning beneath huge pots which rattled as he went. He passed a haggard man with sawn off legs who sold lottery tickets beneath an umbrella hoisted from his wheelchair.

Cyclo drivers here were more energetic than those in Hanoi, and with bare sinewy legs and sweat-stained shirts, their bodies rocked from side to side as they powered down tree-lined streets. Cyclo conversation always began with, 'coos me mam, where you come from?' followed by, 'how many day you stay Saigon?' then 'coos me mam, how many children you hab?' Over lunchtime noodles, one told me how he had been drafted in 1979 and fought in Cambodia, saw his best friend killed by the Khmer Rouge, and then 'escaped'. Using a smattering of English and an on-the-spot 'translator' whose English was not much better, he said his three younger brothers had gone to the US but he was happy to stay here living with his grandmother, although he was 30 and had been a cyclo driver for five years. 'Next year him make wedding,' enthused the translator.

That afternoon Dai the cigarette seller was back at her stand, and eager to take me to the markets, along with several other street-kids including two Amerasian girls. We went to Cho Ben Thanh (known as Saigon Market), a covered market, square and solid, a proper building, not an ad hoc collection of flimsy stalls beneath tarpaulin. The square white clock tower and the tiled cow's head and fish above the arched entrance were reminiscent of a French market place and suggested some semblance of orderliness within. But, oh, what a mistake. This was Vietnam! Amid the shoving and yelling, it was necessary to step around beggars, squeeze through crowded aisles and avoid knocking over the tiny stools of food sellers. Jammed between rows of tall, tightly packed stalls, women sold white leather jackets, lace underwear, perfume and bright coloured umbrellas, everything dreamt of in Hanoi. Rows of colourful elbow-length nylon gloves hanging from rafters offered an amusing sight. I was sure wearing these gloves—so unique to Saigon—was as much a habit as protection against the sun, as some women wore them when ultra-violet rays no longer threatened to darken their skin. (A friend later told me she wore gloves at night to hide her gold jewellery and to protect her palms from the motorbike handlebars.)

Nearby we meandered through what seemed like a maze of open-air markets (I later discovered it was two intersecting streets which we eddied around several times). This was unlike a northern market. Here the produce was not on the ground but on tiered wooden stalls, and the displays were imaginative and colourful—a previously unseen variety of vegetables neatly arranged, freshly prepared food cupped in banana leaves, and an array of bathroom products bound to make a northerner envious. The sheer mass of humanity made it impossible to move at any more than a stilted trudge. People, bicycles, motorbikes and delivery carts, headed in all directions, avoiding, shuffling, bumping.

I bought shirts, sandals, toothbrushes and shampoo for the street-kids with me, then my companions suggested lunch at a crowded sit-down stall serving beef, fish and vegetables—probably their best meal since they took their last foreigner there. That night we were joined by ten more street-kids and trooped off en masse to a cafe specialising in ice cream—another envy of the north, and still a novelty in Ho Chi Minh. (By the following year, ice cream cafes were quite common in Hanoi and Danang, and every second cafe in the south seemed to offer *kem*.)

Several of the street-kids were Amerasians hoping their fathers in America would acknowledge their existence and sponsor them to a better life. One had found her father in North Carolina and was waiting to take her mother and five siblings to join him. Another, a stunning mix of Asian and Caucasian blood, was to marry a French journalist in three months and return with him to Paris. Several hundred of these rejected children of confused identity slept in the park beside the Cathedral, and lived on money sent from abroad—and their wits. ('Amerasian' was a misnomer, as many mixed blood children were not fathered by Americans. Children of mixed blood were not new in Vietnam. After the Americans left, Russians came, hence 'Russasian' children.)

Later at a disco we sat in virtual darkness—I couldn't even see whether my drink was a Coke or a beer—and watched the youth dance to a four-piece band which, judging by the lack of enthusiasm, had done this number too many times. This was one time when the Vietnamese beauties hung up their trousers and donned dresses, most of which fell discreetly just above the knee, although the occasional one reached just below the buttocks. Disco dancing here was not between couples, but a communal affair where several people danced in a circle with one unfortunate dancer in the centre. When he/she had enough, another was pushed into the centre. Sure enough, my turn came, and being the only foreigner there, it came many times.

From the rooftop of the Cuu Long Hotel I surveyed the Saigon River which bowed towards the city then disappeared behind many bends, with only the occasional glimpse of masts and cranes to suggest its course. In contrast to the congestion and commotion on this side of the river, the other bank appeared to be nothing but coconut trees, with just a thin trail of houses visible along the river's edge.

Next morning Dai took me to the other side on a round-nosed blue and white tub-of-a-ferry where passengers, motorbikes and bicycles crammed and stood. On the opposite bank we ate noodles in a partly covered market, where women sat cleaning and chopping vegetables. One woman, revealing just one tooth when she smiled, said she was 90 and earned 2000 dong a day preparing vegetables for the seller (a bowl of noodles cost 1000 dong). I began to speak to some of the other women. One woman, Lien, had worked in the market for 70 years and was now a widow. Her grandfather had been a French shipping merchant, and she had two children living in France. Beside her, topping and tailing beans, was 72-year-old Hieu who said she had lived in seven European countries, the last seven years working as a doctor in Paris with her pharmacist husband. After he died she came back, just before the fall of Saigon. 'The communists jailed me and confiscated our seven houses and two pharmacies,' she said. 'My father and sisters were furious that I had come back and was caught here. Now I have one daughter and son living in Paris, and other members of my family in the US.' But she didn't want to leave Vietnam. 'I'm too old,' she said.

We drank syrup with crushed ice, marinated dates, lychees and slices of white rubbery bean curd, then ventured down a dirt track running parallel to the river. On one side of the path were old French style cottages and houses, delectable little dwellings with shady courtyards, verandahs and tiled roofs. On the other side, wood and bamboo thatched houses on stilts clustered along the water's edge, some as cafes with cane chairs and tables at the front where you could sit and view the metropolis from afar. Rusted freighters languished mid-stream, fishing boats juddered past, gliding sideways against the current, and snub-nosed hulls chugged noisily towards the Mekong Delta carrying glazed earthen pots of fresh water.

The following morning Nhan took me to the Consular Bureau, Deputy Chief Luu Van Tanh who talked about the daunting task of processing applications from people wanting to leave the country legally. In addition to the countless thousands who had left illegally as boat people, 139 000 had emigrated under the Orderly Departure Program (ODP) since 1979. Just over half had resettled in the US, and 20 per cent in Australia and Canada. Another one million were eligible to emigrate specifically to the US. But the bureaucracy was painfully slow, and Tanh admitted that even if only half chose to emigrate, at the current rate, it would take 20–25 years to process them.

In what was once the Greek Ambassador's residence, I found Australian immigration officials Michael Herwig and Tony Le Nevez politely asking Vietnamese families why they wanted to go to Australia. Most of the Vietnamese sat tall and still in their Sunday best, nervously answering questions, hoping their broken English would not fail them. Some said they wanted to study and others to retire, but most wanted to join family members.

That night I dined with the Australian officials at Maxime's, and Herwig joked about the three near misses he had flying with Air Vietnam in the previous 18 months. Ten days later he was killed when an Air Vietnam TU-134 jet crashed in a rice field just before landing at Bangkok airport. Eighty-two others were killed including Vietnam's Health Minister and India's Ambassador. The crash site was littered with Herwig's 22 bags of immigration application papers.

At the Paediatric Centre I met an old revolutionary, Dr Duong Quynh Hoa, who wore her grey hair close cropped unlike other older women who bunned theirs. The shelves of her living room were lined with books. Here was someone different I thought. 'My family was very rich—my grandfather had 1000 hectares and a rice mill in Cuu Long Province—but my father was a teacher of many revolutionaries. They always said you are rich but you don't have any extra rights. I remember when I was about seven I saw a Frenchman get out of a rickshaw without paying the driver. It was the first time I saw the difference between rich and poor. After that it was very easy to join the revolution. I was the youngest of six children, and two of us chose to go with the revolution. My older brother was murdered by the Saigon regime in 1965.'

Hoa was the Provisional Revolutionary Governments' Health Minister. While on the Ho Chi Minh Trail in 1970, she gave birth to her only child, a son who died eight months later of encephalitis. 'After the war I had four miscarriages, then we adopted an eight-month-old girl who was malnourished,' she said, calling her (well-fed) nine-year-old daughter into the study to meet me. Beneath Hoa's no-nonsense look, I suspected a soft soul.

After reunification the Hanoi leaders demoted Hao to Vice-Minister of Health. 'After that I resigned and founded the Paediatric Centre,' she said, denying the move was political, although after the war several southern revolutionary leaders were overlooked by the northern leaders. In 1979, she resigned from the Communist Party saying it had lost touch with the ordinary people.

No trip to Saigon would be complete without a visit to the Chinese district of Cholon, and I discovered the best way was to take the six-kilometre trip by cyclo at night. Saigon at dusk became an invigorating, agitated city: the purr of motorbikes, the incessant chattering of cyclo drivers, the constant horn tooting, the faint beat of a cassette somewhere. It was a city of contrasts: the whiff of festering refuse, the sweet perfume of a dolled-up lady.

Looking up into some flats, I glimpsed laughing faces, slow spinning fans and glossy posters of healthy babies offering hope to young married couples. Repairmen continued working under single light bulbs and pâté sellers under fluorescent bars. Life went on relentlessly. Further from the city, lights faded, street lights became non-existent, and movement was by feel and habit, with the occasional help of headlights.

I could feel and hear Cholon before reaching it. It vibrated, exuding energy. Chinese songs played over loud speakers, cinemas advertised recycled Hong Kong videos. There was the incessant tap tap tap of noodle sellers hitting their sticks, the flip flop of food fryers. Cafes played a mixture of Chinese pop, Vietnamese romance and 1960s Americana. Televisions crackled and blurted out news from the Soviet Union, videos thundered with Hong Kong violence, and somewhere in the night, the faint notes of a flute could be heard.

Colonial buildings with little arches, wooden shutters and wrought iron balconies had been 'modernised' with neon signs and their elegant arches covered with plastic or bars. They had been squeezed between characterless concrete blocks with concrete flower beds on concrete balconies.

Turn the corner near the bus station, and even in the darkness without street lights, you know it's there: the triple-tiered entrance to the Cholon Cho, the largest market in the country, with its masterly clock tower and garish decorative Chinese adornments, majestic even in its emptiness. On either side of the market were once grand terraces, now tatty and shabby with faded signs, broken porticos, dim lights and dusty curtains.

The night offered a pot-pourri of aromas: the unmistakable smell of dry salted fish which characterises Chinese cities, freshly brewed coffee, frying garlic and something akin to poultry droppings. The air had a stale tinge as if the place needed a good wind through it. Pools of water and piles of garbage cluttered wide footpaths, but life went on with a sense of avoidance; after all, this was Chinatown, and like all Chinatowns the globe over, money came before aesthetics.

Seen in daytime, Cholon appeared different. The mystique had gone, replaced by sobriety. The aged terraces, with their red tiled roofs and porticoed verandahs cluttered with plants in old Chinese earthenware pots, evoked images of old Singapore. There were smells of Hong Kong, and faces from every region of China. Yet the wide main street with two lanes each side of a tree-lined median strip, reminded me inexplicably of a has-been English seaside resort.

Outside the market lay three amputees, their festering wounds covered with flies. Oblivious, women squatted in the squalor selling plastic sandals, fruit, coloured rope, spoons, covered coat-hangers, clothes, towels, chopsticks—one breastfeeding while she counted her tattered dong notes. Cyclos, all grey with brown hoods, gathered haphazardly, drivers leaning on seats waiting for customers. Suddenly all were mobile, pushing or dragging their carriages away from the market. They stopped and came back—a false alarm, as the open jeep with traffic police had turned down a nearby street and disappeared. I assumed they were either not supposed to be there or were perhaps unregistered.

Inside the market beneath its lofty ceiling, women sold fruit from glass cabinets carried on poles, Chinese cakes, sweets and sponge cakes puffed up like Grandma used to make them. On

tiny fires, they cooked skewered pork served with salad, bean shoots and noodles.

Visiting the market two years later, I met Tien, a 43-year-old mother of three. For five years she had been selling sugar-coated ginger, sun-dried bananas, spiced lotus, kelp marinated in sugar then dried, sunflower seeds, *ximuoi* (little red cherries marinated in salt water), and prunes from Singapore—altogether 26 products in bowls, jars, bags and barrels, she told me with pride. Helped by her grey-haired mother, her turnover was 40 000 dong ($8) a day with a profit of about 300 000 ($60) a month. 'It's now easier to make a profit. Viet Kieu [Vietnamese living abroad] were coming back with money and giving it to their families,' she said.

Down the street, restaurant operator Hoang also was finding it easier. His business was now semi-private, a joint venture with the State-run Tourist Office. The restaurant would never pass as tourist class, but it did serve delicious boiled spiced chicken. 'When I was a musician, I used to come to this restaurant and I knew the manager. It was State-owned and step by step profits went down, so I suggested a joint venture. It took only two weeks to negotiate and I put in 1.5 million dong. I sacked half the staff because they were not needed. After the rainy season I expect a turnover of 18 to 20 million dong a month, with a profit of 1.5 to 2 million dong. I will put the profits into making the restaurant more comfortable, then buy things for my family—a car, TV, computer.'

By 1989 everyone appeared to be profit driven. And unlike Hanoi, which seemed sometimes to have rejected all offerings from the second half of this century, Ho Chi Minh relished modernity, whether it was little girls in frilly pink dresses, concrete office blocks or mobile phones. Between my visits of August 1988 and the following April, Ho Chi Minh underwent enormous change (Hanoi's transformation occurred the following year). More shops, restaurants and discos opened. Advertisements appeared on television for the first time since 1975—half an hour of back-to-back ads all crammed into the 7.30 p.m. to 8.00 p.m. time slot. It was possible to make international collect calls to some countries and the first fax machines were installed in several city offices and most foreign hotels. The 14-year-old 11.30 p.m. curfew was lifted.

The most obvious difference was in the number and variety of shops, many with freshly painted facades, perspex signs and flashing lights, although flashing neon had not yet made an appearance. The range of consumer goods was endless. It was possible to walk into a camera shop and buy a flashy Nikon complete with a 12-month international guarantee. Chinese consumer goods flooded onto the market after the border re-opened: an estimated 80 per cent of consumer goods originated in China.

As before many aspects of life were illegal but anything was possible. There was always a backdoor, a hand under the table, a relative in a useful position. The blackmarket in dollars flourished and was accepted by the Government. Street sellers flouted registration rules and hurriedly packed up their stalls if the word spread that the police were coming. Prostitution was illegal, but no one stopped the pretty girls sitting along the pavement on their flashy Honda Dreams. Cyclos were forbidden in the city centre so riders pushed rather than peddled their carriages down Dong Khoi and Nguyen Hue Streets. My favourite was the 1989-imposed 'no urinating in public' law, a breach of which supposedly carried a 20 000 dong penalty, yet Vietnam was one giant urinal, from the northern mountains to the farthest reaches of the Mekong.

In January 1989, the Government allowed gold/jewellery shops to open, and 400 sprang up in the first three months. After Tet (February) the price of gold, which was sometimes 30 per cent above the international rate, was closer to the world rate than it had been for many years. By April, the gap between the official and blackmarket exchange rate was the narrowest ever. And inflation, which had averaged 700 per cent for that year, was back to double-digits. It was possible to open a foreign currency account and have money transferred from abroad, although it took about three weeks instead of the usual three days. 'We suspect the bank just doesn't tell you when it arrives so they can use it for a while,' said a Western businessman resident in Ho Chi Minh.

Port facilities included container shipping for the first time and the airport boasted of a new stainless steel luggage conveyor belt—a vast improvement on the chaos that previously greeted arrivees. Posters stuck to trees advertised a rock concert. On the first floor of the old Majestic Hotel, Ho Chi Minh's young elite danced in almost complete darkness to an electronic band.

However, as the economy improved and dong flowed more freely, the gap between the 'haves' and 'have-nots' increased. While the young dancers at the Majestic flashed gold and diamonds, on the street outside 11-year-old Ty, who possessed only the shorts and T-shirt he was wearing and a mouth full of rotting, aching teeth, spread his well-worn mat on the concrete away from the street light and fell asleep as he had done every night for the previous three years.

Late at night, I took a cyclo down dark streets where women swept muddy water with vigorous strokes, amid an odorous amalgam of urine and discarded rotting melons. I passed children asleep in a pavement chair, skinny white dogs with curly tails, a fat Chinese woman clutching an armful of dong on the back of a noisy motorbike, and stylised advertisements for videos of broken hearts and anguished grandmothers. At the back of the palace where the homeless lived, a baby swung in a hammock above piles of rubbish waiting to be sorted.

The city had still not come to terms with its fate, like an adolescent going through an identity crisis. Saigon had fought and lost, but it defied defeat. No longer a political capital—it had reluctantly relinquished that title to its northern sister in 1975—Ho Chi Minh was determined to become the commercial capital. Deals were signed in Hanoi, but they were made here, and executed here. This was the wheeler-dealer's city. Whether you wanted a right-hand drive vehicle, smuggled Khmer statues or a lady for the night, it could be arranged—for a price, of course.

It was trying to be a 1990s city in a 1960s communist straight-jacket. Despite efforts to modernise, tradition lingered. Long-haired beauties with tight tops and bare shoulders scooted past on Honda Dreams, but *ao dai* was still the dress of choice for formal occasions. Arranged marriages were still taking place. Old Chinese people still exercised on rooftops at sun-up, closing their eyes and breathing in the early morning air with the reverence of those who believe in the magic power of exercise.

At the Labour Club (the old Cercle Sportif) young Vietnamese sang, swam, danced and played ball. A generation ago families of French colonists and high ranking mandarins spent their leisure hours here, to the exclusion of ordinary Vietnamese. After 1975 the giant recreation centre was opened to all, and now hundreds of sporty-types in white shorts sat under canvas umbrellas drinking coffee and soft drinks. Tennis courts, once the preserve of the French, were now filled with Vietnamese players. Outside hundreds of bicycles, mopeds and motorbikes were parked in neat rows in a barbed wire compound guarded by three young chain-smoking men.

In an airless room above the main hall, a dance lesson was in progress; a group of diminutive ballerinas in black leotards moved arched lithe bodies in time to the sounds of a piano. Their teachers were Bang, 32, and Tuyen, 25—a husband and wife team who performed their last public ballet in Ho Chi Minh in October 1987 to commemorate the Russian Revolution. As well as teaching ballet and modern dance, Tuyen performed nightly at four or five concert halls. Audiences in Ho Chi Minh rarely saw just one performer, but instead a variety who did one or two numbers then moved on to another venue—a concept apparently unique to Vietnam. I went with Tuyen one night on her moped from concert to concert. She would arrive in time to arrange her costume and make-up, dance, then race to the next hall.

One Sunday Tuyen and Bang took me to their home without my guide, something they would not have considered doing a year earlier. They lived in a two-room apartment, shared with Tuyen's brother, sister-in-law and two small children. Their bedroom doubled as a kitchen, and the downstairs bathroom was shared with the neighbours. To prepare the meal, Tuyen and her sister-in-law squatted on the floor, at the end of the bed, chopping and cooking, on two electric hot-plates which also sat on the floor.

After lunch, from their first-floor balcony, I watched a postman move from house to house, and noticed those who received letters with red and blue striped edges gave him 200 dong. As a friend said later: 'If you have a relative abroad you can afford to "tip" the postman, and if you don't he may be reluctant to deliver next time'.

By 1989 many Viet Kieu were not only sending letters, parcels and money, but returning in person to see relatives who hadn't managed to, or didn't want to, join them in the West. On my 1989 visit, my guide took me to meet her father, Nguyen Ngoc Ha, President of the Committee for Vietnamese Abroad. 'Viet Kieu are important for rebuilding the country,' said Ha. After 28 years in France, he returned in January 1976 to join the communist regime, 'because I was 45 and wanted to spend 15 to 20 years helping rebuild my country, and I want to die in my country.' Now he was responsible for arranging visits for Viet Kieu. 'Some come to help family, some make investment here, but the most valuable for us are intellectuals. Among the two million Vietnamese abroad, there are 300 000 with degrees in modern science, electronics, computers, medicine, law, and they have experience in economics. We consider them very valuable for the rebuilding.'

Several former American servicemen also returned, some to look for their Amerasian children. John Rogers, who spent six years here with the US Army and spoke fluent Vietnamese, had found his daughter 18 months earlier and was back on his 15th trip. After his first visit, he said he was so moved by the plight of Amerasians that he retired after 21 years Army service, and set up a travel agency specialising in trips to Vietnam, as well as FACES, the Foundation for Amerasian Children's Emergency Support, which provided medical support and accommodation for children waiting to emigrate. Officially there were an estimated 17 000 Amerasian children in Vietnam, 8000 to 10 000 of them in Ho Chi

Minh, but Rogers believed the figure was closer to 50 000. He took me to a third-floor apartment where 20 children lived permanently and another 100 visited each day, mainly to shower and cook. He had negotiated long and hard before the authorities allowed him to rent the three-room flat, and was negotiating to open a 300-bed hostel. The following year he was accused by the authorities of siphoning off funds, and was not allowed to return. In January 1990 the Government opened a US Government-funded transit centre which provided free accommodation and food for more than 1000 Amerasians waiting to emigrate.

Other returnees included Vietnamese soldiers serving in Cambodia. Outside the bus station on Nguyen Hue Street, I chanced upon a returned Vietnamese soldier, one whom I'd seen a few days earlier in Phnom Penh when buying my own bus ticket. (Coincidences such as these never ceased to amaze me in a country of 65 million people.) I sat with Du and his friend on the lawn in front of the People's Committee while they smoked (soldiers seemed to be the heaviest smokers) and talked of missing their children and 'smashing the Pol Potists'. Du, 35, was being discharged on health grounds after 10 years as a radio operator at the front line. 'I went to Kampuchea on 1 January 1979 and by 7 January we were in Battambang [in the far northwest]. Early 1979 was the worst time. We were fighting a lot, living conditions were not good and there was not always enough food for our unit. Sometimes orders from above were not very appropriate. The best time was the 1984/85 dry season offensive when we destroyed Pol Pot bases which allowed the Kampuchean people to be very strong,' he said. Now he was returning to his wife and three children in Nghe Tinh province where he would resume working as a farmer. 'I have been fighting for 10 years and I've done my job as an army man, and now I'm going home.'

I had requested to meet some drug addicts, and was taken by a Press Department guide to the New Youth Labour Training Centre to meet Director Nguyen Quang Van. In 20 minutes, through a translator, he gave me an impressively concise and comprehensive overview of drug addiction, complete with figures, a feat rarely achieved in Vietnamese officialdom. The centre was home, school and workplace for 1000 addicts, the majority aged between 25 and 40. 'Since 1975, we've had 22 000 admissions. Seventy per cent come because they are arrested, 20 per cent are sent by their families, and 10 per cent come voluntarily,' he said, adding that before 1975, 90 per cent of addicts in the city were on heroin, now 90 per cent inject liquid opium which is cheaper. He explained that 'before 1975, most were from the army, now the majority are young people, mainly poor people, unemployed and students. The three main reasons they give for starting are the influence of friends who are addicts, to enhance sexual performance, and loneliness. During the war, a big cause of drug addiction was because of social pressure, and after the war it was lack of social activities, and poverty.'

The youngest at the centre was 14, the oldest a 70-year-old man who had been an opium addict during the French time. Only 7 per cent of addicts at the centre were women. Sitting on the steps outside the recreation room, Tot, 39, told me how she began 'using' 12 years earlier. From a poor provincial family, she came to Ho Chi Minh to work as a domestic help. 'Then I started selling fruit at Tan Dinh market and there were many drug addicts there. One day I went to a well-known place and asked for an injection. I wasn't pressured by friends. I had no particular reason. The first time was a very small amount, but soon I was having 5cc three times a week. At the time it cost two dong for 1cc. Now it costs 25 000 dong ($7) for 5cc.'

Tot received massage and medication to help her through the 10-day withdrawal. She was happy living there, she said. 'I don't want to go back to my family, I feel at ease here, I have a lot of friends, the food is good and I have a job.' She washed dishes at the centre for 20 000 dong a month. Tot married another inmate and her second daughter was born at the center. Both children now lived with their grandmother. 'I miss my daughters,' she said.

The An Quang Pagoda was an institution of another kind. The temple was run by the Venerable Thuong Toa, Thich Giac Toan, a stocky 40-year-old monk with bushy eyebrows and short, spiky hair tinged with grey. He was born seven months after his father was killed. 'My parents had only just married when he joined the resistance. The French arrested and shot him.' But Giac Toan held no bitterness towards the French for denying him a father. 'As a Buddhist for a long time, I don't have feelings of hate. It was fate that he was killed.'

Giac Toan decided at the age of nine to join the monkhood but his mother refused to allow him as he was her only son. She died suddenly when he was 14, and two years later he came to Saigon to live in a pagoda. Here, his day begins with pre-dawn meditation, followed by more prayers or administrative work before a 6 a.m. breakfast. 'Because I'm head monk of the pagoda I take breakfast with the other senior monks. We have rice soup or a bowl of soup or noodles with vegetables. I begin work in the office at 7.30 a.m., and depending on the amount of work, I go home at about 10, rest till 12 then have lunch till 1 p.m. Before liberation we only had one meal a day, but now we are doing more work so we need lunch and dinner. The afternoon has no fixed program. I take a rest, read or pray unless there is a meeting. Life for monks is very relaxed,' he said.

Fifteen monks lived at An Quang Pagoda, although in mid-1960 there were 40 to 50 monks. Giac Toan was not saddened by the fall in numbers. 'That is fate. Because of difficulties in our society some have quit the monkhood and married, some have gone to the provinces, and some have been reunited with their families in the US, Canada and Australia. Buddhism has gone through three stages. Before 1975 there were more than a dozen sects in Saigon, all praying to Buddha but sometimes fighting each other. After 1975, under communism there was no religion, but the spirit of national independence was very high. Later, the Communist Party allowed freedom of religion and now Buddhism is on the rise again. We have 3000 to 4000 monks in Ho Chi Minh and more than 20 000 throughout the country.'

One of the joys of returning to Ho Chi Minh in April 1989 was visiting nine-year-old Nguyen Duc. I watched in awe as he abandoned his wheelchair and mounted his crutches as if he had been doing it all his life, then confidently stood on his one leg and counted to 20 in Japanese. With the help of a doctor, he then slowly crossed the tiled floor of the Maternity Hospital, and counted 10 paces—in English. His skinny arms could barely hold his weight and he flopped back into his wheelchair exhausted. 'See, I can do it,' he said grinning, but relieved his morning exercise was over. When I first met Duc, he was lying on a bed, joined to his brother, Viet, from the waist down. They were Vietnam's supposedly 'inseparable' Siamese twins. For eight and a half years they ate, slept and moved as one. Viet and Duc had their own minds, but little else. They shared a single torso, two legs, part of the spine and five organs as well as numerous important arteries. In October 1988 Ho Chi Minh surgeons performed what Western doctors admitted was an extremely difficult operation. Only six similar separations had been reported worldwide, but none as complicated as Viet and Duc's, according to Dr Tran Dong A, the paediatric surgeon responsible for the separation. (The following year when American surgeons separated a pair of Siamese twins flown from Germany, the operation became world headline news, yet Vietnam's feat went almost unnoticed.)

A medical team of 70 worked for 15 hours to separate the twins, and their mother, Lam Thi Hue, cried when she saw them apart for the first time. After 15 days, a beaming Duc was wheeled out of the intensive care unit, to the cheers of hospital staff.

Three months later, just before his ninth birthday, he stood up for the first time on his one leg, and two months later took his first step.

Sadly, while Duc played football with hospital staff, expertly manoeuvering his wheelchair to kick the ball, his brother lay in an adjoining room barely able to move. Viet developed brain damage when he contracted encephalitis before the separation. When I last saw Viet and Duc in April 1991, Duc was going to school, but Viet was still unable to even sit up.

On that visit, I had breakfast at the hospital with Dr Nguyen Thi Ngoc Phuong and recalled how three years earlier she had led me to a locked room where she kept a collection of deformed newborn babies preserved in large jars with black screw-top lids. Rows and rows of them, most with twisted limbs and grotesque faces pushed against the glass—a gruesome sight. It was an ugly reminder of the American–Vietnam War, but on a more practical level they also formed part of her evidence that dioxin (Agent Orange) is responsible for birth abnormalities. 'We know a lot of our data is not scientifically collected, as in the West, but there is considerable evidence to condemn dioxin,' she said, presenting medical studies which linked the chemical to an increase in birth defects, female cancers and Siamese twins. Even in the West, two per cent of babies are born with abnormalities, and some specimens in Phuong's jars may have been natural occurrence, but she believed the incidence of abnormalities in Vietnam since the war was much higher.

One little publicised side-effect of dioxin is on women's reproductive health. Vietnamese and Western researchers have linked dioxin to benign hydatidiform moles which form in the uterus during an abnormal pregnancy, and can develop into a cancer, choriocarcinoma, which can be fatal. 'The incidence of hydatidiform moles in other Asian cities is about one per 200, here it is one in 25. Before the war the incidence of choriocarcinoma was about one in 200 which is the same as in other Asian countries. Now it is higher,' said Phuong. 'In a study of villages sprayed with dioxin, the incidence of deaths *in utero* was 40 times higher than in non-exposed villages, the miscarriage rate was eight times higher, the rate of hydatidiform moles and choriocarcinoma was four times higher and the rate of birth defects was three times higher. We identified five kinds of birth defects: cleft palate, Siamese twins, and defects of the nervous system, sensory organs (ears, nose and throat) and limbs.'

Phuong had a double career, as she was also the only woman Vice-President of the National Assembly, making her the second most senior woman politician. The eldest of 12 children born to plantation labourers—'we were very poor, but happy'—Phuong's involvement in the communist movement was largely influenced by her father who became a Viet Minh soldier and was jailed by French authorities for three years for being a suspected communist. Phuong joined the resistance when she was a medical student in 1967 and then joined the Party in 1982, the year after she was elected to the National Assembly.

Phuong could be living in comparative luxury in Paris. She had the chance to leave before the fall of Saigon with her husband, but she decided to stay, 'to serve the poor people'. 'I have been to Paris, and it's very nice but it's not mine. I've been to many countries, even the US. I went to Las Vegas in 1987 for a dioxin conference and it's such a strange city. People come from around the world and gamble for 24 hours a day—and get married in one hour!'

At La Bibliotheque (the Library) restaurant, I met a former parliamentary vice-president who also had French connections and could have left had she chosen to. Madame Dai—she always used her husband's family name—trained as a lawyer in Paris, married a doctor and returned in 1952 to South Vietnam where her husband later became Vice-Dean of Medicine at the Saigon University and she was appointed one of five vice-presidents of the Senate.

She was the first woman admitted to the bar, but after 1975 she became a restauranteur. 'My husband was jailed for a month, because he has a very big mouth and he liked to criticise the new regime, and I opened a cafe with friends in my front yard.' By the late-1980s La Bibliotheque was a well established restaurant, often frequented by Westerners. With a colonial period pressed-tin ceiling, decor included old Chinese chests, Vietnamese paintings, Thai fans, Khmer busts, and two walls of bookshelves crammed with such tomes as *Applied Anatomy, After Vagotomy, Medical Care in Developing Countries* and *Les Maladies de l'Anus*.

Madame Dai invited me to dinner, then spent most of the evening in the kitchen, as was her habit. 'I'm happiest in the kitchen,' she said. Out the back in the large dark smoky kitchen, she fried prawn crackers with chopsticks and joked about her daughter in Canada sending her a microwave.

On that 1989 trip, I was to meet one more woman of the revolutionary generation, Nguyen Thi Thi, who a month earlier had appeared on the cover of *Asiaweek* as 'Vietnam's Queen of Capitalism'. She was a diminutive, gently spoken woman. What she lacked in business-like appearance, she made up for in astute transactions. As a teenage revolutionary she fought against French 'colonialism' and American 'imperialism' (appropriately, the inlaid scene in her reception room was of warriors). Half a century later she was running two of the largest State enterprises in Vietnam, and was planning a third—all on capitalist principles.

During the American–Vietnam War, Ba Ba Thi, as she was known to friends, was an executive of the Women's Association and the National Front (Viet Cong) and was a key player in the 1972 exchange of American and Viet Cong prisoners. At the end of the war, and after losing 23 members of her family, including her father, brother and husband, she was appointed Vice-Director of the Government's Food Service which distributed rice to State employees. The Government faced a desperate shortage of food in 1978 because it set the price of rice so low that farmers hoarded it. Against much opposition, she persuaded the Government to set the price according to market demand, a system still used. 'People didn't believe I could settle the food shortages, but I proved them wrong,' she said.

With profits from her Food Company, and using mainly French equipment and expertise, in 1988 Ba Ba Thi established Saigon-Petro, Vietnam's first oil refinery, with herself as president of the company's management committee. Her next project—three times larger than SaigonPetro—was a food production enterprise capable of processing 600 tonnes of rice a day. 'I have been in the Party for 53 years. To say I am "The Queen of Capitalism", is not correct because these are State enterprises,' she said, taking me by the hand down a flight of steps.

We stood in the courtyard while men stacked sacks of rice in a nearby warehouse. 'I became a member of the National Assembly in 1987, first for my country, second for the family I lost. Our first priority after independence was to have good living conditions for the people, and many colleagues helped me achieve that goal. We are not starving but there are still many poor people here. Fourteen years ago, if the Party hadn't made any mistakes we could have solved many problems, but now our Government is struggling. Bureaucracy and the subsidised system are hampering the economy, and I want to change that. I am the woman who brings the most money for the country—but not for myself; my salary is very minimal, about 50 000 dong. I have been successful, because I embrace *doi moi*,' she said.

By 1990 *doi moi* had brought further changes to this forever evolving city, and they became more apparent during each of my three visits that year, in April, July and December. The number and variety of shops and consumer goods was phenomenal. Glass fronts replaced grilles. Photo and photocopy shops were everywhere. Civil servants were abandoning their 70 000 dong a month jobs to set up businesses or joint ventures with foreigners. The stamp-and-coin seller I had known before as a destitute, wore smart new clothes and a gold ring. My 1988 guide Nhan had moved to a bigger house.

Bathroom products from Thailand were everywhere. Nguyen Hue Street now had video hire shops as well as camera outlets, and shops along Ham Nghai Street were crowded and stacked high with imported electrical goods. Walking beneath Dong Khoi Street's tamarind trees was no longer a pleasurable stroll, as the pavement had become a place to park motorbikes. The faded postcards of Dalat, which looked as old as the buildings on them, were no match for the classy elongated cards of Nguyen Hue Street taken with a wide-angle lense. Cigarettes and nut stands now offered 'superior quality electronically tested' condoms. Air Vietnam had opened a fancy new office in front of the People's Committee building. Japanese-style Kareoke bars were the new rage. And a private university—Saigon's first since 1975—offered three-year MAs for 700 000 dong ($100) a year.

The work ethic was still strong; the desire to make money stronger. From my hotel balcony, night after night, I watched the man opposite sewing shirts and trousers, bent over his treadle machine like one possessed, from dawn until way after his daughter had gone to sleep. Even on Christmas Eve when others were celebrating, he was still there, sewing, forever sewing.

The city was like a fortress at night, everything locked behind grilles. Even cyclo drivers slept in their carriages. The only sounds were of a lone motorbike, the massage man making his way through the hotel gently, rhythmically clanking metal to attract attention, the noodle sellers tapping sticks as they worked through the night, and the wailing of boys selling sticky rice in banana leaves. At 3 a.m. trucks from the provinces came to unload produce at the market behind the hotel. When the light was still faint, cyclos buried under baskets of green leaves or slithery fish, moved silently, eerily, through the streets, usually with a woman balanced precariously atop the pile. By 6 a.m., the first motorbikes and motorised cyclos appeared, and declared that the city was awake.

Ho Chi Minh had its peculiarities. Each morning, the hotel receptionist knotted his tie over his knee, then slipped it over his head. The waitress brought me bread and French cheese wrapped in silver foil—and a small meat cleaver with which to spread it. I was invited to the engagement of a Vietnamese friend to his

Western boyfriend, a union that required incense to be burnt for the ancestors—who were probably turning in their graves and wondering what else the 1990s would bring. According to a book I had been given by a scientist, the present research ranged from work on superconductors and nuclear reactors to preserving pig semen in hen's yolk and the use of solar energy in sexing cucumbers.

The Continental Hotel, the grand old dame of Saigon, was again receiving guests. Once the bastion of French colonialists and their fine ladies, during the American era it became the in-place for officers, journalists and spies who gathered on the renowned terrace at dusk to swap gossip and news of the war. After the Americans left, it became army offices, until the Government decided to restore it as a first-class hotel. Now businessmen and travellers were sitting under the electric chandeliers and ornately carved wooden ceilings. In the spacious 'souvenirs shop', the in-house tailor worked from a beautiful old wooden table surrounded by wall-to-wall suit material imported from France. As the brochure said, the Continental was 'a romantic combination of classical style architecture and modern comforts'.

On Sunday nights, thousands of would-be-yuppies cruised the city block on motorbikes, down Dong Khoi and up Nguyen Hue, around and around, bumper to bumper, hour after hour. This was the *chay vong vong*, the big run around, a new phenomenon that gave the young and chic the chance to dress up in denim or lace and release caged spirits, to flaunt and flirt.

In the two years since my first visit, the *ao dai* had come back into vogue, and was not only worn for formal occasions but also by receptionists, in hotels, banks, offices, even at the bus station ticket office. It was easy to see how French men, and later Americans, fell in love with young Vietnamese women in those simple but stunning dresses. I was reminded of Anthony Grey's description of two teenage Americans arriving in Saigon in the 1920s: 'Among the slow moving crowds slender, graceful Annamese girls wearing traditional silken *ao dai* caught their eye again and again. The pastel coloured costumes were at once demure and provocative; fitted tight from throat to hip, they clung to every line of the delicate, high-breasted figures, heightening the allure of slender shoulders, tiny waists and the swell of young flanks; below the waist, however the gossamer-light side-split skirts and billowing trousers of white silk shrouded legs and thighs in secrecy, and to Chuck and Joseph the exotic girls of Saigon seemed not to walk but to float gently beneath the tamarinds on the evening breeze.'

But 1990 also saw arrests and detentions. Western friends talked of the 'hardening-up' period, and some cited examples of surveillance. For some, the bureaucracy was inexplicably slow, while others had their negotiations or contracts delayed or cancelled without legitimate reason.

General Manager Patrick Imbardelli told me how, while establishing the Saigon Floating Hotel, he communicated with his head office using secret codes which were changed each week; how papers were taken from his hotel room and two weeks later reappeared during negotiations with his Vietnamese counterparts; how he was given a photocopy of an incoming fax instead of the original; how he used cyclos and back doors of hotels but was still monitored. 'One time I had dinner with friends until 1 a.m. and at 7 a.m. met with my Vietnamese counterpart who asked how I enjoyed the meal with so-and-so.'

Chancing upon a Vietnamese friend from the Hanoi Press Centre, I took him to the Caravelle's top floor restaurant, where, amid blue and cream 1960s decore, one could order 'grilled deer with five tasties'. We talked earnestly of contradictions and conflicts, of the lingering past and uncertain future. The wall had come down in Eastern Europe, and the underswell of anti-government sentiment was making itself felt in Vietnam. Calls for more democracy were growing louder, there was talk of free elections in Cambodia. 'The leaders are worried about losing power,' he said in a moment of frankness. 'This is what Ho Chi Minh fought for, this is what the revolutionary struggle was all about. They are not going to let go now after 50 years of fighting.'

No matter what Uncle Ho stood for, capitalism and bourgeois ideas were reappearing. Even official gambling had returned; the old racetrack near Cholon once again had horses and jockeys, due largely to the efforts of Philip Chow, a Hong Kong-based Vietnamese–Chinese businessman and racehorse owner. He left Saigon as a teenager and returned in 1987 with a fistful of dollars and a burning ambition to revive horseracing in Vietnam. We were sitting in the official's pavilion watching tiny horses race around a dusty track with jockeys as young as nine. Below, thousands of men and boys in shorts merged in a scruffy brown mass. The only women were selling food from baskets on the ground, already littered with betting tickets which sold for 1000 dong from a window with rusty grilles. The huge old French-built stadium, faded and flaking, emitted the stench of urine and old bananas. It was vastly different from the multi-million dollar Happy Valley and Shatin tracks Chow usually frequented in Hong Kong. He said he wanted to impart some of the Hong Kong sophistication, but admitted it would be a major task.

'I came back 50 times in the first three years and now I have a joint venture with the Sports Department,' said Chow. 'When the People's Committee asking me to start horseracing again, I put in $150 000 and got it all back in eight months. On the first day, betting totalled 30 million dong. Now it's 30 million dong per race and there are six to eight races a day, three times a week. The Sports Department and I get 8 per cent each, and the rest goes to tax and charity. Now we want to build a $6 million stadium to seat 10 000.'

This was July 1990, but when I tried to contact Chow five months later, I drew a blank at the racetrack, found a British businessman living in his apartment, and heard unflattering rumours about the horse man.

Another noticeable change was the increase in visitors— 104 000 foreigners came through Tan Son Nhat airport in the first six months of 1990 according to Saigon Tourist. The authorities rather misguidedly designated 1990 as 'Visit Vietnam Year', following Thailand's success three years earlier with the same theme. The difference was that Vietnam didn't have the facilities or personnel to cope with such an influx. Nevertheless, the visitors came. Businessmen, tourists, overseas Vietnamese, and former American servicemen. Backpackers were noticeable for the first time. They trudged the streets seeking a bed for $3 a night, then hired motorbikes and roared off to the Mekong Delta.

I met many businessmen and visitors who all had stories to tell. One was a German security consultant who lamented that the city authorities had bought fire engines from a German Viet Kieu for three times the price they cost in Germany. On another occasion while chugging down the Saigon River on a cruising restaurant I met an American veteran who had reclaimed his Amerasian son, and had then adopted three more Amerasian children. When I met him he was giving his extended family of 22 a night to remember. At a hotel restaurant I met an Australian so-called 'exporter' slouched over his beer lamenting a lost love and a lost deal. I had met him in Hanoi several months earlier, and here he was again still talking about 'deals', but never saying exactly what he did. This time his partner had skipped through to the US with film of military installations and had not been heard of since.

Other 'businessmen' included smugglers from Cambodia who used a well-known hotel near the airport as their base for handing over stolen cars brought from Bangkok through Phnom Penh to Ho Chi Minh. The hotel was the site of many shady deals. It also arranged visas for people who arrived without one—for a price of course—provided they stayed at the hotel. 'The racket is run by a manager whose sister works in immigration,' whispered one of those 'in the know'.

With the return of visitors, Saigon Tourist began converting war-time buildings into hotels. 'The Spring Hotel, famous in the American time, is used for industry offices but will be renovated and re-opened as a hotel,' said Saigon Tourism's Tran Huu Phuoc, a neatly dressed officer in his mid-40s. He made a striking contrast to the foyer of his building which was bare, dirty and covered in cobwebs with faded maps and curled up postcards in a cracked glass cabinet. 'The Eden Rock and Plaza Hotel, which are now student hostels, will become hotels, and we are making a joint venture with a French company to build a seven-storey hotel in Le Duan Street opposite the American Embassy. Le Loi Hotel will be expanded from 75 to 600 rooms, and we plan to build a 1000-room hotel in Ton Duc Thang district.' By 1995 these six hotels would give Ho Chi Minh an additional 2245 rooms for foreigners. 'Before liberation there were 65 to 70 hotels with more than 6000 rooms. Now, Saigon Tourist has 18 hotels for foreign guests, the Restaurant-Hotel Company has 40 for foreigners and locals, and there are 140 small private guest houses.'

Several new hotels were run by private businessmen. One of them was 62-year-old Luong Xuan Hy. A former construction engineer, he came out of retirement and persuaded the city authorities to lease him the triple-storey radio station building opposite the ferry wharf. With money inherited from his mother, he converted the building into the 10-room Saigon Mini Hotel.

While we talked, he smoked from an old blue porcelain pot with a silver handle and trim, sucking noisily through the long thin bamboo stem. 'We thought it would take 800 million dong, but when we started renovating, it went up to 1.5 billion. Half of that came from the bank, and the other half from my family. My wife had to sell her gold and diamonds.' I noticed he was simply dressed and lacked the flash watch and gold chain so often seen on the new vogue businessmen here. 'The Government owns 35 per cent and they get 35 per cent of the profits. We expect to get back the 1.5 billion in three years,' he said. As I left, he offered me his business card which was identical in colour, design and logo to that of Patrick Imbardelli of the Saigon Floating Hotel, the five-star monolith moored on the river 100 metres from Hy's more humble establishment.

The Saigon Floating Hotel was the city's *piece de resistance*, an oasis of luxury where you could buy international magazines, sit on deck and order a bottle of Australian red wine with Italian salami and French cheese, while the Business Centre transmitted a fax for you, and all of this charged to your Visa credit card. One resident of the hotel, a commodities trader, conducted his business beside the pool, calling around the world with a remote phone—a concept not even imagined two years earlier. Imbardelli, a former Hilton manager who at the age of 28 became the first Westerner to run a hotel in reunified Vietnam, told me, 'This is the only floating hotel in the world, and we were the first in Vietnam to have buffet meals, hotel fax, Visa and IDD [International Direct Dial]'.

Described as the most well-travelled hotel in the world, the 'Flotel' was hauled to Vietnam from the Australian Great Barrier Reef where it had been a financial disaster. In Ho Chi Minh it not only offered first-class accommodation for a city starved of luxury facilities, but it also provided a training concept previously un-heard of here. 'We took on 300 trainees, and deliberately chose 90 per cent unemployed because we didn't want them to come with bad habits,' said the Food and Beverage Manager, Rodney Hawker. 'They had to learn everything from personal hygiene —some had never even worn shoes before—to carrying a tray of drinks up and down stairs. And we had to gradually get them used to working eight hours without a siesta.' Three months later, the Floating Hotel turned out alert, immaculately groomed, English-speaking receptionists, waiters, bar attendants and room servants. Within six months, other hotels were poaching their elite workers, and their training manuals.

On the seventh floor of the Bong Sen (Lotus) Hotel, I break-fasted with ten American academics—specialists in Asian re-ligion, social studies and international relations. The group was led by American peace activist John McAuliff, founder-director of the US–Indochina Reconciliation Project, which promoted academic exchange programs between the US and Vietnam, Cambodia and Laos. 'Reconciliation means a process going both ways, and at first the Vietnamese had problems with the term. They said, "what do we have to reconcile with?" ', said McAuliff who had returned 15 times in as many years.

His first trip was in 1975 with a small group of anti-war activists. They arrived in Hanoi on 30 April just as the last US helicopters lifted off the Embassy rooftop in Saigon. 'We had no idea the war was ending, everyone was surprised it happened so fast.' Much had changed since then, he said. 'People are much more out-spoken, much more critical. In the past there was a theoretical "we ought to have better relations with other countries", but it was confined to the socialist bloc. Now it's not. In 1975 the Party was everything and the National Assembly was a rubber stamp operation; now it's a real factor in decision making. The process of elections has been democratised, and the next elections will be broader with fewer Party members.'

National Assembly member and senior economic adviser to the Government, Nguyen Xuan Oanh, agreed there had been many changes, but lamented that not all had worked. I had met Oanh many times—in Hong Kong, Hanoi and Ho Chi Minh—and he always talked of the future with hope, but this time breakfasting on the top floor of the Cuu Long, he seemed to lack enthusiasm, as if his dream was fading. He had just returned from the mid-year session of the National Assembly which gave Vietnam its first maritime law, introduced taxes on luxury items, personal income and company profits, and further liberalised the foreign invest-ment law. 'Economically the Government is getting more liberal. But the foreign investment code has not been that successful. Only $1 billion has been invested by foreign companies—$400 million of it in oil exploration—when we expected $2 billion. We are still quite green,' he said. 'The National Assembly reviewed the past six months, and I think we have done quite well, but it's hard to switch from a centrally planned to an open market system, and we have a banking crisis. A banking decree is coming out, but I think it's much too late, the damage has been done. The credit crisis is basically a problem of managing the banks and the need for banking legislation and regulation. It's not a shortage of money in the coffers, it's a management problem, but we don't have qualified personnel for banking.' He fell silent and I knew what he was thinking: he could do the job, but the governor of the bank had to be a Party member, which Oanh was not.

Oanh, the only Harvard-educated economist in the country, once ran the central bank of South Vietnam. After studying and working in the US for 15 years he returned to Vietnam in 1963, became Governor of the bank, and was twice Acting Prime Minis-ter. Under the new communist regime, he spent almost 10 years in the political wilderness, before being called on to help shape Vietnam's economy. He had been one of the main architects of the Foreign Investment Law introduced in 1987 aimed at attracting foreign capital to boost Vietnam's flagging economy. He was now Chairman of the Vietnamese Economic Association, Director of the Bureau of Economic Research, Executive Vice-President of the Industrial and Commercial Bank, and Managing Director of the Investment and Marketing Consulting Corporation.

I thought about Oanh and others who had swapped political caps for the sake of trying to improve their country. I pondered over the idolising and ideology of Uncle Ho. He had wanted the best for his people, and his people made him into a national hero and idolised him. Finally, after half a century, the standard of living was improving, but now the people wanted more than material improvements, they wanted more freedom. Communism in Hungary, Poland, Czechoslovakia, and East Germany had capitulated, tanks had been used in Tienanman, Gorbachev was struggling. For how much longer could Uncle Ho's successors hold on to power? I looked at the cafe with fancy new chairs and umbrellas, the Mercedes outside the Cuu Long, the hotel I had stayed at in 1988 and now renamed the Majestic. Not long, I thought. A freer economy nourished a freer mind.

I also thought how everything seemed harsher here, less refined than across the border in Cambodia. There was killing and suffering in Cambodia, but the people retained their dignity and manners. Here, the cyclo drivers were rude and pushy, the hawkers more persistent.

Unlike Oanh, some people still thought of greener pastures beyond Vietnam. A restaurant owner, a woman with 12 children, told me how her two sons escaped eight months earlier and were in a camp in Thailand intending to go to Australia because 'it's difficult to live and work here'. She was serving a Canadian businessman who came with dreams of sending home artwork, furniture, silk and handmade lace.

The Amerasians were still waiting for someone to send them to their dreamland. One street-kid I had known for more than two years found me at the hotel, greeted me as a long-lost friend, and as usual called me 'adopted mother'. I had been generous in the past, but when I told him I couldn't buy a house for him and his mother, he left dejected, and I didn't see him again. The mother of an Amerasian I had met on previous visits watched me having coffee with a colleague, then followed me to my hotel room. She showed me photos of her daughter at a transit centre in the Philippines and in the US with her adopted father, then she asked for money. A few nights later, a youth with nimble feet attempted to rip a gold chain from my neck. Having someone groping at my throat in the dark was more terrifying than losing a piece of gold, and the feeling of those hands around my throat stayed with me for several days. On my last night in December 1990, my hotel room was broken into, my case slashed and $2000 worth of saleable goods taken. This was Saigon, not the Ho Chi Minh I had known in 1988.

The Ho Chi Minh to Phnom Penh bus

Rice fields were turned to mine fields.
Kim Hang, deputy Party Secretary

In 1988 the usual way to leave Ho Chi Minh was by plane to Hanoi or Bangkok; the unusual way was by bus to Phnom Penh. This regular passenger service, which linked two of Asia's most interesting cities, had been barred to foreigners since the end of the American–Vietnam War. The 13-year ban ended in August 1988 when I made the 10-hour journey along with Vietnamese and Cambodian passengers. A few months earlier, aid workers and journalists had been allowed to travel by government car between Ho Chi Minh and Phnom Penh at a cost of $300 for car, driver and guide—the bus ticket cost 3050 dong or less than $1. The Vietnamese authorities gave me permission to go by bus and the Cambodian Consulate not only approved but an official took me to the bus station to buy the ticket. Yet when I arrived in Phnom Penh, Foreign Affairs authorities wanted to expel me on the spot because it was unacceptable for a foreigner to travel by public bus. I was saved because a consulate employee had taken me to the bus station and I already had permission to be in Cambodia. However, having set a precedent, I was later allowed to do the trip several times, once, in 1990, with an overnight stop in Svay Rieng.

At 6 a.m., six times a week, a large overcrowded bus pulls out of the downtown depot next to the Rex Hotel, and heads for Cambodia, usually arriving in Phnom Penh at 2 or 3 p.m., although sometimes not until 7 or 8 p.m., depending on the vagaries of border and river crossings, and immigration, customs and tax officials, not to mention accidents and breakdowns. Drivers alternate between being either Vietnamese or Cambodian, and they supplement their pitiful Government salaries by earning money on the side.

The bus I took in August 1988 was a not-so-old wrong-side-drive Bulgarian model with a front and side door, and dusty pink and purple cloth flowers hanging from the windscreen mirror. I arrived at the depot just after 5.30 a.m. to find a chaotic scene: boxes and other cargo being stacked on the roof, under seats, and in the aisle. Bus Number 1 was not just a Ho Chi Minh to Phnom Penh passenger bus, but also a goods transporter, although cardboard and thick black nylon sacking hid the contents so I had no idea what we took—or smuggled?—into Cambodia. Loading was orchestrated by the conductor, a wiry character with a furrowed face and a cigarette drooping from the right side of his mouth. Smoke clung to him like mist. With a hoarse voice, he yelled at his two helpers, who later rode with the roof-top cargo. It was like watching ants building a castle, and the pile on the roof grew until everyone was satisfied.

Inside, passengers climbed over luggage and seats, squeezing into what space they could find, and men called noisily to each other while arranging their belongings. The only other females besides myself were an ageing portly Vietnamese woman who, exuding determination, used her bulging string bag to muscle her way into a front seat; a domineering woman, who told others where to sit, before finally settling next to the portly woman; and a young Vietnamese girl with curly hair who nervously clutched a designer bag with a 'Disneyland' sticker. I was squeezed into the front seat beside her, with one bag under my feet, another on my lap, and the metal door guard rubbing my knees. Between the feet of a man behind us lay a limp bundle of speckled hens tied together by their ankles. Occasionally, one raised an alert head and jerkingly looked around.

Only 12 passengers were civilians, the rest were uniformed Vietnamese soldiers returning to Cambodia after their vacation, all looking young and smoking heavily. They were going to fight in someone else's war. Serving in Cambodia was part of their compulsory three-year military service, avoided only by those able to gain university admission or bribe their way out of the army.

We set off with people still standing on seats, and baggage unsecured. It seemed half of the passengers were to stand in the aisle, and some were to travel on the roof for 250 kilometres. Several blocks later, the exasperated conductor was still rearranging luggage and passengers—men next to men, women next to women, chickens and baskets on the floor, and bags on the overhead luggage racks. Apparently soldiers could only occupy spare seats, otherwise they stood in the aisle or sat on squat stools up front; some sat on the doorway steps—all trying to position themselves before the long journey ahead.

Driving out of Ho Chi Minh on Highway One at 6 a.m. through the western suburbs, the poverty of daily life became evident—the substandard housing, the old men poking in rubbish piles, cyclo drivers with threadbare shirts, children and pigs roaming the streets.

As we headed towards the border, passing the airport with its rows of disused concrete hangars, suburbia gave way to a string of roadside villages. There were markets, outdoor cafes crowded with men, rice paper drying on bamboo racks, neat cemeteries, jumbled scrapmetal yards, mud-splashed buffaloes, long rows of yellow flowering acacias, and large billboards encouraging productivity and discouraging drinking (part of the Government's crackdown on alcohol consumption).

We stopped to take on another four soldiers who crammed into the centre of the bus through the side door, while an officer with four stars and a red cross on each collar stood in the aisle watching. Further on, a latecomer hailed the bus from the back of a motorbike. He climbed aboard—sporting striped trousers, a white shirt, black brief case and long manicured fingernails—and fought his way to his reserved seat, grudgingly vacated by a soldier. The driver put on taped Western music—'I love him, I love him, I love him, I'll follow him forever, forever'—although the soldiers were attempting to sleep whether sitting, standing, or slumped across comrades.

During these last hours in Vietnam, I saw more modes of transport than in the previous month: an old wooden-wheeled dray left beside a straw stack; a pony-drawn taxi with a tarpaulin shade; a dainty little cart, pulled by a skeletal cow; an old bus, fueled by burning wood and cooled from a water tank on its roof; an overcrowded Desoto bus on its way to Tay Ninh with motorbikes neatly parked on its roof; an open-air jeep driven by a young man wearing a multi-coloured shirt and baseball cap; a Honda motorbike ridden by a boy in an over-sized floppy hat who only seemed to be about eight years old; and a woman's bicycle pedalled by a tiny girl who straddled the V-bar. While an old yellow and green bus was travelling ahead of us, two youths on the roof were rearranging the cargo which included half a dozen bicycles, one of which was wheeled from the back of the roof to the front, the youth being oblivious to the motion of the bus.

Leaving the cluster of roadside villages, we headed out into the open countryside with grey mist and heavy dew covering the fields of sugar cane, sweetcorn, lotus and rice. Traversing the southern corner of Tay Ninh Province, we passed through Go Dau, the last Vietnamese town on Highway One before the border. The main street was dominated by the impressive twin-towered temple of the Cao Dai religious sect. Cao Daiists worship the gods of all major religious groups, including Christ and Buddha, as well as secular figures such as Joan of Arc, Victor Hugo, Sun Yat Sen and the Vietnamese writer and astrologer Nguyen Binh Khiem. Founded after World War I by a spiritual medium Ngo Van Chieu, it is partly modelled on the Catholic Church and encompasses aspects of Confucianism. By 1938 it claimed 300 000 devotees and was politically influential. During World War II, Cao Daiists and the followers of Hoa Hao, another southern sect, sided with the Japanese occupiers. At the end of the war they fought against the Viet Cong in a futile attempt to gain control of Saigon, but later joined the Viet Cong to fight the American and South Vietnamese forces. Regarded as obscure, members conduct elaborate rites, wear distinctive long brown robes and broad-rimmed brown hats. Their headquarters is a rococo-style, almost grotesque, temple in Tay Ninh town.

At Go Dau, Highway One turned west and headed towards the Mekong River. Leaving town, we crossed a long single-lane bridge over the Vam Co Dong River. Part-way across, two well-dressed young women on a motorbike stalled in front of us, panicked, then abandoned their bike, much to the amusement of our driver and front-seat passengers. From here to the border, the road became much narrower, and an almost continuous stream of bullocks, drays, cyclists and foot traffic, forced the bus to slow. At one point, we rode the verge to pass an oncoming truck.

The border, 50 kilometres from Saigon, was marked on the Vietnamese side by a boomgate and a small wood and bamboo hut where passports and papers were processed by uniformed officers of Vietnam's Immigration Department. They worked with proficiency commensurate with the heat of the day and seemed to take half an hour to complete each document. Customs took another half hour.

While waiting, peddlers offered cold black tea or coffee in plastic bags with ice, fresh rambutans, citrus fruits, custard apples and steamed sweetcorn. When we left, the road was littered with empty cigarette boxes, rambutan shells and spent sweetcorn cobs. Littering was not seen as wrong in a country as poor as this. The two-hour wait was spent buying food, sitting in the shade, smoking, and watching border guards search the many large bags tied to bicycles that were pushed across the border in both directions. The soldiers congregated in one group and civilians in another. One, a young Cambodian man who spoke some English, introduced himself to me and said he was studying at the University of Ho Chi Minh. After doing two years of an economics course, he was returning to Phnom Penh because his father was ill. Thousands of Cambodians were sent to Vietnam each year for academic and technical training. Hok said he didn't want to go to Ho Chi Minh but had been picked from among Phnom Penh's top economics students. His scholarship covered textbooks and accommodation at a university hostel, but his family had to send him 'living' money.

Later, when the driver joined us, squatting in the shade of the bus, Hok asked him questions for me and translated the replies. By the time he finished his second cigarette, it transpired that our 45-year-old charge had driven buses for eight years before joining the Phnom Penh to Ho Chi Minh Bus Company the previous year. As a State employee he was paid little but would not say how much he earned on the side, and didn't want to damage his clean record by carrying smuggled goods. What he earned was enough to feed his family which included five children aged between 2 and 18.

Another Cambodian who spoke English listened to our conversation for some time, before asking me what I considered to be too many personal questions. The latecomer with the manicured fingernails joined us. His first question was whether I was a journalist, and I wondered if I was under surveillance. He was a civil engineer from Phnom Penh but said he made more money conducting private maths lessons and helping his wife run a shop selling watches and shirts. I also learned the bossy woman was a Vietnamese army officer's wife and was on her way to visit him in Phnom Penh.

Long queues of trucks waited on both sides of the border and between the two frontiers in no-man's land. Most of those heading for Ho Chi Minh were loaded with food, and those leaving Vietnam carried mainly consumer goods destined for the markets of Phnom Penh. Drivers slept on mats under their trucks, or in hammocks hanging from the rear of the vehicles. Women were cooking food for them or serving noodles from baskets carried on poles.

Vietnamese women could be recognised by their straw hats, Cambodian women by bright coloured checked scarves wrapped around their heads or necks. There was no shade in the large barren area between the frontiers, nor on the Cambodian side, so trucks languished in the sun for hours.

Returning from the immigration office I found a chunk of

unwrapped beef hanging from the ceiling of the bus, as this was apparently the way to transport a piece of meat you had just bought. The bullish Vietnamese woman pulled several whole dried fish from her string bag, alighted and returned a few moments later tucking well-worn Cambodian riel notes into a hidden pocket. People stood on each other's luggage to get in and out of their seats, regardless of what might be inside. The customs inspection disturbed the hens which responded with loud squawking.

With Vietnamese formalities completed, the bus moved to no-man's land while Cambodian immigration and customs officers inspected documents and searched the bus inside and out. Packets of cigarettes changed hands along with passports and papers. Boxes and bags on the roof were inspected first—a time-consuming task—then I was called inside the bus to open my bags, although the other passengers remained outside while their goods were scrutinised. As I was the first foreigner to pass through by bus, I was prepared for problems, and hoped I would not be responsible for delaying the bus. The customs form required details of consumer goods, jewellery and foreign currency, and I had to produce the items one at a time. When the man with the white uniform counted the money, he found $100 more than I had declared. Not wanting the other passengers to see, I had counted the notes without taking them out of my travel pouch—and miscounted. I held my breath while the officials talked among themselves. After a few moments, he made a notation in Khmer on my form and returned it with an awkward, 'Thank you'.

Finally the guard lifted the red and white boomgate—which was weighed down at one end by a rusty old one-metre-long artillery shell—and we were free to pass under the huge wooden arch marking the Cambodian border. (When I came through in July 1990, the arch which depicted five Angkor Wat temples had been repainted and two bright white ceramic lions sat erect at each base of the arch. A new toilet block and a brick administrative office had been erected and a small private cafe opened nearby, although shade had still not been provided.)

The bus reloaded and set forth for Phnom Penh, but was stopped a few hundred metres from the border while huge black bags were hauled onto the roof by ropes. It took a considerable amount of time, and everyone became hot and sweaty and kept pointing at the clock. Later when the conductor inspected our tickets one man couldn't find his, so the driver stopped once more, causing great consternation, and again everyone pointed at the clock.

The first Cambodian village was a small cluster of thatched cottages surrounded on three sides by a neat row of eucalypts. The houses were set further back from the road than in Vietnam. Some houses had small ponds beside bare yards where children played in the dust. A man swung from a hammock beside his house. Washing, including a red and yellow Cambodian flag, hung over a bamboo rail. It was a peaceful setting, and in many ways a microcosm of rural life in Cambodia. At the next village, a solid square Soviet-built Kamaz truck looked out of place parked beside the flimsy thatched shops lining the road.

This was Svay Rieng Province. It has an area of 2966 square kilometres, and a population of 382 000 making it among the most sparsely populated of Cambodia's 22 provinces. It covers a vast rice-growing plain in Cambodia's southeast corner, where the rainfall is low and forests almost non-existent. Half the province protrudes into Vietnam, and despite traditional antagonisms, many Vietnamese live in Svay Rieng and neighbouring Prey Veng Province.

The landscape was vastly different from that of Vietnam: flat land as far as the eye could see, randomly dotted with tall sugar palms, unlike most trees in Vietnam which were planted in rows, usually along the road, around villages or between rice fields. And Svay Rieng had few of the imported eucalypts, acacias and casuarinas, so common across the border. Sugar palms were so typically Cambodian that Cambodian people regard any land growing them as part of their country, and there was a clear distinction along the border area between palm and non-palm land.

Only about half the land here was under production, growing mainly rice and maize. There were fewer motorised vehicles, and bicycles outnumbered motorbikes. Most houses were of mud and thatch. Some larger timber homes were built on stilts providing an open-air living area under the house, as well as shade for families and animals.

The fields were almost deserted—such a contrast to the industriousness in Vietnam. Occasionally children could be seen riding on or washing buffaloes, while small groups of women worked the fields, each with a *krama*—the traditional Cambodian checked scarf—wrapped around her head, rather than a conical hat. The *krama*, woven from rough cotton, was one metre long and worn by men and women. The most common image of a Khmer Rouge soldier is with a red and white *krama* around his neck, yet many other Cambodians wear red and white ones, and the scarves come in many colours, some quite vivid. The *krama* was a symbol of being a Cambodian, and it was extremely versatile—I once listed 25 functions—used most commonly to shade head and neck from the sun, and to absorb perspiration. It could be used by a mother to carry a young child on her back, or as a hammock for a baby to sleep in, or wrapped in a tight bun to balance a flat tray of food on the head. Around the home, to bath in or to do hard physical work, men wore a *krama* tied at the waist so it just covered the knees. Wealthy men wore bright coloured silk *kramas*.

When not wearing trousers, country women donned a loose cotton sarong, a length of cloth with the ends sewn together, which was held in place by a knot at the waist. City women working in offices wore a straight-fitting tailored *sampot* which had a waistband and clasp replacing the knot.

The bus trip was not as fast nor as nerve-racking as I expected, although the narrow road forced vehicles onto the verge when passing. I suspected the driver had been told to drive cautiously on account of 'the foreigner'. For the most part the road was in good condition, although at times it almost brought the bus to a halt, and having driven this route many times before, he slowed down before reaching rough patches.

Travelling ahead of us was a mini bus, which had a man riding with one leg and half his body hanging out of the window to cool himself. There were no people in the fields and only a few cycling on the road. I wondered if children were able to attend school as the homes seemed so far from any town. Electricity wires on rusty poles cemented into the ground were the only symbol of 'technology' or anything remotely modern.

Further on, a billboard featured a man holding a machine gun against a backdrop of a Cambodian flag; another depicted two hands holding a hammer and sickle. A shirtless youth with a red, orange and yellow *krama* around his head drove a relatively modern red Soviet tractor pulling a bright orange trailer. Two more tractors passed shortly afterwards. That was three tractors in half an hour, as many as I had seen in a whole month in Vietnam. (A long-term Westerner in Cambodia later said she had seen lines of 10 to 15 Soviet tractors at the border waiting to cross into Vietnam.) A more familiar sight was a pig upside down on the back of a bicycle, mud covering his belly to protect him from the midday sun.

Nearing Svay Rieng, the capital of the province, spindly eucalypts had been planted between the fields and beside the road. At times, thick clusters of palms, eucalypts, jackfruit and bamboo trees gave the impression of driving through a small forest interspersed with little mud and straw houses. (Private selling was always tolerated, but after the Government sanctioned private enterprise in 1989, many of these roadside houses began selling drinks, and a rather pathetic collection of household goods, such as washing powder, cigarettes, matches, instant noodles and sugar coated nuts.)

Several bombed buildings and bridges remained as ruins—a stark reminder that Cambodians had been fighting foreign forces and each other for 20 years. Svay Rieng and the other eastern provinces bordering Vietnam were heavily bombed during the Vietnam–American War, and were the first liberated by the Vietnamese when they drove out the Khmer Rouge in 1979. As the Khmer Rouge army retreated they blew up bridges, the remains of which can still be seen along the highway—the rebuilding of Cambodia had been slow and was still far from complete.

Since gaining independence from the French in 1953, Cambodia, under Prince Norodom Sihanouk, adopted a policy of neutrality. During the Vietnam–American War, however, Sihanouk allowed the North Vietnamese and the Viet Cong to use Cambodian jungles along the border as a sanctuary. And, as parts of the Ho Chi Minh Trail crossed into Cambodia, his country became an important link in the communist's supply lines. To wipe out the bases and disrupt supplies, the US began its infamous secret bombing campaigns instigated by President Richard Nixon and Secretary of State Henry Kissinger. The first, the 1969–70 Menu strikes, were concentrated on the Ho Chi Minh Trail and were codenamed 'breakfast', 'dinner', 'dessert', 'snack', 'supper' and 'lunch'. The US Air Force did not restrict its operations to the border; by 1973 virtually all of Cambodia except the far west, had been bombed.

The eastern provinces were devastated, agricultural production came to a virtual standstill and more than two million people (a third of the population) left their villages to fill refugee camps in Phnom Penh. Cambodia's neutrality was lost, and Sihanouk became an 'enemy' of the US.

While on a trip to France in March 1970, Sihanouk left Defence Minister Lon Nol in charge of running the country. Supported by Sihanouk's cousin, Prince Sirik Matak, Lon Nol mounted a bloodless coup in which the National Assembly passed a vote of no confidence in Sihanouk and replaced him with Lon Nol as Head of State on 18 March. There was widespread conjecture, but no proof, that the CIA was instrumental in the coup. Nevertheless, the following month the US began a massive military build-up in Cambodia and gave Lon Nol's government financial, military and diplomatic support. The deposed Sihanouk spent the next 21 years under house arrest in Phnom Penh or in exile in Paris, Beijing and the North Korean capital Pyongyang—until he returned to Phnom Penh in 1991.

The US bombings and the emergence of a pro-American government in Phnom Penh strengthened the Khmer Isarak, an internal independence movement—more anti-imperialist than pro-communist—which had begun after World War II when the French returned to govern Cambodia. Gradually there emerged a communist group which Sihanouk called the Khmer Rouge, meaning Cambodian Reds. Once coined, the name remained, although not all Cambodian communists joined the Khmer Rouge, and not all members of the present-day Khmer Rouge army were communists.

Sihanouk mounted an aggressive anti-communist drive in the early 1960s, forcing the communists underground. Leaders such as Pol Pot, Khieu Samphan, Hu Nim, Hou Yuon and Ieng Sarey later fled to the jungles of the north and west, where they received support from disadvantaged, disillusioned hilltribes. They re-emerged in 1970 to mount guerilla attacks against the Lon Nol and American armies. The Khmer Rouge that we refer to now began in the 1960s as a small band of communist guerillas living in jungle bases.

Paradoxically before 1970 Lon Nol had been Sihanouk's deputy and the Khmer Rouge his adversaries, but after being deposed, Sihanouk reversed his alliances and formed a government in exile with the Khmer Rouge and called on the people of Cambodia to fight the 'imperialist' forces of Lon Nol's 'American-installed' Government.

Civil war raged for five years, with the Khmer Rouge progressively taking ground from the Lon Nol forces. By 1973 much of the countryside was under Khmer Rouge control. On 17 April 1975, the guerillas, wearing black 'pyjamas' (which Cambodian peasants wore to work in the fields) and checked scarves, victoriously entered the capital. They were welcomed as liberators, but within hours they began emptying the city at gun-point, and marched the entire population into the countryside. It was the beginning of what later became known as 'Year Zero'. A new agricultural based society was established, in which all aspects of modern society were obliterated. The Khmer Rouge abolished education, religion, Western medicine, private ownership, currency and commerce. Children were separated from their parents; intellectuals executed; and industry abandoned; and schools, hospitals and temples destroyed or turned into prisons. Virtually everyone—doctors, civil servants, children and the elderly—was forced into hard labour working 10 to 14 hours a day in rice fields. During the four-year Khmer Rouge rule more than one million Cambodians are said to have been killed or died of torture, starvation or disease. The Khmer Rouge 'killing fields' left an indelible physical and emotional scar on a society where virtually everyone lost at least one, and sometimes a dozen family members.

The Khmer Rouge atrocities ended when Vietnam invaded in December 1978 and drove out the Khmer Rouge who fled to the Thai border. The Vietnamese invasion was sparked by repeated attacks into Vietnam in 1977 and 1978 by the Khmer Rouge who were attempting to regain parts of southern Vietnam which they believed historically belonged to Cambodia. The most devastating Khmer Rouge attack resulted in the massacre of hundreds of Vietnamese villagers in Tay Ninh Province in December 1977. As a result, Khmer Rouge and Vietnamese forces frequently clashed along the border, and the Vietnamese Army made several incursions into Cambodia. On Christmas Day 1978, Vietnam finally mounted a full-scale retaliation, and Highway One became the main route for the invasion.

The further the Vietnamese troops advanced the more horrors they saw. They are said to have discovered mass graves so fresh that bodies had barely started to decay. These were the 'killing fields', later found all over Cambodia. The Khmer Rouge horrors had until then gone virtually unnoticed by the rest of the world. A Yugoslav television documentary showed forced labour, and some refugees who fled to Thailand told horror stories which the West generally refused to believe, even though US intelligence reports including satellite photos showed empty cities and huge work forces toiling on irrigation schemes. Having just lost the American–Vietnam War, the US administration apparently wanted to forget Indochina regardless of what horrors may be occurring there.

As a result of the brutalities during the Khmer Rouge rule, thousands of people from Svay Rieng and neighbouring provinces fled across the border to refugee camps that the Vietnamese authorities had established. One escapee was Sam Tha whom I met in 1990 as a senior Communist Party official of Svay Rieng. He was a 23-year-old student in Phnom Penh when the Khmer Rouge arrived in April 1975 and evacuated the city. He walked to his home village in Svay Rieng, but the next day was arrested. 'The Khmer Rouge leaders responsible for this zone applied part of the Maoist theory that if you destroy a regime you must also destroy the individuals who belong to that regime,' he said. Sam Tha was jailed with 800 prisoners, and forced to work 'without anything to eat in the morning'.

On 1 September 1975 the Khmer Rouge leadership proclaimed the foundation of the Revolutionary People's Party of Kampuchea, a new constitution was decreed, and prisoners were released. Sam Tha spent the next two years of forced labour digging irrigation canals as part of the Khmer Rouge's plan to turn the countryside into vast rice fields. Eleven months later, he escaped across the border with a group of friends. 'At the time, Vietnam had very strict control at the border, so we chose another route which meant going through a lake. It was reasonably shallow, so in some places we could walk, hiding behind tall grass. We walked and swam for 25 kilometres, through the whole night. At 6 a.m. it was light and we were still in Cambodia but fortunately we were in an area with high vegetation, so it was easy to hide.' The small group crossed into Long An Province, west of Ho Chi Minh. Through a friend, they arranged to live with a Vietnamese family, working the fields in return for food and lodgings. Having learnt Vietnamese, Sam Tha worked as an interpreter in one of the refugee camps, and was soon placed in charge of a camp of 2000 Cambodians. Later, he was appointed assistant to the Refugee Committee. 'An old Vietnamese man, Nam Long, was in charge of the Committee. He was born in Svay Rieng and he had a Cambodian wife. By 1978 there were 10 000 refugees in camps in Long An, and many more living with Vietnamese families.'

Sam Tha's colleague Bun Sophal, Svay Rieng's Chief of Cabinet, also fled to Vietnam with the Vietnamese army. The Khmer Rouge had turned his village of Santhor—29 kilometres from the border—into one of the notorious killing fields. 'The Khmer Rouge began killing their own officers in the village in 1976 because they thought they were opposing them. After killing military people, they began killing people involved in the Lon Nol regime. Then they started accusing people of being Lon Nol supporters or Vietnamese supporters, and killed them. Every day we saw people killed. We waited for the chance to flee. In early November 1977, the Vietnamese came into Cambodia and fought the Khmer Rouge for about 10 days then withdrew. When they came to my village more than 5000 people from our commune decided to go with them as they withdrew. About 200 people didn't want to cross into Vietnam, so they turned back, but the Khmer Rouge caught and killed them.'

Bun Saphal was also placed in charge of a refugee camp and while in Vietnam met Cambodia's future Prime Minister Hun Sen who had crossed into Vietnam in July 1977 and the soon-to-be President Heng Samrin who crossed 14 months later. 'When Heng Samrin came to Vietnam, I and my group went to Tay Ninh to work with him because he planned to liberate Cambodia from the Khmer Rouge. People in Vietnam started organising an opposition force in early 1978. Hun Sen went around the camps and gathered up all the men who could fight, and they were regrouped in one camp and trained. Hun Sen was military commander, and there were 5000 soldiers including some from his own unit who came to Vietnam with him. After training, they were sent to join Vietnamese units.'

It was 1990 and we were having lunch at the Party guesthouse in Svay Rieng town. At the same table a year earlier I had lunched with Prime Minister Hun Sen and Heng Samkay, Svay Rieng's Party Secretary (the province's most powerful official) who was also the elder brother of President Heng Samrin. It was 17 April, the anniversary of the Khmer Rouge takeover, and perhaps Hun Sen had consciously chosen to be out of Phnom Penh that day.

The Prime Minister had told me how as an 18-year-old he took up Sihanouk's plea to join the fight against Lon Nol. He soon rose through the military ranks, and in April 1975, at the age of 23, was commander of a battalion. The day before the Khmer Rouge victory, he was seriously wounded in a heavy battle which cost him his left eye and rendered him unconscious for 10 days. When recovered he was made a commander of the Eastern Zone which included Svay Rieng.

The Khmer Rouge is believed to have been made up of several factions, and in early 1977 one led by the Marxist Pol Pot gained full control and began eliminating its opponents. As the purge heightened, Hun Sen said he realised he could be next. So when he received orders to attack Lok Ninh village inside Vietnam, he stalled and used the time to arrange escape plans for himself and his men. 'I was not a Pol Pot officer but no-one knew I was against the Pol Potists because I worked in secret.' Eighteen months later, he returned to Cambodia with his troops riding Vietnamese tanks. When the Khmer Rouge were driven out, Hun Sen was made Foreign Minister in the new government, and in 1985 at the age of 35 he became the world's youngest Prime Minister.

Over lunch at Svay Rieng, away from the pressures of politics in Phnom Penh, he had talked openly about his personal life. He told how, under the Khmer Rouge regime, he was part of a mass wedding. 'It was 5 January 1976, and we were married with 13 other couples.' He agreed it was hardly romantic, then admitted that years later he and his wife, Bun Sam Hieng, dressed in traditional wedding costume to have their photos taken. He told me how he didn't see his eldest son until he was 18 months old. He had fled to Vietnam four months before his son was born and it was two months after liberation before he first saw him. 'I had been told my wife and son were killed by Pol Potists, and my wife thought I was dead. The first time I saw my son he called me uncle [meaning close family friend]. He continued to call me uncle for the first two months, and he didn't want me to stay in the house or to be with his mother,' he laughed. Hun Sen and his wife went on to have another four children, two boys and two girls, then adopted a young girl from an orphanage in Phnom Penh.

After lunch and a short siesta—wearing a white singlet, checked *krama* and no glasses the Prime Minister was barely recognisable —he had straddled a motorbike and ridden 40 kilometres to visit a remote border area, returning before dusk. His entourage was small and security was minimal, but Svay Rieng was probably the safest province. While the government forces continued to fight the Khmer Rouge, and the two non-communist factions in the north and west, Svay Rieng, by being surrounded on three sides by Vietnam, was the first province to declare itself Khmer Rouge-free and to lift its curfew in 1981.

Svay Rieng was also the first to become self sufficient in rice, although it was difficult, according to Deputy Party Secretary, Kim Hang. 'This province is based on rice production only. Under Pol Pot manpower was expelled or killed, and fields were abandoned and turned into mine fields to prevent the Vietnamese coming into Cambodia. After liberation, people started coming back but there was a lack of manpower, equipment and food, and nearly all the people were exhausted or affected by malaria, especially those coming from the west. We started clearing the land mines and bamboo sticks, and in the first year we were able to plant 38 000 hectares of rice, most of it by hoe because we didn't have ploughs.' Eight years later the area under rice had quad-rupled, but it barely reached the level it was in the 1960s—more than two decades had been lost.

Another legacy of the Pol Pot era was a phenomenal number of orphans. Most were adopted by surviving families, and some were taken to an orphanage in Svay Rieng town. When I visited, the Director, Sem Sakhin, was happy to announce that after 11 years only 41 Pol Pot orphans remained, although children from poor families have since been brought under his care. All six of his own children survived the killing fields—'I'm the luckiest man'—and he didn't mind how many other children were added to his 'second family'. Here, they combined schooling and occupational skills, as was evident by the cacophony resounding from the metal workshop where teenage boys were making buckets with rusted pieces of metal. Outside, one boy expertly bent strips of metal around a tree trunk to curve them, working with the ease of one accustomed to monotonous tasks. In the sewing room, 11 girls were making *sampots* on Taiwanese treadle machines donated by a Swedish aid organisation. Overseeing the work was Toch, 40, who told me how her husband and both children died under Pol Pot. 'I remarried and we've been trying to have children but can't. I would love to have one. Give me just one,' she laughed, obviously embarrassed by talking about something so intimate in front of her students. Her colleague, Ung Phon, 51, who learnt his craft in the 1950s from an old Hong Kong tailor, taught the girls how to make trousers. Toothless, with stubble on his chin and with exceptionally dark hands, he joked that he had no teeth because he used them to cut the thread. In reality, they fell out when he became ill while working in a Khmer Rouge labour camp.

After 1979 re-establishing schools and hospitals was as important as replanting rice, yet 11 years later, the Svay Rieng hospital —like many others—was still sadly lacking in all aspects, despite assistance from the Red Cross and Medecins Sans Frontieres (MSF) Holland–Belgium. I commented on the filthy walls. 'You can't wash them because the paint comes off, then they crumble,' said MSF doctor Kevin Yuen. 'One of the biggest needs was to help train surgeons—there hadn't been any really well trained doctors here for quite awhile—and to get the theatre operating. There was not much operating equipment, nor electricity. In the year before we came they did less than a dozen operations, now they do about 20 a month,' he said. In the men's ward, five of the six beds were occupied by soldiers with malaria. Down the corridor, two women with chronic bronchitis lay on woven mats with small dirty pillows; another lay lethargically with TB, which was more common in Svay Rieng than in any other province. A shirt hung on a pole at the end of her bed, and a hat the other end. A husband prepared food in a pot on the floor. Relatives often supplement the hospital's two rice meals a day.

In the intensive care ward—usually occupied by motor vehicle and gunshot victims—lay a man with typhoid, and beside him a young boy dying of diptheria. 'There is nothing more we can do for him,' said Kevin, who had received the best that Western training could provide. The number of children in hospital was double the norm, he said. 'Between the dry and the start of the wet season, food and water supplies are at a low, so a lot of kids are malnourished and dehydrated, which makes them more susceptible to infections. It's also the dengue fever period, and we've had quite a few kids over the past month with meningitis or encephalitis,' he said pragmatically.

Villages were served by very rudimentary district hospitals, so only serious cases were brought to the provincial hospital, but transferring patients from outlying country areas presented numerous problems. An ambulance was not always available, might not be working, or might not have a driver. 'Then there are problems with blood,' said Kevin. 'You need a laboratory that's working and a donor, and the current price for blood if you don't have a family member is nearly 10 000 riel [two and a half month's salary for a civil servant], so it's really a gamble whether you're going to live or die.'

More often than not, there was no ambulance, and patients travelled by oxcart or *remorque* (motorised trailer), sometimes taking more than a day to reach a doctor. Hospitalisation put extra financial strains on the family and disrupted family life, as at least one relative always had to live at the hospital to cook and care for the patient. Medication was not free, and they had to buy food including the staple rice at market prices when they would otherwise take it from the land.

Bernadette Glisse, MSF's midwife, worked closely with rural women and her objective was to keep childbirth at home but in better conditions, rather than have deliveries in hospitals. She did this by improving the skills of midwives and birth attendants. 'There are not many women here,' she said as we walked passed empty beds in the obstetrics and gynaecology ward. 'Only those with complications come here—and sometimes it's full. It is the tradition to deliver at home, so we focus our project on educating midwives and birth attendants at the commune, village and district level. We have to change traditions like putting ash or mud on the baby's umbilical cord which can lead to tetanus.' Other people told me that the umbilical cord was sometimes cut with black Chinese scissors or a piece of tile, then medicinal roots placed on the wound to aid healing.

Born and trained in Belgium, Bernadette spent seven years working with Cambodians in refugee camps on the Thai–Cambodian border before coming inside the country in 1988. 'I'm 41, single, and free to go where I need to be. I'll stay till there is peace,' she said. (Peace was a long time coming, and Bernadette left Cambodia in March 1991.)

Kevin and Bernadette were among the few Westerners living in rural Cambodia. Their nearest Western neighbour was an agronomist Mark Hickey, working on an Australian Catholic Relief program in Takeo, west of Svay Rieng town. 'It's on the site of an old Pol Pot system which was badly designed—canals go uphill,' he said with unconcealed contempt. Some irrigation canals built during the Khmer Rouge rule followed a grid pattern rather than contours, so many flowed contrary to design. Mark's 'home' was a room he shared with his Cambodian driver in Takeo's only guesthouse. His four Cambodian colleagues lived in a thatched hut built to store rice, water pumps, oil and diesel, sleeping together on a bench of bamboo slats. He breakfasted at the market with his Cambodian friends. 'The others have a bowl of noodles, which is one thing I can't handle, so I have bread. We eat at a rotunda-style cafe—it's left over from the French time—and eating French bread at a French-style cafe in the middle of Takeo market is very strange.' Reaching the cafe meant passing through the market. 'A couple of pig heads mark where the pork section begins, and one woman always seems to be butchering the head of the beast, splitting it down the middle with an axe. All the offal is sold in a separate section and there are usually twice as many people there because it's cheaper. I certainly haven't increased my intake of beef or pork since going to the market.'

I came through here again in 1990, but this time going in the opposite direction, to Ho Chi Minh. On this trip I couldn't help noticing the obvious increase in consumer goods. Cartons of 555 cigarettes were carried on bicycles, in the back of cars, and in the rear of our bus. In what appeared to be an isolated area, a video blasted loudly from a house on stilts with bamboo walls and corrugated roof, crammed with people all engrossed in the audio-visual import from Ho Chi Minh—or Thailand or Singapore.

A young man sitting behind me sported a flash black-and-gold Rado watch and a smarter shirt and trousers than anyone else on the bus, and he listened to taped music through headphones. Judging by his appearance, I guessed he spoke some English —and I was right. In halting dialogue—suggesting he had reached Streamline English Book Four—he told me how he ran a business importing ready-made clothes from the Cambodian port of Koh Kong, paying 1000 riel ($2.06) to take a crowded taxi from Phnom Penh to the seaport, then 10 000 to 20 000 riel to bring back six to eight sacks of clothes, calculated to be worth 50 riel per shirt. He was 26 and had finished secondary school two years earlier. (As children missed four years of schooling during the Khmer Rouge time, the Government set up special classes for older students, many of whom finished their schooling at the ages of 20 to 24.) Now he was taking his mother-in-law for medical treatment in Ho

Chi Minh where she would stay with his sister and her Vietnamese husband.

The first time I came through Svay Rieng, the bus stopped here for lunch. The driver, who had been told to take care of me, took me down an alley to the back of the cafe where other passengers were washing their hands, face and feet. They stood in a concrete yard and used a plastic bowl to scoop water from a square waist-high concrete tank, then with a *krama* they dried themselves. No bathroom with brass and tiles and fluffy towels could have done a better job of washing away six hours of heat and dust. It was totally invigorating.

The cafe had stools around a circular bar and a giant palm-leaf umbrella shading the area. It reminded me of an open-air beach-side bar. Soldiers and civilians sat in a semi-circle to eat bowls of noodles and to drink beer. Opposite, an old man with a wispy beard watched from his doorway. Several nearby shops were closed, their concertina grilles padlocked. Others sold a pathetic selection of home cooked food, household goods and bicycle parts. Many buildings remained in ruins, and the town had an eerie deserted feeling. Two years later, I found old buildings were being painted, and new ones erected, including a four-storey hotel. As in other rural towns, the streets were deserted around midday, but lively in the afternoon and evenings when food and drink stands appeared and videos were switched on.

Svay Rieng to Phnom Penh normally took four to six hours by bus. We passed the town's monument—a man with a gun and hoe beside a woman, signifying unity between the people and soldiers—and were making good progress, when we heard an explosive sound from the rear of the bus, then the unwelcome sound of rubber flapping on the road. To inspect the damage, the driver climbed out the window instead of clambering over bodies to reach the door. The driver and conductor decided to continue to Phnom Penh—at 20 kilometres an hour—rather than replace the tyre, which was surprising as the Vietnamese and Cambo-dians are remarkably good at repairing and improvising.

The countryside was vastly different from Vietnam's—not a hill or a mountain in sight, only tall palms scattered over untilled fields. Groups of houses, set among coconut, palm, banana and jackfruit trees, constituted villages rather than towns. There was no impression of sophistication—instead a sense of near-poverty; not of hopelessness, but of despondency. Life had been tough, and it was evident on the faces, furrowed and often toothless. Children laughed as they clung to the backs of buffaloes or splashed naked in canals, unable to conceive what their parent's generation had endured.

Under a huge arch bearing 'Long Live the Revolutionary People's Party of Kampuchea', and over a small narrow bridge, we entered Prey Veng Province, famed for dry-season rice and ortolau, an immigratory bird from Siberia. The road was raised above the fields virtually all the way, and was narrow and rough with broken edges which meant we had to almost stop to allow other vehicles to overtake us.

A disabled truck, parked on the verge with passengers sitting in its shade, displayed on its door a distinctive blue and white UNICEF sticker. It was one of the more than 100 trucks sent to Cambodia during the 1979/80 emergency. In 1979, as a consequence of the US bombings, the civil war and the Khmer Rouge rule, Cambodia came close to the brink of irrecoverable tragedy. Reports reaching the West estimated two million people, a possible third of the population, faced starvation, although the figure was later lowered. The outside world was only made aware of the 'killing fields' and the plight of the Cambodian people after the Khmer Rouge were driven out by the Vietnamese in January 1979. Vietnam, the Soviet Union, East Germany and Cuba began sending aid to their communist colleague, but the first Western relief officials were not allowed into Cambodia until July 1979—and then, for only 48 hours. A representative each from the UN, Unicef and the International Committee of the Red Cross (ICRC) witnessed appalling conditions, and immediately made an international appeal for help. The first Western food aid arrived in October. A consortium of 34 aid agencies organised by Oxfam UK, sent 43 barge loads of food, seeds, fertilisers, agricultural equipment and vehicles, and raised more than $100 million which was channelled through Western aid agencies. Foreign governments also donated considerable sums, despite pressure from the US not to help the Vietnamese-installed communist Government of Heng Samrin. This massive effort saved many thousands of lives and helped Cambodia begin the long road to recovery. The West condemned Vietnam's invasion and refused to recognise the Government in Cambodia, so both countries were denied bilateral aid. In addition, a US-instigated trade embargo isolated Vietnam and Cambodia from international markets, forcing them to turn to the Soviet Union and other socialist bloc countries for trade, and economic and military assistance. The direct result of the embargo and non-recognition was to force both countries deeper into a communist bloc—the opposite of the US's aim in the American–Vietnam War—and to deny more than 60 million people in desperate need of aid.

Non-government organisations (NGOs) such as Oxfam stayed on after the emergency period and set up small humanitarian projects in agriculture, health and education. Ten years later, there were more than 60 NGOs from non-socialist countries. They included world bodies such as the International Rice Research Institute and World Vision, and some set up especially for Cambodia, such as Enfants du Cambodge (Children of Cambodia). More than a dozen countries were represented, including Australia, Belgium, Canada, France, Japan, Hong Kong, the Netherlands, Norway, Sweden, Switzerland, West Germany and the UK.

Several American agencies worked in Cambodia—including American Friends Service Committee, Church World Service and the Mennonite Central Committee—although the US Government did not recognise the Heng Samrin Government. Nor did the United Nations, although Unicef started providing aid in 1979 and in 1990 spent more than $6 million on programs designed to improve conditions for women and children. This was done under political constraints which discouraged development assistance. Programs varied from installing hand pumps, water jars and household latrines, to teacher training, textbook printing and sawmilling, and a mammoth program aimed at immunising all children under one against six preventable diseases.

According to Susanne Wise, Unicef health program officer for three years, the task had not been easy. 'The normal things you would expect are missing; even when you have a building you don't always have electricity, water, basic equipment or drugs. There is an enormous shortage of trained manpower because doctors, nurses and trainers of health workers were targeted by Pol Pot or left the country, and books and training facilities were destroyed. Cambodia doesn't have a normal health profile—there is a high proportion of children and female adults—60 to 65 per cent of adults are women, 30 per cent of households are headed by a woman, and 45 per cent of the population are under 15. And there has been a lot of moving about because of the war. Although infant mortality has come down drastically, it's still very high. Birth rate and population growth are very high.'

Everywhere in Cambodia I was reminded of the devastation wrought by civil war and the Khmer Rouge rule, and of the considerable progress made since the end of the 'killing fields'. The enormity of destruction to agriculture was hard to comprehend, and when driving past still-abandoned fields, it was difficult not to think of the Pol Pot philosophy as anything but absurd. Even buffaloes and bullocks were killed, making it impossible for the country to grow enough rice. Before 1970 rice exports was the country's largest foreign exchange earner—in some years it had accounted for up to 60 per cent of export revenue—yet in 1979, one to two million people faced starvation. Since then rice production had increased almost four times and in 1990, for the first time in two decades Cambodia produced enough to feed its population which was estimated by the Government to be 8.4 million.

Teachers were considered to be intellectuals and were therefore killed—15 000 of them, two-thirds of the total. For almost four years no children sat in classrooms; instead schools were destroyed or turned into Khmer Rouge headquarters, communal kitchens, storehouses, pig sties, prisons and torture centres. When the new regime began rebuilding the education system, not only did it face a critical shortage of buildings and trained teachers, but basics such as pens, pencils, paper, chalk, blackboards, desks and chairs. By 1987, more than 50 000 teachers had been trained or retrained, and there were 5600 schools with 1.3 million students, a revived Medical School, a School of Fine Arts, a Technology Institute, an Institute of Economics, an Institute of Agricultural Technology and a College of Languages. The literacy rate was the highest it had ever been—even higher than in Sihanouk's time. The Government claimed the literacy rate reached 93 per cent by the end of the 1979 to 1988 national literacy campaign, although Western aid agencies put the figure closer to 70 per cent.

Achievements in health were similar. A mere 45 doctors and fewer than 500 midwives were left to serve the whole country— and 20 of those doctors fled within the next three years, leaving just 25 doctors for a population estimated to be six million. By the late 1980s there was a hospital in each of the 22 provincial capitals, more than 150 district hospitals and 1400 commune clinics. The number of doctors increased 16-fold in five years.

At the busy town of Neak Loeung, the most famous highway in Asia crossed the most famous river in the region—the mighty Mekong, which began its 4025-kilometre long course in the Tibetan mountains. The longest river in Southeast Asia passes through China, forms the border between Burma and Laos and between Laos and Thailand, then meanders through Cambodia and Vietnam. Approaching the South China Sea, the Mekong splits into nine rivers, hence its ancient name Cuu Long, meaning Nine Dragons. It divides southern Vietnam into four provinces and forms the great Mekong Delta which covers 25 000 square kilometres. As the snows of the north begin to melt, the Mekong swells downstream to more than 2 kilometres in width, spreading over thousands of hectares of rice fields.

The Mekong has always been a main route for transporting goods to and from Phnom Penh. In 1988 most cargo vessels came from Singapore where goods were unloaded from ocean-going container ships and transferred to smaller vessels for the trip to Phnom Penh. Laden with food, machinery and consumer goods, they passed through the silted mouth of the Mekong then began the last leg of their journey up the river to Phnom Penh, all passing through Neak Loeung. Queen of the Mekong was the *Mekong Express* which in 1988 arrived in Phnom Penh twice a month, amid great anticipation. At this time, life in the capital revolved around the once-a-week Kampuchean Airlines flight from Ho Chi Minh and the arrival of the *Mekong Express* which came laden with everything from cement to Heineken beer. Four years later, there were 17 direct flights a week to Bangkok and at any time six to 10 freighters were anchored at Phnom Penh port.

Our bus reached the Mekong as the 60-tonne cross-river ferry slid off its ramp and began hauling a load of trucks across the river. The current was such that the ferry traced a huge arc, and the river so wide that buildings on the opposite bank were barely distinguishable. Long queues of cars, vans and trucks languished in the midday heat on each side of the river waiting to be transported to the other side. Most were topped with boxes, bicycles, tyres and jerry-cans of fuel. Occupants sat in the shade of their vehicles or at nearby cafes where women wrapped in *kramas* served food and drinks under tarpaulin or palm-leaf shades. Fresh coconuts were drunk via straws, as were bottles of bright coloured Cambodian-made cordial sold from little two-wheel blue wagons.

A couple of cows wandered among people and vehicles. Vietnamese women cooked food in metal pots, or sold home-made food from trays carried on their heads. Chickens lay on the ground, feet bound, awaiting a sale. Teenagers moved between vehicles offering coconut cakes, home-made samosas, grilled chicken legs, cold beef kebabs. A 13-year-old girl was selling hot corn (10 riel a knob) because it was school holidays, she said. Another girl, 17-year-old Tey, said she had been selling cakes at the crossing since she was 11. Her five brothers and sisters also sold cakes—made by her sister at home—and in three days each earned a third of a civil servant's monthly salary, working from early morning till the last ferry at about 6 p.m.

Money traders mingled with sellers, offering dong to Vietnam-bound travellers and riel to those heading for Phnom Penh. Hoa, a 33-year-old Vietnamese born in Neak Loeung, had been selling money here for two years. He bought dong from one of many merchants who came from Ho Chi Minh bringing with them between one to two million dong a day. His male friend flashed two long little-finger nails painted bright pink with silver sparkle.

In 1988, Helene Hege, a doctor with the American-based Mennonite Central Committee, was the only Westerner living among 800 000 Cambodians in Prey Veng Province. She lived and worked at the provincial hospital 30 kilometres from Neak Loeung. Although she had running cold water and electricity four hours a day, sending a message to Phnom Penh meant going to the Neak Leoung ferry and finding someone prepared to deliver it. I wondered why a 29-year-old single woman would swap the good life in France to work in the heat and dust of a provincial town in one of the world's poorest countries. 'Many of my friends went to work in developing countries instead of doing military service, and I thought I could do the same. My Christian belief taught me to be willing to share my life and skills with poorer people. It's very interesting and I live more closely to Cambodian people than it would be possible in Phnom Penh.'

Three years later several Westerners were living in Prey Veng and Svay Rieng, including an agronomist, a rural nurse, an agricultural development officer, an anthropologist and an eight-member MSF medical team. Dutch couple Evert Van Bodejom and Sita Van Der Veer twice a month came down to Neak Loeung to cross the Mekong en route to Phnom Penh. They were the first foreigners in

25 years to live in Romeas Hek district of Svay Rieng near the Vietnam border. 'We were like monkeys in a cage,' said Evert. 'In the first few weeks they were really astonished to see us, and everyone came to look in our house. They are pleased foreigners are living here because it's a sign of being recognised; sometimes they think they are forgotten by the world.'

He and Sita spent three years in Mozambique before coming to Cambodia to oversee rural development projects for Padek (Partnership for Development in Kampuchea), a consortium of five NGOs. At Romeas Hek they established an extension (advisory) service for farmers. 'It assesses needs of farmers and introduces new methods. Farmers have many problems and we want to be sure new species and the results of research and new technology reach them.' Evert and Sita enjoyed living in a Cambodian house and eating only Cambodian food, although Sita admitted she sometimes dreamt of cheese fondues.

Crossing the Mekong in April 1989, a smartly-dressed, English-speaking cadre told how he had been sent to the northwest of the country, to the new province of Banteay Meanchey. He had made his mark as a young ambassador in East Germany several years earlier and since the Party decided in 1985 to strengthen its bases in the provinces, he was one of many senior cadres sent to the countryside. He hoped his one-year stint in the northwest would not be extended, he said, because he didn't like being separated from his family who remained in Phnom Penh. (Standing on the tarmac at Phnom Penh airport in early 1991, the newly-appointed Deputy Foreign Minister, Phy Thach, introduced himself and reminded me that we had met on the Neak Loeung ferry two years earlier!)

While waiting to cross the Mekong in 1990, I met a Californian anthropologist working as a technology transfer specialist. Somewhat reluctantly abandoning the novel he was reading in the air-conditioned comfort of his Landcruiser—the standard agency vehicle in Cambodia—he said he was concerned that the forthcoming rice harvest would be down due to a lack of rain and fuel for pumping. For the 1989 planting season farmers paid the State 16.5 riel per litre for fuel. Twelve months later, he said, they were forced to pay 70 to 100 riel (14 to 20 cents) a litre on the open market, because the Government had removed subsidies and the Soviet Union had withdrawn its fuel supply to Cambodia. He was critical of rural development centres being set up by several relief agencies at the request of the Government. He warned that when the NGOs stopped supporting the centres, they would collapse.

During my first crossing, as vehicles and passengers streamed off the ferry, an aged fuel truck stalled several times while trying to ride the muddy incline. Apparently, the driver couldn't engage first gear, and twice found reverse by mistake, sending people scurrying as the vehicle lurched backwards towards the ferry. The brakes locked and the truck skidded to a halt. The driver tried again, and again it slid uncontrollably towards the river. People stopped and watched, holding their breaths, while he found the right gear and slowly hauled the truck to the top of the bank.

After almost an hour of waiting our bus, now partly emptied of passengers, gingerly eased down the huge metal ramps to the sturdy old ferry to be taken across the murky Mekong. Foot-passengers crammed on, squeezing their bodies and baskets between vehicles.

As the river level was down and the exit ramp steep, the under-carriage of the bus scraped noisily across the ramp as it left the ferry. The Phnom Penh side of the Mekong had as many vehicles waiting, and hawkers selling their wares. The crowds on this side were held behind high gates until the ferry was ready to receive them. Once opened, the gates released a human torrent which surged onto the ferry, carrying bags, pushing bicycles, and hauling boxes.

This is the way the Vietnamese entered—and left—Cambodia. The number of Vietnamese soldiers in Cambodia reached a peak of 200 000 in 1982. Troops were progressively withdrawn from then until the final pull-out in September 1989. (Despite repeated claims from Phnom Penh and Hanoi that no troops remained after the final withdrawal, some units are said to have stayed on ᴜ returned soon after. In early 1991, US intelligence sources said they believed at least 2000 Vietnamese soldiers were still in the country, most acting as advisers. When the United Nations began disarming Cambodian soldiers in June 1992 as part of the UN peacekeeping operation, the Khmer Rouge refused to cooperate because they said the UN had to verify the complete withdrawal of all Vietnamese troops. The Khmer Rouge, however, did not say how many Vietnamese soldiers they thought remained in Cambodia, and failed to produce evidence to support their claims.)

During the two largest withdrawals, in June 1988 and September 1989, hundreds of trucks loaded with troops rolled down Highway One, across the Mekong to Ho Chi Minh, then up Highway One to other cities in Vietnam. I was in Cambodia during the 1988 pull-out when the Neak Loeung ferry worked from 3 a.m. to 11 p.m., transporting more than 50 000 Vietnamese soldiers.

The road between the Mekong crossing and the capital was lined with hundreds of Cambodian flags, which then were bright red with the yellow five-tower outline of the main Angkor temple. (From May the following year, the lower half of the flag was replaced with blue representing democracy.) Flags were flown for the two major withdrawals. Officially it was to thank the Vietnamese for keeping the Khmer Rouge at bay and helping rebuild the country; at a more grassroots level it reaffirmed Cambodian patriotism and independence.

On the road to Phnom Penh we passed cactus hedges in front of small thatched homes, each with a large unglazed earthenware jar to collect rain water. A van with a dozen passengers on the roof and a dusty horn-tooting Mercedes forced us on to the verge. Taxis ranged from old white Peugeots to motorbike-drawn trailers where people sat along the sides. Everywhere, men and women had red and white checked scarves around their heads or necks. Smoke wafted from windows of thatched houses. Dozens of live chickens hung upside down from the tailgate of a truck—a mass of speckled feathers and splayed feet.

As the bus crawled towards Phnom Penh, some passengers on the left hung towels over the windows to block the sun, and a baby (whom I hadn't noticed before) began crying. Most people slept—or tried to—in the last two hours before reaching the suburbs.

At a customs check point, we were stopped by two young officers in olive green short-sleeve uniforms, one with an AK47 hanging from a thick shoulder strap. The driver took several packets of cigarettes from a locked compartment above the

ı, and gave them to the conductor who spent ten
egotiating with the officers. He returned, collected
re packets, and we proceeded.

through the same area two years later, my Ho Chi Minh-
; was stopped by a mobile tax unit. A young boy had
ᵇᵉᵉⁿ sitting beside the driver on a cardboard box which was
promptly turned upside down and torn open to reveal about
20 000 riel ($41) in small notes banded in large bundles. Twelve
bundles were given to the tax collectors 'to facilitate the trip'
because on board (crammed in the aisle) were several untaxed
motorbikes.

Much of the terrain to the north of here was scrubland
stretching to the horizon without a house in sight; fallow land
which in Sihanouk's time grew maize and some tobacco, but had
not been put back into production since the Khmer Rouge rule.
The Hungarian Government had partly helped revive tobacco
production, and rows of new brick kilns with shiny galvanised
roofs were a testament to their effort.

Crossing the Mekong put us in Kandal, neither a rich nor poor
province, which extended south of Phnom Penh and was dissected by the Mekong. Land here was expensive, as the fertile
plains along the Mekong supplied Phnom Penh's markets with
fruit, flowers and vegetables—mainly banana, mango and corn,
also tomatoes and beans as subsiduary crops. In Kien Svay
town—capital of the famous mango growing district—there was
a beautiful double-storey white colonial building, and a once-
elegant pagoda. To me they represented the two influences which
have most shaped Cambodian society in the past century: the
French era and Buddhism. The pagoda, presumably sacked by
the Khmer Rouge, had not been restored yet and stood among
banana and jackfruit trees and tall grass. At the top of the columns
could be seen carved figures, once brightly coloured but now
faded. Nirothreanthey pagoda, just outside Phnom Penh, had
been restored, and it looked splendid. In Sihanouk's time it was
famous for curing children who were brought from all over the
country to be bathed by the monks who performed a sermon for
them. On 17 April 1975, Nirothreanthey became the temporary
home for thousands of people pushed out of Phnom Penh by the
Khmer Rouge. They walked the five kilometres from the city and
spent their first nights in the expansive grounds under the shade
of the huge trees, where today chickens scratch.

Phnom Penh: a city revived

I came to see communism at work, but it's all gone.
Former US Senator Dick Clark

Arriving in Phnom Penh at the end of a hot, jolting 10-hour bus trip, was not the ideal way to experience the city for the first time, yet as we crossed Monivong Bridge my deadened senses immediately came alive. The first impression was of a vibrant city, showing little signs of war. The streets were wide and tree-lined, busy yet virtually devoid of cars, trucks and buses. From a small settlement in the early 1800s—well positioned on the confluence of the Tonle Sap and Mekong rivers—it had grown to a beautiful city, although by 1988, after 20 years' conflict, much of the beauty had faded. It was a distinctly Asian city, yet the French influence was pervasive, from the circular gendarme traffic stands in the middle of intersections, to the window arches on colonial-built homes.

Cyclists and cyclos jostled with motorbikes. Street-side vendors sold cigarettes, sugar cane, tea, noodles and bananas. Shops offered beds, furniture, earthenware pots, fire wood, pharmaceuticals, shoes, cloth and bicycles. Bright coloured cyclos were everywhere, driven by men with bronzed muscular legs, with *kramas* wrapped around their heads or necks. There were women in sarongs, children in shorts, men in squat turned-up hats and traffic officers in olive green uniforms which had replaced the white French uniforms of former times. The bus passed the drab looking Olympic Stadium built by Sihanouk for the 1966 Ganefos Games, then we stopped opposite a military school where young men marched in line, many wearing mismatched uniforms and plastic sandals.

In the late afternoon the long wide main street designed by Sihanouk and named after his grandfather, King Monivong, was thick with people. Some women balanced huge flat trays on their heads offering home-prepared food including rice cakes wrapped in banana leaves. Others, in patterned sarongs, carried children on their hips. Children carried younger children on their hips. Cyclos and motorbikes carried piles of produce as well as passengers. Young women, wearing dark blue *sampots*, made a striking picture in thick bright fluffy hats, as they sat upright to peddle smart new Thai bicycles.

Shops along the Monivong Boulevard looked remarkably normal compared with Vietnam's hotchpotch of stalls and drab retail outlets. The wide footpaths were devoid of peddlers, and shops stretched for several blocks, side by side, all the same width, each with a similar neat blue and white sign above the door stating the shop number and address. There were tailors and hairdressers and a variety of small retailers. A few shops stacked old silverware behind windows, and exchanged money behind counters. One American dollar bought 85 riel which in turn bought a pack and a half of imported cigarettes. (This was August 1988. By July 1990 one dollar was worth 485 riel on the blackmarket, or 380 at the official rate, yet one dollar still bought the same number of cigarettes. In November 1991 the exchange rate fell to 1200 riel, one-twelfth of what it had been three years earlier.)

The row of shops ended at the Monorom Hotel where the top floor restaurant offered panoramic views for those prepared to climb six flights of stairs. (Even in 1991 the lift worked only on disco nights, and then only stopped at the sixth floor. On a rare occasion when it operated 'normally', a group of Japanese women were stuck between the second and third floors and became hysterical.)

Just past the Monorom was the 1930s-built railway station where three mornings a week, at 6 a.m., an old steam train left for Battambang 300 kilometres away. Before dawn, the platform became a jostling mass of people eating, selling, carrying. Women served steaming bowls of noodles from portable stalls, others plied the platform with trays of food balanced on their heads, amputees swung down the platform with their empty trouser legs flapping. One carriage towards the rear carried a rotating artillery gun manned by half a dozen armed soldiers. Free passage could be had on the first carriage which acted as a buffer if the train hit a landmine, and despite the risk, it was always crowded.

Further down the north–south Monivong Boulevard (although renamed Achar Mean many people still used the former name) was the site of the old Catholic cathedral, also built by the French in the 1930s. After prohibiting religion, the Khmer Rouge pulled the cathedral apart brick by brick. In 1988 a Soviet satellite station which beamed all Cambodia's phone calls through Moscow, Ho Chi Minh and Hanoi was built on the site. In August 1990 Australia's Overseas Telecommunications Corporation (OTC) installed a satellite next to the Soviet satellite station site, giving the country its first international direct dial system.

The satellite station stood at one end of a beautiful wide tree-lined east–west boulevard, with Wat Phnom at the other end. This concrete conicle pagoda (*wat*) dominated the city from the top of a small rounded hill (*phnom*). According to legend, while an old lady, Daun (grandmother) Penh, bathed in the nearby river, a branch floated past carrying a small Buddha statue. To protect and preserve the statue, she built a pagoda on top of a man-made hill.

Around the base of the artificial hill I found a children's playground and the city's only zoo, which had a pathetic collection of bears, antelopes, monkeys, otters, owls and various birds. In the early morning amputees from the nearby Military Hospital, the country's second largest hospital, milled around the Wat, many in pyjamas, smoking and talking, or just watching the passing traffic. They were a pitiful collection of has-beens, social rejects who had served their purpose in war and were now homeless and aimless. They were also a reminder that this country was littered with landmines.

North of Wat Phnom, the city's northern boundary was marked by the 'Broken Bridge', a four-lane concrete arch which once spanned the Tonle (River) Sap. The centre span was blown away in 1973 by the Viet Cong who along with the Sihanouk-led resistance forces were fighting the 'US imperialists' and the Lon Nol army. South of Wat Phnom, at the other end of leafy Tou Samuth Boulevard, stood the dominating five-tiered Victory Monument built in 1960 to commemorate liberation from the French in 1953. The city's other landmark of the French era was the Samaki Hotel. Built near Wat Phnom in the 1930s as Le Royal, it was known as Le Phnom in Lon Nol's time and in 1979 renamed the Samaki, meaning solidarity, in recognition of the new Cambodian–Vietnamese solidarity. By 1991, it was once again known as Le Royal.

Dinner on my first night was with a Samaki Hotel resident, a Western aid worker. Sitting on the balcony of a restaurant overlooking Boeng Kak Lake on the northern edge of the city, she ordered *soupe de crevettes a la citronelle* and *poisson elephant sauce piquante* from the French-speaking waiter who inclined his head in respect then backed away. His colleague, a 22-year-old orphan, said he was going to be a soldier 'to end the bloodshed between Cambodian and Cambodian'. Riding back to the Samaki, side by side in cyclos, we talked of how much the city had changed in the 18 months she had been here.

It was hard to imagine that 13 years earlier these streets were virtually deserted. This city of parks and beautiful French villas had no people, no cars, no animals. The Khmer Rouge entered on 17 April 1975 and the angry young men, wielding US-made M16 and Chinese AK47 rifles, emptied the city of all its inhabitants, who then clogged the roads as they trudged slowly to the country-side. Some were told to leave for just three hours, so the guerillas could eradicate the last of Lon Nol's Government forces; the majority left because they were told the city was to be bombed by the Americans; none imagined it would be three years, eight months, and 20 days of unbelievable death and tragedy before survivors could return.

Phnom Penh—once the favourite of France's Indochina cities —retained splashes of Frenchness, mixed with traditional Khmer, and to a lesser extent Chinese and Vietnamese influences. Reminders of a past glory were plentiful: the wide streets with aged trees and huge median strips, the triple-storey terraces and grand public buildings, and of course the Royal Palace, a fine example of traditional Khmer architecture. Its gracefully curling tiled roofs rose above its protective wall, and took on a rich golden hue in the early morning light. The interior—out of bounds to commoners while the royal family lived there—boasted a well-preserved collection of buildings and gardens and the Silver Pagoda which featured a floor of solid silver and housed a much revered jade Buddha.

Cambodian monarchs had lived here since 1821 when the Cambodian capital moved to Phnom Penh from Udong just 40 kilometres to the north. The monarchy ended when Sihanouk's father died in 1960, although Sihanouk continued to live here until his dismissal in 1970. He was then held prisoner here by the Khmer Rouge from September 1975 until January 1979, with just his wife, Princess Monique, and his Khmer Rouge guard. The palace then remained deserted for 13 years until the exiled former king made his historic return in November 1991.

Riding through the streets at 5 a.m. on my first morning in August 1988, I saw what made it such an interesting city. Once-fashionable hotels stood deserted. Once-beautiful villas crumbled at the edges. Amputees on crutches and piles of refuse mingled with colourful markets and crowded outdoor cafes. Pedestrians, cyclists, cyclos, trucks and cars threaded their way across busy intersections, unaided by traffic lights. Children carted water from open street wells. At the Tonle Sap market, long wooden boats bobbed and jostled side by side at the foot of the steep riverbank, while baskets of bananas, bags of rice, and barrels of fuel were unloaded and carried up the steep steps, almost at a running pace.

Nearby, an old Buddhist temple had been converted to a wood yard. A faded wooden sign above an arched doorway was the only reminder that a derelict building had once been the old 'Grand Hotel': in 1988, it was no more 'grand' than a worn-out brown paper bag. French villas now housed three or four, and sometimes ten families. Pigs and chickens foraged where gardens had flourished. It was sad to see all this and think what it had been in former times.

The cyclo driver took me to O-Russey (The River of Bamboo) Market, a haphazard collection of stalls held together by iron roofing and torn tarpaulins, under which women sat on small raised platforms in the stifling heat to sell beautiful silk *sampots*, or squatted in the muddy aisles awaiting buyers for their home-prepared food. Live fish were thumped over the head with a wooden club before being expertly gutted and dissected, and I watched in amazement as a young woman squatted in the mud and skinned live frogs which then had their hind legs removed with one swift blow of a meat cleaver. The smell of motor oil and metal from the mechanical parts section mingled with that of dried fish and raw meat. Women squatted to eat hard-boiled, almost-ready-to-hatch eggs spiced with salt, pepper and lemon juice. As they pushed their tiny spoon into the shell you could see the solidified young chick, just days from hatching.

At the Tuol Tum Poung Market, in the southern suburbs, I found old Cambodian wares including small silver betel-nut boxes, Buddha statues and bronzed Khmer lions, between stalls offering sapphires and rubies, cloth, clothes and food. Here were Wilkins & Sons' Apricot Preserve, Suzie Quatro's Greatest Hits and exotic condoms (popular among the Soviets, I was told), amid Australian beer, tins of French butter and canned Russian caviar (for $3, one-tenth of the cost in France). I even found Canadian IUDs which women would take to a doctor for insertion. I bought a 'bronze' lion, and several months later a hind leg broke and dirt and tiny pebbles trickled out of the thin metal mould; I didn't know whether to cry or triumph at having discovered the maker's secret.

In 1988 it was apparent that this was a city undergoing a huge but slow transformation, from a ghost town left virtually deserted by the Khmer Rouge, to a lively city of approximately 800 000 people. By 1990 the change was even more dramatic, and Phnom Penh was almost back to what it had been in the early 1970s.

Pam Harrison had lived in Phnom Penh in the early 1970s, helping in refugee camps while her engineer husband worked on the Mekong irrigation project. They returned in 1990 and she recalled what it had been like twenty years earlier when, she said, Phnom Penh was larger, dirtier and less peaceful. 'I had four young children and I was scared most of the time', she said. After the 1970 coup the city was under the constant threat of attack from revolutionary forces wanting to overthrow the Lon Nol Government. 'There were always the sounds of war. You could see tracers in the sky, rockets came close to the city, and we had a curfew. It's so peaceful now.' Paradoxically, we were sitting in a cafe just off Monivong Boulevard and the overwhelming sound was of motorbikes and tooting horns.

In the late 1960s and early 70s, as a consequence of the US bombings and fighting between Government and resistance forces, the rural economy virtually collapsed and refugees streamed into Phnom Penh which grew from one to almost three million people. Like many Western wives at the time, Pam Harrison helped look after women and children in refugee camps and orphanages. She recalled seeing the refugees arrive. 'I went to Michaud's, a French deli, to get something special on Christmas Day. Sitting on the footpath was a filthy baby covered in sores, and beside her an old woman. I was so stunned. The next day I went back with a plastic basin, and my driver and I sat on the footpath bathing this baby, while my children looked on in amazement.

We discovered the woman was 49, had never had children but had accepted this baby as hers. We took them both to a refugee camp. Two days later I was told that instead of using the money we gave her for food, she got drunk, then beat the baby. Gaetana Enders, the wife of the American Charge d'Affaires, was going to Switzerland a few days later to see her children who were at school there, so she took the baby with her. She would be 20 or so now, and is probably skiing down the slopes of Switzerland.' Pam Harrison left Phnom Penh in 1973.

Two years later the Khmer Rouge—also called Pol Potists— arrived in the capital. It was 17 April 1975, and Ngak Chhay Heng, caretaker of the city's parks and gardens, was at his home in Tuol Svay Prey, a southwest suburb, with his wife, four children (aged 4 to 15) and parents-in-law. 'It was the [Cambodian] New Year holiday so everyone was at home. The Pol Pot soldiers came at 9 a.m. with guns and told us we had to move out for a few hours only because the Americans were going to bomb the city. We put our things—some clothes, food, plates—in our small Honda taxi truck and pushed it. We couldn't drive because there were too many people. By 10 a.m. the roads were already crowded and it took one hour to move one kilometre. People were carrying possessions, pushing carts, all kinds of people—young children and new born babies, old and sick, some in wheelchairs, some with walking frames, some using hammocks to carry sick people. Some Lon Nol soldiers had taken off their American uniforms and left them laying beside the road. And so many dead people beside the road . . .' he trailed off. 'About 12 kilometres from Phnom Penh, we stopped at Chruoy Ampil Pagoda and camped under the trees with around 8000 other people. After 20 days there, Pol Pot said everyone had to return to their birthplace.' Heng's family went by boat up the Mekong to Rokar Koang, then took an ox-cart to his native village of Trapeang Kak in Kompong Cham, near Skoun. 'We put our possessions and the children on the cart and we walked.' They reached the village 32 days after leaving Phnom Penh. 'When we arrived everything had changed. Pol Pot had moved all our houses about 600 metres back from the road, some houses were destroyed, and they had changed the name of the village.'

During the Khmer Rouge rule from 1975 to 1979, Heng worked in the fields near his village. 'We worked all day and sometimes at night—we couldn't see where to plant the rice, so we had to measure the distance by hand, and there were lots of mosquitoes. We worked 18 hours a day. The men, women and older children were always segregated, so husband and wife never worked together. They had "schools" but the children learnt to carry cow dung, not to read and write.' Heng came back to Phnom Penh after the Khmer Rouge were driven out in 1979.

One young couple, Eth Sary and his wife Mou Bun Tha, were among the few who stayed in the city during the Khmer Rouge time. Sary remembers it as a quiet city with no cars, buses or bicycles; no markets or cafes. It was devoid of life, although people were living there. 'It was a sad city,' he said. 'The roads were empty. There were no gardens. Pol Pot destroyed all the gardens then planted banana and coconut trees. We could only eat at the communal kitchen, there were no shops. And no cigarettes, but some people smoked the leaves of papaya trees. In the former regime, we could go anywhere, but Pol Pot wouldn't let us go to another part of town.'

We were sitting on a bamboo bench outside his small house of woven bamboo walls and palm-leaf roof on the outskirts of the city. Nearby was the former Youth College (now the School of Fine Arts), where Sary and more than 1000 people lived in cramped conditions during the Pol Pot days. Each morning workers had stood outside in neat queues waiting for a truck to take them to a workshop or rice fields. Those who worked near the college, walked in regimented single file. Sary worked at the power station in Phnom Penh, and his wife-to-be, Tha, was taken to fields near Cheoung Ek, where more than 100 mass graves were later found.

Sary and Tha had seen each other, but had never spoken—'Men and women were not allowed to talk to each other'. Then one day in 1978 they and ten other men and women were given the names of their future spouses and told they all would be married the following evening. 'Everyone must obey the Pol Potists, and when they say you must marry someone, you must,' said Sary. He and Tha had five children—and no regrets, he said.

The Khmer Rouge rule came to an end when the Vietnamese arrived in Phnom Penh on 7 January 1979. They found an almost deserted city, with neglected houses and piles of rubbish. Animals roamed the streets and banana trees grew wild. There were no cars, no industry, no public amenities. Cars were stacked in piles near the airport, or in warehouses, along with refrigerators and airconditioners. (Some were seen being transported down Highway One towards Ho Chi Minh soon after the Vietnamese arrived.) As the Vietnamese advanced the Khmer Rouge fled, killing or taking with them what little population there was in the city. On that first afternoon the Vietnamese found more than 500 prisoners being herded down Highway Four towards Kompong Speu, many barely able to walk.

On the first day they also discovered Tuol Sleng concentration camp, a former high school transformed by the Khmer Rouge into a torture centre and the largest prison in the country. For some reason, on my first trip to Phnom Penh I avoided visiting Tuol Sleng, and when I finally saw it in 1989, I knew why. It was a grotesque institution, comparable with Hitler's or Idi Amin's torture chambers. On display, as a testament to the murderous regime, were tiny cells, torture instruments, dossiers and documents, books of victims' names, victims' photos, their clothes and belongings, even blood-stained floors.

It was not the blood nor the barbaric torture instruments that upset me the most, but the photos of child victims, and the hollow, lifeless eyes of hundreds of men, women and children photographed before their death. One remains in my mind: Chan Kin Sron, holding her baby with a desperate, penetrating look. She was the wife of Van Piny, Sihanouk's Vice-Minister of Foreign Affairs. He and eight other members of the cabinet and diplomats came back to Phnom Penh with Prince Sihanouk in September 1975, and were later murdered by the Khmer Rouge, while the former monarch was held under house arrest. The chilling black and white photos represented a fraction of the more than 20 000 victims imprisoned and exterminated at Tuol Sleng.

Methods of torture are said to have included lashings, water baths, extraction of finger nails followed by the pouring of alcohol on the injury, ducking victims face-down into a water barrel, suspending them from a beam by their wrists, pinching the nipples of women with red-hot pincers and pouring water onto a victim's face covered with a cloth until he was unable to breathe. Other victims had their necks broken with thick bamboo sticks or hoe-rings, then their gall bladders extracted. Infants are said to have been massacred by striking them against trees trunks or poles.

No class or profession were spared, everyone suffered at the hands of the Khmer Rouge: peasants, workers, technicians, engineers, monks, ministers, Khmer Rouge cadres, soldiers, doctors, teachers, students, even foreigners, including several Americans and one Australian. At Choeung Ek village just outside Phnom Penh, I found a skull said to be that of the Australian—identified by a hand-written label—along with thousands of others neatly stacked side by side behind glass. The new Government had built a towering four-sided glass monument on the site of mass graves to remind future generations of 'the Killing Fields'.

I was introduced to former sculptor Icm Chan who was in Tuol

Sleng when the Vietnamese arrived. He had survived the torture techniques but was unable to walk. As the Khmer Rouge fled they gathered together seven survivors from Tuol Sleng and five from other prisons and forced them onto the road, but Chan could only crawl—his ankles had been wrapped in iron chains for too long. 'We had irons on our wrists and ankles and 20 of us were joined together at the ankles by a steel rod that ran through the irons.' Chan attempted suicide twice—'every day I wanted to suicide'—by wrapping a *krama* around his neck, and the second time by using a mosquito net. 'When the guard saw me, he beat me and I was interrogated,' he said, his hand shaking as he tried to write on my notepad.

The interrogation technique Chan hated most involved filling the lungs with water. 'They spread us out on our backs and put our wrists and ankles in irons, then put a cloth over our face and poured water onto the face, so the water went into the lungs. When we didn't move they knew we were unconscious, then they put a foot on our stomach to force the water out.' Chan became very emotional, and jumped when a door closed nearby. 'For other prisoners they used a knife to pierce the wrist. They removed nails from the pointer finger, and every day . . .' he didn't finish. Before the Khmer Rouge rule Chan had spent 10 years helping restore Angkor Wat with Andre Groslier, the renowned French archaeologist in charge of restoration. Chan's once-artistic confident hands were now only capable of producing Angkor-style sculptures for a Government-run shop.

While Chan was enjoying his first days of freedom from Tuol Sleng, Ngo Dien, a former Vietnamese journalist who was chief of the Press Department in Hanoi during the Vietnam War, arrived in Phnom Penh to help set up the new government's Ministry of Foreign Affairs. At the end of 1979 he was appointed Vietnam's Ambassador to Cambodia until January 1992.

When Dien arrived in January 1979—by helicopter from Ho Chi Minh, a few days after liberation—Phnom Penh looked like a city that had been struck by nuclear warfare which had killed everyone, but had left the houses untouched. 'From the airport to the city there was nothing, only my car and the army men. In one house a meal had been prepared and was still sitting there, solidified, just as the occupants left it. The most horrible thing was the smell of dead bodies.'

He visited many houses but one had a more lasting effect than others. 'I saw a blackboard, a table, a bed, and the shoes of a little girl. On the blackboard she had written in French, "I love my house",' he paused, thinking hard, ' "the birds are singing on the tree in front of the house." I took the blackboard back to show the men and said, "look what has happened, this is the remains of her family, it was a peaceful life and now . . . " '

Dien never forgot what he saw in Kompong Speu, west of Phnom Penh, soon after he arrived. 'As the Khmer Rouge fled they forced people with them. Mothers who could not feed their babies put them under trees and made prayers to Buddha,' he said, pressing his palms together and bowing his head. 'The commander of the Vietnamese unit ordered his men to split into small groups, gather up the babies and children—some were two, three, four years old—and take them to the hospital. A medical team from southern Vietnam set up a small hospital in Kompong Speu. There were wounded and sick people in the hospital, and under the trees because there were not enough places. And I saw the babies,' he said, making a 'tut' sound and shaking his head. 'They had no flesh, only bones, and big heads. And big eyes just staring.' Dien was obviously moved. He often paused as he recalled what he had seen 11 years earlier, several times inclining his head and swallowing hard. 'Some men adopted these children as their sons. We decided to set up orphanages in Phnom Penh for these children, and took over schools or big houses. We had four or five orphanages and some still exist today. We called them "lotus centres" because lotus is the symbol of something pure and fragrant, it's born from mud but it's very clean and beautiful.'

The first orphanage was run by Pum Si Chan, a formidable yet motherly woman who a decade later was a senior official in the Municipal People's Committee. It was there that I found her one afternoon. She professed not to speak English until it became apparent that her grasp of the language was better than her interpreter's. A former teacher, she survived the Pol Pot days planting rice in Battambang Province. After liberation, she sold her previously-hidden earrings to pay someone to find her children and then spent a month walking with them from Battambang to Phnom Penh. 'I had a little gold and paid for my youngest daughter to ride on a cart.' In Phnom Penh she found notices calling on people with education or expertise to help re-establish social order. 'They asked me to open the orphanage. The Vietnamese army collected children and they came from all over the country but most from Battambang. They were all very thin and sick. The number increased every day and when we had 500, we opened the first orphanage—it was 1 June, International Children's Day,' she said.

'We had great difficulties, we lacked everything, so the [Vietnamese] 24th division, known as Cuu Long, supplied us with rice, sugar, milk, clothes, all brought from Vietnam. Each day the children became stronger, and out of 500 only two died. The number coming continued to increase and when we had another 500 we opened another orphanage, until we had four in Phnom Penh, plus ones in Kompong Speu, Kompong Som, Takeo and Kompong Cham.'

One orphanage was named Cuu Long, although the original was unimaginatively called Orphanage Number One. (It seemed to be the socialist custom to identify establishments by number rather than name. Phnom Penh's streets were numbered—my address was House 29, Street 200—and the three main hospitals were 2 December, 7 January and 17 April, all commemorating recent Cambodian events.) I went with Chan to Orphanage Number One which in the early days was home to 560 waifs of the Pol Pot era, half of whom still lived there 15 years later. The others had married or found jobs and moved on. Only 17 of the current orphans were born since the Khmer Rouge time. Most were left at hospitals by single or destitute mothers, like eight-year-old Peoteth, who wore a dirty yellow T-shirt and cheeky smile, and followed me around the courtyard.

Kang Uanreun, 20, had been living there since the centre opened. She worked at a nearby hospital as a trainee and would not earn a salary until next year, when she hoped to move out and be independent. Until then, she shared a dirty, poorly-lit room with nine other working girls. As in homes, clothes hung on bed poles and on wire strung across the room. The walls were partly covered with old newspapers, and a glass panel in the door had been replaced by plywood boards. Chickens could be heard outside and I could smell where they had been inside. Next door, builders were working on an extension, funded by Medicins du Monde, one of the many Western aid agencies based in Phnom Penh.

From the end of 1989, the Government allowed foreigners to adopt orphans, and in the first six months, six couples and three single women did so. According to a Cambodian doctor, Party officials used to say that Westerners could not adopt Cambodian children because they would take them away, bring them up and send them back as spies. 'But I never believed that,' he said.

While Pum Si Chan was setting up orphanages, Western aid workers began coming to Cambodia in the latter half of 1979. Onesta Carpene, an Italian with remarkable devotion and endurance, was among the first to live here. She arrived in February 1980 on a three-month assignment to administer the distribution of emergency aid. Twelve years later she was still here, running projects for Australian Catholic Relief, after working eight years with CIDSE Cooperation International pour le Development et la Solidarite, a consortium of 14 Catholic agencies.

In the first few months of 1980 she travelled the countryside extensively to assess the need for projects and the distribution of aid. 'On my first trip in March I went to Siem Reap and Battambang (in the northwest). I didn't see any animals, not even chickens. I thought the countryside would produce something but there was nothing, not even birds. It was the dry season, so it was brown everywhere, and you couldn't find water. When we asked a family for a drink, they went to a coconut tree and got a drink for us, and were very upset that we offered to pay. These people were poor, and they gave what they had, and didn't want anything in return.'

Phnom Penh didn't look like a capital city then. 'There was no water—even the hotel had to bring in four truckloads every day. There was dirt and rubbish everywhere because there was no collection, and hordes of flies in the market. There were people cooking in the streets; a lot of people moving. Some were looking for jobs or houses, or just passing through the city on their way to other provinces. I remember huge queues of ox-carts coming and going, stacked with all the family's possessions. I thought it was the countryside. There were no motorbikes or cyclos, few bicycles and just a few cars of agencies and socialist embassies.'

By the time I visited in 1988, the city had been gradually rebuilt, physically and spiritually. Once again there was peak-hour traffic, and the street lights, which had lain dormant for years waiting for a repairman, functioned, although still subject to breakdowns. For the first time in almost 20 years, people were doing up their houses which had been deserted, run-down, overcrowded and abused.

The number of cars plying the streets increased—probably ten-fold—from 1988 to 1990. Among the first to appear were 'Phnom Penh cars'. Custom made from scrap metal and odd car parts, often topped off with a Mercedes insignia, these creations cost about $700 in 1987. Then old Peugeots and Volkswagen Beetles were brought out of hiding after more than a decade of gathering dust, and mingled with the occasional Soviet-made Lada used by diplomats from the socialist bloc. These old remnants were soon dwarfed by flash Japanese models (mainly Datsuns, Toyotas and Nissans), along with less-numerous Mercedes, BMWs and Peugeots, all imported via Thailand, Singapore and Japan.

By early 1989 many public gardens, parks and the median strips between the lovely wide tree-lined streets had been renovated; the wrought-iron fences of public buildings, and many buildings themselves, had been painted, and abandoned cars removed from the streets. Much of the new look came as a result of the '7 January celebrations' which marked 10 years since liberation. A lot of this was superficial—structural changes came only after the Constitution was amended in 1989 allowing private ownership. People then started renovating and building.

Returning to Phnom Penh in 1990, I was amazed by the changes. Scanning the streets from the sixth-floor balcony of the Monorom Hotel in mid-1988, it was possible to spot just an occasional car among the hordes of bicycles. By mid-1989 on average there was about one car per block. Now there were hundreds. Many of the occupants were young, wore sapphires and designer jeans, and belonged to Phnom Penh's emerging upper class. They cruised past shops which sold televisions, stereos, videos. They dined at floating restaurants, and later went to discos. At home, they had a bottle of Hennessy on the shelf.

Private enterprise had always existed but on a relatively small scale, and without Government sanction until April 1989. Since then hundreds of shops, restaurants and private enterprises had opened. Several hotels had been built or renovated. Buddhist temples were reopening. The markets had a phenomenal range of consumer goods, imported mainly from Thailand and Singapore. It was now possible to buy almost anything found in Robinsons department store in Bangkok—cosmetics, stationery, clothes, toys, electronic goods, sports wear. (The exceptions were bleach, soft washing powder, decent batteries, good cork screws and books. By 1992, all these were available except the last, for Phnom Penh still had no bookshops and the only foreign language books were English and French dictionaries.)

Pavements along the main streets were now dotted with street vendors, offering everything from cigarettes and mangos to fluffy toys. Central Market had spread beyond its original boundary, and stalls outside the circular covered area sold food, clothes, stationery, footwear and luggage. The drab State-run stalls inside had been replaced by glistening displays of gold jewellery. At the larger, more free-wheeling O-Russey Market, stalls were stacked high with colour TVs and videos. The range of household goods was mind-boggling.

While the governments of Thailand and Singapore continued to enforce ASEAN's strong political stand against the Phnom Penh Government, Chinese–Cambodian traders were busy importing goods—by the ship-loads. The most noticeable arrivals were cars and motorbikes. Phnom Penh had become a staging post on the 'Hun Sen trail'—to avoid tax and trade restrictions with Vietnam, vehicles from Singapore were sent to Vietnam and China, via Cambodia. They were shipped up the Mekong, or through Kompong Som port, to Phnom Penh, taken by truck to Ho Chi Minh (where some were sold, for more than double the price in Phnom Penh), then by train to Hanoi, and eventually to China. While waiting to be transported out of Phnom Penh, many cars were driven around the city, adding to the impression of prosperity.

Although profits were filtering through the community, it was generally only traders who benefited—the majority of Phnom Penh residents still lived in sub-standard conditions. As one Cambodian reminded me, 'Phnom Penh is not Cambodia—out in the country it is a very different story'. With the city's flashing lights and gleaming chrome, it was easy to forget a civil war raged in the north and west of the country. The resistance factions—the Khmer Rouge and those led by Sihanouk and former Prime Minister Son Sann—stepped up their attacks on Government forces after the Vietnamese withdrew in September 1989, and fighting in the northwest was intense, especially in Battambang and Bantey Meanchey provinces.

The recent and obvious consumerism was a facade. Underneath, the economy was being squeezed by the war which swallowed 30 to 40 per cent of the country's budget. In mid-1990 the Government was rumoured to be on the verge of bankruptcy. With the economy so fragile anarchy broke out in February 1990, when rumours in Phnom Penh suggested the Khmer Rouge were approaching the capital. Inflation shot up 500 per cent overnight and economic panic continued for two weeks. In May police were brought in to control the price of rice at some markets. In Kompong Som soldiers raided the market and helped themselves, saying they had not been paid and couldn't afford the high prices.

Despite changes seen on the street, the economy was only functioning at 60 per cent of the level it was in Sihanouk's time, and the port at Kompong Som operated at one-third its capacity. A report by the Swedish International Development Authority in 1989, revealed that more than 600 000 hectares of agricultural land had yet to be reclaimed, half the country's tractors lay idle due to breakdowns and shortage of spare parts, and the country's rice yield was among the lowest in the world; that life expectancy was 48 years, and infant and child mortality remained among the highest in the world.

Industry was still almost non-existent. It suffered from lack of modern machines and electricity, which worsened after the Soviet Union reduced fuel supplies in 1990. Although five new fuel-driven power plants (one large one in Phnom Penh and four smaller provincial ones) came on line in 1989 and boosted electricity production by 11 per cent, it was still far short of the nation's needs. Blackouts—day and night—were routine in Phnom Penh, and some provincial cities only had electricity for one to two hours a day.

The capital was still far from normal: the majority of houses remained in disrepair, only a quarter of the population had access to safe water, there were not enough desks for school and university students—not even one book for four pupils—medical supplies were needed, and it was often easier to hand-deliver a message than to use the telephone.

Poverty was still rampant, and may in fact have increased in the previous two years. While the rich became richer, the poor remained poor, and Phnom Penh had become home to an increasing number of beggars and shanty dwellers as more peasants migrated from the countryside. The beggars—with grubby clothes, pathetic eyes and outstretched hands—loitered around hotels, restaurants and shops frequented by foreigners. They included women, children, those born with deformed limbs, and legless veterans. Many amputees also 'begged' from shop-keepers, who were forced to give five or ten riel or risk having their wares smashed by a flailing crutch, in what had become a small-scale, but well-organised racket.

Amputees were only one aspect of the war. The fighting may not have been in the streets of Phnom Penh, but it touched every-one. People feared the return of the Khmer Rouge. They knew their sons and brothers might be conscripted at any time. They saw victims and occasionally heard explosions. Mig fighters took off with brain-splitting roars from the airport. There were fewer men in the countryside. Inflation was high and Government spending was being cut. Electricity blackouts, fuel shortages and the 9 p.m. curfew were daily reminders of the war.

Traditionally the population of Phnom Penh would swell from December to April when an estimated 100 000 to 250 000 people came from rural areas in search of work during the dry season when they could not plant or harvest rice. They crowded in with relatives or built primitive shelters of woven palm on the footpaths or in a backyard. When the 1989 and 1990 rainy season started many did not return to plant rice, preferring to eke out an exist-ence in the capital. For the first time, homeless people began sleeping in parks.

As the civil war intensified in 1990 and the guerillas spread their influence over a wider area, Phnom Penh became a sanctuary for those displaced by the fighting. (Tens of thousands of others moved into camps on the Thai–Cambodian border and centers erected by the Government in several provinces.) And Phnom Penh also became 'home' to an increasing number of widows forced off their land inadvertently by the 1989 land reforms, which benefited most families but made it difficult for those without male labour to survive financially.

An increasing number of young women were also coming from the countryside and joining brothels. Until the last Vietnamese troops and advisers left in 1989, the Government maintained that the only prostitutes were Vietnamese girls who were periodically rounded up and sent back across the border. Within a year of the

Government sanctioning private enterprise, more than 150 similarly-built houses along the dyke on the northern outskirts of the city were operating as brothels. They were not bright and garish like brothels in Bangkok or Manila—most were of timber and thatch, and had a simple naked light bulb. They looked like ordinary homes, with pretty girls in mini-skirts sitting on the front verandahs.

At one I found four girls who all came from the provinces believing they could earn more here. They made 500 to 1000 riel a day (from one or two clients) and paid half to the brothel owner, the 34-year-old wife of a policeman. Two young Cambodian (male) journalists had taken me there and we sat around a rickety wooden table, drinking beer and eating dried squid dipped in fish sauce. A child slept in a hammock in a corner and another was curled on a floor mat. Gradually, the girls started to tell their stories.

Thy, 18, said she came because she was told she could make more money here than in the countryside. Now she missed her mother and wanted to go home, but she had borrowed 4000 riel ($8.25) 'from the rich people' to buy suitable clothes, and would have to repay 6000 riel over the next two months. Ra, 22, was sending 2000 riel a month to Kompong Cham to support her younger brother and sister (we spent that much on five beers). Mom, 30, had not heard from her husband since he left for the US in 1985. She arrived at the brothel four months ago from Kandal, with her 7-year-old son and 10-year-old daughter who lived here with her. Run, 20, burst into tears when asked why she had come. Eventually she admitted her husband had been jailed for smuggling goods across the border to Thailand and to repay his debts his brother had sold her to the brothel.

This was Street 273, and activity here continued beyond the 9 p.m. curfew, but the rest of the city had shut down and the streets were almost deserted, except for small groups of police who manned the main intersections with AK47s slung over their shoulders. Curfew ended at 4 a.m., when each morning the intersection of Monivong Boulevard and Achar Hemcheay became a brief and illegal bus/truck station. Government and private trucks, carrying fuel and other supplies to the provinces, stopped here to take on province-bound passsengers who squeezed into cabins and piled on top, and travelled—in uncomfortable circumstances—for slightly less than the bus fare.

Government drivers, who, like other public servants, were paid 3000 riel ($6.20) a month, could earn that amount each day by carrying passengers. Although illegal, such activities were tolerated because of low Government wages. One morning, in the darkness, I watched police officers wander along the lines of trucks. One told a driver four times to move on, which he did only after there was no more room for passengers on top of his fuel tanker.

Each day at 5 p.m. the same intersection was crowded with bicycles, cyclos and horn-tooting motorbikes and cars. Seen from the sixth floor of the White Hotel it was a bustling melting pot of swirling colour. From this level, the city took on a completely different perspective. From here you could see rooftop life: the children playing games, women cooking dinner, men swinging lazily in hammocks, a student writing on a blackboard—all as if they were at ground level. Directly ahead, 40 kilometres away, I could see the magnificent pale blue mountains of the Kompong Speu range. Directly below, I peered into back alleys.

At street level, shops sold gold jewellery and imported goods. But enter the lanes behind them and you entered another world—rarely seen by non-residents. Near-naked children played among piles of rubbish, open drains carried black sludge. Beggars and the homeless squatted. Women cooked on open wood fires. Travelling hawkers called their wares. Small businesses—repairers, barbers, tailors—proffered their trade.

I was invited by a Khmer friend to a home off one of these dark alleys. It meant picking our way through rubbish and water then climbing six flights of stairs in virtual darkness. The overpowering smell was of urine, dampness and food. Her 'home' was a small room with a bed, a coal-cooker and a huge pile of mangos ready to sell at the market the next day. It was impossible for two people to be in the room with the mangos, so we retreated down the stairs, which, although I couldn't see them, felt as if they were covered in pork fat.

The first time I went to a home for a meal was Khmer New Year 1989; until then foreigners were not allowed in Cambodian homes. I first encountered 16-year-old English-speaking Sop at a restaurant hawking maps to foreigners. He lived with his mother and 15-year-old sister in two rooms of a large house which once housed just one family and was now shared by four. Sop's family cooked and slept in the same room, and used the second room to eat and live in. The 'bathroom' was a one-metre high concrete tank of water in the corner of the front yard. The family shared a toilet with eleven other people. Their only furniture was a wooden table in one corner and three wooden chairs.

At meal time two mats were spread on the floor and we all sat down—men crossing legs, women tucking them under—to eat copious rice, fish and vegetable soup, cooked cucumber, and pork in batter, followed by fresh sliced mango. Coke was poured into glasses with blocks of ice which seemed to leave little room for liquid. (A block of ice had been bought at a local 'shop' and smashed into bits with a lump of metal.) It was an extravagant spread turned on for the foreigner. And it's one meal I will long remember for its originality and hospitality.

More than 20 family members and neighbours crowded into the tiny room to watch me eat. I was given, and shown how to tie, a Cambodian sarong which is worn around the home—the tailored *sampot* is for the office and outings. On each subsequent visit to Sop's family, I was taken into the second room where I swapped trousers for sarong.

One afternoon Sop's family decided to take me to the cinema. The film was about love and death, heroes and villains, patriotism and capitalism. *Don't Forget the Pol Pot Times* was barely-concealed government propaganda with a strong anti-Khmer Rouge message, yet it was also sensitive, funny, and included a surprisingly traumatic post-rape scene.

Being the only foreigner in a hot, airless cinema, with mum, two teenagers, two aunts and the next door neighbour's three-year-old boy who cried at inappropriate times, was an experience—to say the least. I sat between Sop and a friend both of whom interpreted, neither of whom apparently had any sense of co-ordination between seeing and hearing. As a motorbike passed across the screen, they said: 'a motorbike is going down the road'. No matter how many times I told them I could see what was happening but couldn't understand what was being said, each time the heroine entered a hut, they would duly inform me that the heroine had entered a hut. The dry comedy in the film and their visual interpreting combined to make it one of my funniest trips to a cinema.

In 1989 it was possible to visit Khmer homes, but in 1990 I was able to stay with a Khmer family rather than in a hotel, and became the first journalist to do so. This was only one of many examples of social and political change. Aid worker Susanne Wise had lived in Phnom Penh since 1987 and talked of the many changes. 'Now you can visit Cambodian homes and have a personal open relationship with people you deal with, which includes the woman who cleans your house and people in Government departments. We can now drive ourselves, and go to appointments without a guide if we want to, but we still have to get permission to go to the provinces. It's not always been like this. A few years ago, a technical consultant was allowed to visit the project she was working on once a week—for 20 minutes on a Friday afternoon—such was the level of rigidity. At that time you had the feeling it was a really weird place. I was very conscious about doing everything—you didn't just do something, you had to consider whether it was right, whether there would be consequence. There weren't any rules, so you were never sure what you could and couldn't do. One time, a German woman returned from a boat trip and was informed if she went on the river again she would be deported. Now we can hire a boat and go anywhere, anytime.' Sunday cruises on the Mekong were in fact common among the international community, and the highlight, the bi-annual Australia versus The Rest of the World cricket match was played on the sandy banks of the Mekong, 15 kilometres upstream from Phnom Penh.

When I arrived in Phnom Penh in 1988 there were only 130 Westerners including children. They all lived and worked in the two main hotels, the cramped drab Monorom and the much more sprawling Samaki which included several bungalows and boasted one of the city's few swimming pools. Some Westerners had their office in the Samaki and apartment in the Monorom, or vice versa, and commuted between the two by cyclo. 'Apartment' here meant a hotel room where residents paid $16 a day and washed their dishes in the bathroom sink. Over the next three years the number of Westerners more than trebled and they moved into rented villas (foreigners could not buy houses) spread around the city.

From 1 May 1989 Cambodians automatically had the right to own the house they lived in, on that day. At the same time, the last Vietnamese advisers were leaving, and vacating dozens of large villas which the government then allocated to senior officials. In the new spirit of capitalism, these instant home owners—seeing flashing dollar signs—made their new homes available to foreigners, while they crammed their families into less palatial dwellings, or used the rental advance to build a smaller house at the rear of the villa or in the outer suburbs.

Unicef, the International Red Cross and most of the 30 aid agencies working in Cambodia concentrated on agricultural, health and to a lesser extent education and women's programs. They contributed significantly to rebuilding Cambodia, although it was not easy and not all projects were as successful as hoped. Unicef program officer Brigitte Sonnois, believed insufficient understanding and planning on the part of the agency, poor communications, and lack of management, supervision and training meant many programs did not reach their target. 'You always go with a government counterpart, and as few aid workers speak Khmer, you have to go through an interpreter, which doesn't help communications, which are already difficult because of cultural differences. We make assumptions, they make assumptions, and we think we have correct information but we don't. And because of what happened in the past 20 years some people tell you what they think you or government counterparts like to hear.'

The National Paediatric Hospital in Phnom Penh was among the largest aid projects. In 1989 I found the corridors strewn with bodies. Women and children lay or slouched on flimsy mats on the floor, some sleeping, spoon-feeding young children or breastfeeding naked babies. The hospital Director, Dr Ho Bun Hong, squatted among them, checking, reassuring, offering advice.

Hong was one of 25 doctors left after the Khmer Rouge rule. Being thin had saved his life, he said laughing. 'My parents were farmers and because I knew how to plant rice and ride a cart, and because Pol Pot expected doctors to be fatter than I was, they didn't think I was a doctor.' He witnessed with horror family members and fellow doctors being killed. 'One of my friends was thrown into a pond with crocodiles. They killed the rest of my family with guns.' Hong returned to Phnom Penh after liberation, and in June 1980 was appointed hospital Director.

The hospital was built for $1 million in 1975 by World Vision, a US-based Christian aid and development group, yet it never opened because of the war. The Khmer Rouge used it to house animals and prisoners and to store ammunition, and in early 1979 it was used by the new regime as an army barracks. In less than four years this modern hospital, which was going to be the best children's hospital in Southeast Asia, was turned into a derelict, almost useless collection of buildings needing major renovations. 'There was no furniture, no medical equipment, only the excreta of animals and humans,' said Hong. 'There were shrubs growing all over the hospital—you could hardly see the buildings—and you could see the sky through the holes in the roof. I was the Director but there were no patients, no furniture and no supplies.'

Seeing their showcase in ruins, World Vision set out to rebuild it with $3 million from the US Government. World Vision staff tell how President Stan Mooneyham came to Foreign Minister Hun Sen in January 1980 to ask permission and said, 'Don't look at my face, you will see an American, an enemy—look at my blood,' then he cut his wrist with a knife. Hun Sen gave permission for the hospital to be rebuilt and it opened later that year.

Across a cracked concrete yard from the medical and surgical wards, a group of women stirred six large pots boiling above wood burners. Outside, chickens ran around a netted yard next to a garden plump with green vegetables and pumpkins. Inside, mothers sat on the floor feeding naked pot-bellied babies. This was a centre for RINE—rehydration, immunisation, nutrition and education—where malnourished children were treated while their mothers were taught basic child-care. They learnt about hygiene and nutrition, and how to grow and prepare nutritious food using local products. In the adjoining vaccination-education centre Leiv Sary, who had adopted three 'Pol Pot orphans', immunised up to 1000 babies a month against the six preventable childhood diseases: measles, polio, diptheria, tetanus, whooping cough and TB.

At the provincial hospital in Kompong Speu, 40 kilometres west of Phnom Penh Chris Drummond told me how she was part-way through an operation when the last theatre light bulb blew. She finished the operation under torchlight then drove 80 kilometres to Phnom Penh and back to get a new bulb. I watched a young boy—no one could tell me his name or age—slowly lift the banana he had been clutching all day and begin peeling it. Several of the hospital staff cheered. He had severe malnutrition and the banana was the first food he had attempted to eat for several days. It was a long-awaited sign that he was improving. He was only one of thousands of children in Cambodia who suffered from malnutrition. With distended bellies and unsmiling faces, they lay on bamboo woven mats, usually covered with flies that no-one could control. But he was one of the lucky survivors—each week at the Kompong Speu hospital three or four children died before they peeled their bananas.

Each week, two or three people were treated for horrific injuries from land mines, some of which dated back to the 1970s, although most had been recently placed. The victims were almost always farmers working in fields, often women. Patients sometimes took days to reach the hospital, by which time their injuries became infected. Amputations were standard. (In 1992 the UN began training former soldiers to clear some of the estimated four million mines just as UNHCR began repatriating the 350 000 refugees on the Thai–Cambodia border and the 170 000 internally displaced living in Government-run camps.)

Neville Henry, one of two Red Cross doctors stationed at Kompong Speu told how one man did not reach the hospital until seven days after losing his leg. 'He had been seeing a traditional doctor, and arrived here in a terrible state, with tetanus and gangrene.'

The most amazing of my many coincidences in Vietnam and Cambodia was meeting Neville. After he showed me around the hospital, we returned to the bungalow, and sitting around the kitchen table having a cup of tea, we talked of home and family—and I discovered his father's brother had married my father's sister!

Back in Phnom Penh, I was invited to lunch with Sisowath Lida, better known as Princess Lida. She and her sister Neary, both cousins of Sihanouk, were the only members of the royal family who remained in Cambodia after the 1970 coup. Twenty years after Sihanouk left, she was working for the Government he was fighting against. She was a member of the National Assembly (parliament) and Vice-Director of International Relations for the National Front.

She said her Khmer Rouge days, spent in the fields in Battambang, reinforced her faith in Buddhism and confirmed her commitment to remain in Cambodia. 'When I was young, during Sihanouk's regime, I liked to shoot birds, and because I'm Buddhist, I thought the Pol Pot time was my punishment. My husband and three daughters died and after liberation I said, "Buddha gave me my eyes, my face and what's important, my culture, so I must give my eyes, ears, hands. I must stay in Kampuchea to help make life better for my people".'

Lida was not an ardent royalist, nor an anti-royalist, yet she kept alive rare court dances. Four times a year she performed a unique dance for the gods, and said she was the only one to do this as other members of the royal family no longer recognised these religious days with dance. Watching her, I was almost mesmerised by her Jekyll and Hyde character as she switched from loud, aggressive chanting (and yelling at her staff to bring or light more candles) to sweet, soft singing. Chanting in Sanskrit, she prayed for peace. Like the dancers of the royal palace, she curled her fingers, arched her back and balanced delicately on one foot. But Lida had learned to dance only three years earlier. 'I was 43,' she laughed, sweat dripping after the all-consuming one hour dance. 'I didn't learn in the palace because when I was young I didn't like dancing. But now I must do it for my people, to bring peace for my people.'

If she had danced as a young girl, her teacher would probably have been Chea Samy, a favourite of the royal court. Born in Kompong Cham, she was brought to Phnom Penh by a dance teacher at the age of five, and joined about 500 young dancers at the Royal Palace. She began dancing at seven, and teaching at 30. At 73, she was still instructing young dancers, and helping revive classical Khmer dance, characterised by elaborately-decorated costumes and dramatic masks. This ancient, graceful, art form,

which dates from 802 AD and at its most complex, involves more than 3000 gestures, is an important symbol of Cambodian culture. 'In Sihanouk's regime I went everywhere: India, the Philippines, France, Indonesia, Singapore, Czechoslovakia, the Soviet Union, North Korea,' said Chea Samy, while dressing a young dancer for a special performance at the School of Fine Arts. On the wall behind was a photo of her star student, 20-year-old Yim Devy. 'She is not perfect yet. She has been dancing for ten years and needs another five to be 100 per cent,' she said.

After the Khmer Rouge wiped out 90 per cent of the country's artists, there remained only a handful of dancers, three costume makers and two dance instructors who knew all of the 3000 gestures (Chea Samy and Ros Kong, also in her 70s). Chheng Phong, a former instructor who became Minister for Culture, began reforming the dance company. By the mid-1980s it had been rebuilt, and began touring socialist-bloc countries, but the international isolation of Cambodia made it difficult for them to perform in the West. In June 1990 the national ballet toured Europe and became the first Cambodian cultural group to perform in the West in more than 15 years. The one-month trip was followed by a three-week tour of the US by a second dance group. At the end of the highly-acclaimed tour, six members, including the star Yim Devy, were persuaded to stay in the US by political groups opposed to the Phnom Penh Government.

In 1990, helping to document all the dance gestures before Chea Samy and Ros Kong became too old, were Australian ethnomusicologist Bill Lobban and American anthropology student Toni Shapiro. After spending time with Cambodians in refugee camps in Indonesia and on the Thai–Cambodian border, Toni was amazed how much time and energy they devoted to performing and teaching each other to dance and play music. 'I was intrigued by the importance put on performance in these precarious and dangerous conditions: why, wherever they are, is performance, especially dance, a priority?' This is what she hoped to answer in her dissertation.

While dance was being revived, so too was religion. During the Khmer Rouge rule, all religion was banned; temples and churches were destroyed or turned into store houses or prisons; all monks were derobed, and thousands executed. Buddhism, the religion of 90 per cent of the population, was the core of Cambodian life; more than anything else, it drew the people together. From early childhood—consciously or subconsciously—it influenced almost all their thoughts and actions. Hun Sen laughed when I asked him one day whether the Government would consider family planning to limit the extraordinary population growth of 2.8 per cent per annum at a time when the country couldn't grow enough to feed its population. 'In Buddhist teachings, people are told they should not kill, and family planning has the intention to kill life. I would be voted out of power if I suggested that,' he said. The Government had become acutely aware of the power of Buddhism as a vote winner.

The Venerable Um Sum, the country's second-most senior monk and a National Front executive, told me Buddhism was reborn on 7 January 1979 and that Buddhists were then free to worship. However, most people agreed religion was still restricted, and was not officially sanctioned until Cambodian New Year (April) 1989, when Heng Samrin, Hun Sen and former monk-turned-Communist Party leader Chea Sim officiated at a ceremony during which the ashes of one of Buddha's fingers were placed in the Sakyak Mony Chedey stupa in front of the railway station. From early morning thousands of worshippers, most dressed in white, shuffled behind saffron-robed monks in a three-kilometre procession around the city's main streets. I was photographing the procession from various balconies en route; it was an overwhelming sight.

Since then Buddhism has flourished: many more pagodas have been repaired and rebuilt, young men once again join the monkhood, and the Buddhist Institute has been re-established. Until 1989 only men over 50 could become monks. By mid-1990, Un Sum estimated 10 000 and possibly 15 000 boys were living in temples. 'Before, young boys were not able to become monks because they were needed to defend and rebuild the country,' he explained, while offering me Coke and ice in his small room dominated by the universal colour photograph of Heng Samrin. 'After liberation there were many problems: to protect the country from the Khmer Rouge, then to improve the economy. Now the economy is stable, so the young boys can become monks again,' he said, repeating the Government's line.

Christianity was officially recognised in April 1990, exactly a year after Buddhism, although a group of Vietnamese Catholics had been holding services—in a Buddhist temple—and the Western community held weekly services at the Samaki Hotel. The first public service was in the National Theatre, officiated by Father Tom Dunleavy, an American priest resident in Phnom Penh, and a visiting French priest, Father Emile Destomes. In front of Westerners of all denominations and 2000 Cambodians including high-ranking representatives of the Government, the Communist Party and the Buddhist hierarchy, Dunleavy, dressed in long white robes with a gold embossed stole, held a tall white candle while it was lit by Destomes. It was 8 a.m. on Easter Saturday, and it marked the rebirth of Christianity in Cambodia. The country's estimated 10 000 Christians—the majority of them Vietnamese —could now officially practise their religion freely.

The other main social change stemmed from the 1989-amended Constitution which stated all people were free to return to Cambodia without reprisals. Exempt were the eight hardcore Khmer Rouge leaders, known as the 'Pol Pot clique', including Pol Pot, Ieng Sary, Ta Mok, Son Sen and Nuon Chea. Overseas Cambodians had started returning in small numbers in 1988. Among the first was Californian psychologist Seanglim Bit who came back to see his two children for the first time in 13 years.

Somaya was two and her brother Ketya was three when their father left Cambodia in 1975. Like many thousands of others he fled across the border to Thailand, leaving Somaya and Ketya to be brought up by the parents of his wife, whom he said had died during the Pol Pot rule. They had not seen their father since they were infants—although in later years they sent letters and photos—until they met him in the foyer of the White Hotel one morning in August 1988. It was an emotional, but guarded, reunion between a man who was virtually a stranger to his own children, and teenagers who had grown up in a society totally different from his. While they lived in uncertainty and survived on few resources in a country stripped of almost all its infrastructure, Bit earned a doctorate in education at the University of San Francisco, bought a house in El Cerrito, and set up a psychology practice.

Returning to Phnom Penh, he was saddened to see his once beautiful city still in a state of decay, but was impressed with how much had been achieved. 'They score a lot of points for improvements between 1979 and now. It's a city now, not a ghost town,' he said. He was surprised by the availability and variety of consumer goods and the amount of disposable income that some people had. 'I imagined there would be more modesty than you see in the streets. Sometimes in restaurants they play Western music which was a surprise. I thought they would stay with the revolutionary songs, but it seems that only the national radio does. But people keep reminding me that it is only recently that the Government has relaxed and allowed a free economy.' During Bit's one-week stay, the Cambodian Government gave permission for Somaya and Ketya to go to the US. It took almost a year to get permission from the US and to finalise details. In June 1989 they flew to San Francisco—the second and third children since 1975 to officially emigrate to the US from Cambodia, although thousands had been admitted as refugees from camps along the Thai border. In 1992 Bit was one of more than 20 overseas Cambodians who returned and set up political parties to contest the UN-supervised elections.

Others who had fled in the 1970s also began returning. The first prominent American–Cambodian to come back was In Tam, the former President of the National Assembly in the Sihanouk and Lon Nol Governments. He returned in January 1989 for six weeks, and impressed by what he saw, accepted the Government's invitation to sit on the Constitution Commission which, among other things, changed the country's name, flag and anthem. The People's Republic of Kampuchea (PRK) became the State of

Cambodia (SOC), blue was added to the flag to represent democracy, and the new anthem became less revolutionary.

Sitting with him on the Commission were two other prominent overseas Cambodians who returned in 1989, former Sihanoukists Pung Peng Cheng, 72, and his wife Tong Siv Eng, 71. They left Cambodia when Sihanouk was deposed and lived in exile for 20 years, following him between Paris, Beijing and Pyongyang before retiring in Paris. Siv Eng, who in 1955 became Cambodia's first woman politician and the following year the first woman minister, was also private tutor to Sihanouk's children. Pung Peng Cheng, who had been Sihanouk's Director-General of Education, Education Minister and General Secretary of the High Council, became Chief of the Cabinet in exile.

The couple had worked closely with Sihanouk for 26 years until 1982 when he signed a pact with the Khmer Rouge and Son Sann's faction to form the Coalition Government of Democratic Kampuchea. 'We refused to work with the Khmer Rouge,' Pung Peng Cheng said. In a politically expedient move, Hun Sen appointed Siv Eng to the eight-member Council of State, and asked Pung Peng Cheng to be a Minister Assisting the Prime Minister. Why did two loyal Sihanouk aides change sides and work with the communist regime? 'I came back for nostalgic reasons—after 20 years abroad I wanted to see what my homeland was like,' said Pung Peng Cheng. 'I was very impressed with what I saw—the country has been rebuilt. I'm not a communist, but I'm a Minister in a communist government, and this is good because I can introduce liberal ideas.' Added Siv Eng, 'I am like the salmon—they are born here, grow up and go away, then come back to die.'

Although overseas Cambodians made up the bulk of visitors in 1989 and 1990, tourists and businessmen also began to arrive. Japanese, Chinese, Taiwanese, Singaporian, Thai, French and Australian businessmen came to discuss or set up investments. The first joint venture was between the Government and a Singaporian company to complete the huge luxurious Cambodiana Hotel. Begun by Sihanouk in the late 1960s, it finally opened in July 1990. Under other contracts, logs were going to Thailand, agricultural products to France and scrap metal to Singapore; a Thai company was bottling mineral water, a French company was freezing fish and Coca Cola was talking about rebuilding the soft drinks factory.

Investors had been encouraged by the political stability and economic improvements as well as by new policies which promoted private enterprise and foreign investment. The economy still had not recovered to the level it was in the 1960s, although there had been considerable progress. Agricultural production was up, exports resumed, and compared with the rest of the country, Phnom Penh was booming. For the first time in almost 20 years, Cambodia was producing enough rice to feed its people, and this had been a major moral, as well as economic, boost to the country.

According to Un Buntha of the Ministry of Planning, despite the continuing civil war, significant amounts of foodstuffs and other products were being exported. 'In 1989 we had a remarkable result, especially in food and rubber production. Rice production has reached self-sufficiency. We produced 2.5 million tonnes, up 5 per cent on 1988. And now we have begun exporting soya beans, maize, tobacco leaf, resin, timber, sandalwood, mattresses, bicycle tyres and soyabean sauce,' he said. 'The State now allows families to own part of the rubber plantations so they can restore them and boost production.' The Government also allowed farmers to buy tractors from the State, although few could afford to do so.

While economic and social-cultural liberalisation continued, the Government instigated a political crackdown which became public in May 1990. The most notable victim was Khieu Kanharith, an intellectual who founded and edited the Government-run *Kampuchea* newspaper and voiced liberal views which included calls for political reform. He was dismissed by the Politburo, but declared he would remain as outspoken as before. At the same time, Men Sam On was dismissed as chief of the Party Organisation Commission, although she retained her post as the only woman member of the Politburo.

In the previous month, Transport Minister Ung Phan and six senior Government officials were jailed for attempting to form a political party when the Constitution only allowed for a single party. Reportedly, up to 100 others were questioned and an unknown number detained. This marked the beginning of a tighening-up period by the Communist hardliners set on stamping out the seeds of liberalisation and anti-Communist sentiment. Targeted were those who supported democracy and a multi-party system, and there were obvious parallels with the situation in Vietnam at that time. Both the dismissals and arrests were said to have been instigated by Vietnamese authorities who were worried about the possibility of anti-Communist or subversive activities across the border in Cambodia. While visiting Hanoi in May, President Heng Samrin was told by Vietnamese authorities that they had a list of Cambodians whom they considered were associating with or receiving assistance from the West, especially the US. They told Heng Samrin that Kanharith's name was on top of their list. Four weeks later he was dismissed.

Ung Phan and his six colleagues were released in October 1991, and the former minister was expected to test the new political climate by setting up a party but after his release he kept a very low profile. In a rare interview in January 1992, he criticised the Government for corruption, and said he would set up a party when the UN Transitional Authority in Cambodia (UNTAC) was established. The following week he was shot in his car on the southern outskirts of Phnom Penh. The attempt on Ung Phan's life came less than a week after the killing of Tea Bun Long, a Government official whose bullet-ridden body was found 30 kilometres south of Phnom Penh. The following month, the deputy editor of an opposition newspaper survived a shooting after publishing anti-Vietnamese articles. It was not clear that these three were political shootings or whether they were related, but either way, they underscored the fragility of the political environment. Phnom Penh officials and intellectuals warned that there could be more political assassinations before the UN arrived. They were worried that Ung Phan's colleagues might be next.

Mid-1990 was a turning point for Cambodia—not a sudden turn but rather a gradual curve to the right. Attitudes started to change. Peace talks were underway—although not achieving a great deal, the factions were at least talking. Hun Sen's economic reforms were starting to bear fruit. Western and Asian governments were not as hostile to the Phnom Penh regime as they had been. Nevertheless, I had strong views about the injustice of international politics, and little hope of a peace settlement. Like many people, I thought it wrong that the Khmer Rouge-dominated coalition continued to occupy Cambodia's seat at the UN despite the fact that the Phnom Penh regime had been in power 11 years and controlled 80 to 90 per cent of the country. The threat of a Khmer Rouge return came closer to reality than in the previous decade. Perhaps spurred by this, several Western governments started to recognise that the Phnom Penh Government had been in power more than a decade; had made a commendable effort at restoring the country; that it was less socialist and more capitalist; and its economic reforms were working—but still none reestablished diplomatic relations or provided bilateral aid.

The country urgently needed a massive injection of funds for infrastructure redevelopment, especially for roads, railways, ports, telecommunications and irrigation systems which had been largely untouched since damaged during 20 years of war, and for health and education services. The Government was looking for assistance from Western governments and development agencies, such as the United Nations Development Program (UNDP) and the International Monetary Fund (IMF), as well as international investors. But this was denied in order to apply pressure for a political settlement.

While the West and ASEAN refused to recognise the Phnom Penh regime and provide development aid, neighbouring countries experienced an economic boom: Thailand boasted economic growth of 9 per cent per annum, while Cambodia failed to reach its 1960s status. If development aid had been provided when needed—and not prevented by international politics—it could have saved thousands of lives and immeasurable suffering.

'It's all games. And the Cambodian people are the pawns. They are still being punished,' said Eva Mysliwiec, long-time Western relief worker and author of the 1987 book *Kampuchea: Punishing the Poor*. 'The international community keeps saying the time is not right. Now they want to focus on Eastern Europe,' she said. Although Cambodia had come a long way since the Khmer Rouge days, the rebuilding of a nation is a slow process, and Eva believed it would take more than a generation to restore Cambodia to even its pre-war status, especially if the West continued to deny aid, as it was doing in 1990.

The US-imposed embargo was to be lifted with the final Vietnamese troop withdrawal, but after the withdrawal in September 1989, Washington announced the embargo would remain until there was a peace settlement. Disheartened, the Government continued its peace negotiations; then the US said the Hun Sen administration had to be dismantled as part of a peace settlement. Rules were constantly changed and new obstacles raised. Meanwhile, the war went on, Cambodians continued being killed, displaced and humiliated. China said it would stop supplying the Khmer Rouge if the Government allowed the UN to verify that no Vietnamese troops remained. The Government not only agreed, but asked for international verification. China continued supplying the Khmer Rouge.

China and Thailand were key players in keeping the Khmer Rouge alive—China by giving political and military support, and Thailand by allowing the guerillas to set up bases inside Thailand and to transport Chinese arms and supplies through Thai provinces. Although fiercely anti-communist, Thailand was not prepared to force the Khmer Rouge back across the border because they did not want to fight the Khmer Rouge; the guerilas provided a useful buffer between themselves and the Vietnamese; and the Thai army received a proportion (reportedly 10 to 15 per cent) of all arms supplied to the Khmer Rouge. Even if China stopped supplying arms, the guerilas were said to have stockpiled two years supplies. They also had the ability to buy from elsewhere (even from Phnom Phen Government forces, such was the level of morale and pay in the Cambodian People's Armed Forces) with the millions of dollars they earned from lucrative timber and gem mining in areas they controlled along the border.

Some analysts believed that if the Khmer Rouge lost the UN seat and China's support, it would eventually disintegrate into small bands of guerilas capable only of lightning strikes, and in 10 to 15 years might disappear altogether. However, a peace settlement without them was unlikely. One reason was Sihanouk's inextricable ties to the Khmer Rouge and Beijing. Founding-director of the US–Indochina Reconciliation Project, John McAuliff, believed the US could, and should, have broken those ties. 'The US forced the marriage of Sihanouk and Son Sann with the Khmer Rouge, and we should now force the divorce. This could be done in less than 24 hours, by stating that we withdraw support for him unless he ends all military and political co-operation with the Khmer Rouge. We are the ones who gave the Khmer Rouge legitimacy through their marriage with Sihanouk, now we should reverse that. Even people in Congress and the Administration have come to recognise the Phnom Penh regime is more than a Vietnam-puppet government, that it has earned the right to govern. And to take away their right to govern would be very dangerous in practical terms—it could allow the Khmer Rouge in. At the very minimum we should now do five things: drop the trade embargo and allow the existing unofficial connections and investment opportunities to expand; stop opposing IMF, World Bank and Asian Development Bank assistance; develop direct dialogue with the Phnom Penh Government; stop undermining Thailand's efforts to end its role as a supply line for the Khmer Rouge; and stop voting for the coalition seat at the UN.'

The West had criticised the Government without recognising the considerable achievements of the previous decade. The Soviet Union and Eastern Europe were praised for their liberal moves, but not Cambodia, although economic reforms and privatisation were introduced here before the eastern bloc. The West focused on negative aspects, such as corruption (which was, in 1990, far less here than in other Asian countries) and ignored the fact that society was being restored, that the economy and living standards had improved, despite the war.

The Khmer Rouge, Sihanouk and Son Sann's Khmer People's National Liberation Front (KPNLF) had won comparatively little ground militarily or politically during the previous decade. They did not contribute at all to rebuilding the country—on the contrary, they considerably slowed it by continuing the fight. If there had been an end to the fighting, the trade and aid embargo would have been lifted, and if the Government attempted to commit 40 per cent of its budget and thousands of men to the war, that recovery may have been complete. While the opposition remained outside the country, the Government attempt to return a semblance of normality to a decimated country. After 11 years in government and after re-establishing a functioning society, the Hun Sen administration had more right to govern than any other faction. Yet the fighting and negotiating continued. For too long there had been talk but little action: the West had done virtually nothing to stop the Khmer Rouge, the coalition still occupied the UN seat and was still being provided with arms, the embargo had not been lifted, and economically, Cambodia was still isolated. The people were still suffering. When would we put human suffering above politics?

Finally, in the second half of 1991, the ball started rolling. Sihanouk stepped down as resistance leader, handing over to his son Prince Ranariddh. Sihanouk invited Hun Sen to Beijing and Pyongyang, and the Prince accepted the Prime Minister's invitation to visit Phnom Penh later in the year (ostensibly to return the remains of his mother-in-law who had died in January). In June, during peace talks at the Thai seaside resort of Pattaya, the four factions accepted a voluntary ceasefire and agreed to base the Supreme National Council in Phnom Penh with Sihanouk as President of the SNC. At a second Pattaya meeting in September the four leaders agreed to demobilise 70 per cent of their respective armies, and on 23 October, the four Cambodian parties and 18 other nations signed a comprehensive peace agreement. Within three weeks the ruling Communist Party officially threw out socialism, changed its leader, name, flag, emblem and philosophy, adopting liberal democracy with a multi-party system. The UN began arriving, and on 14 November Sihanouk returned to Phnom Penh in triumph.

The peace agreement paved the way for a permanent ceasefire and for an interim UN-administration to disarm and demobilise the four armies, then prepare for UN-supervised elections. But the historic signing went virtually unnoticed in Phnom Penh. There were no celebrations (until the following day when the Government organised a rally); no one except Westerners seemed to be even talking about it. The public reaction was similar to when Sihanouk was deposed in March 1970—it was as if the people were waiting for a directive, but none came, and there was no spontaneous response. Perhaps Paris was too far away for it to seem real, or after 12 years of war and four years of peace talks the Cambodians were tired of having their hopes raised then dashed.

However, an extraordinary Party Congress the week before was much more obvious. Blue and white banners flapped across the city's main streets everywhere, proclaiming peace and reconciliation. Conspicuous for their lack of (revolutionary) red, they advertised an unwritten message: out with socialism and the revolution, long live liberalism and democracy. The Communist Party had ruled unchallenged since 1979, under a system where suppression and the Constitution allowed for only one party. Democracy was the new catch-cry. Former US Senator Dick Clark of Iowa State, an observer at the historic Party Congress, commented, 'I came to see communism at work, but it's all gone'.

Some analysts saw the reforms as close to self-annihilation by the Party; others said it was only window-dressing and that not enough real changes would take place. The party appeared more liberal and less socialist, which the Government hoped would translate into votes. However, personal freedoms were still limited, and the hardcore revolutionaries who formed the party and the government in 1978–79 were still firmly in control. The People's Revolutionary Party of Kampuchea became simply the Cambodian People's Party; the inner cabinet—the Politburo—was given the non-socialist name of Permanent Committee, but the members remained. The Party was almost certainly pushed into reform in order to present a more appealing face for the election; as one former senior Government advisor commented: 'The white on the flags is not for freedom—it signifies fear. The Party fears that unless it changes it will lose the election.' The peace agreement had prompted the rulers to change their shirts but their hearts and minds were still in the old mode, and they were determined to stay in power by whatever means.

The peace signing made way for the UN to send its advance mission ahead of the peacekeeping force. First to arrive was a 40-man Australian communications unit, followed by a 117-member French aviation team with a C160 transporter and four helicopters, and 20 New Zealand mine-clearing trainers. The sight of blue-beret soldiers was such a novelty in Phnom Penh that on the first afternoon onlookers blocked Achar Mean opposite Kalmet Hospital where the Australians were crammed into a double villa, and continued to cause traffic jams for three days. 'We were like monkeys in a cage, and they wouldn't go away until the police moved them on,' said one Digger.

The UN troops arrived in time to form a guard of honour for Sihanouk—along with the aid and diplomatic community and hundreds of Cambodian women in colourful royal silk *sampots* —beneath a 10-metre high portrait of Sihanouk looking 30 years younger. The deposed leader had fled Phnom Penh on 6 January 1979, the day before the Vietnamese entered the capital, aboard a Beijing-bound Air China 707, and returned 11 years later aboard an Air China 707, underscoring Beijing's support for, and influence over, Sihanouk. He fled with his Khmer Rouge guard who became his private secretary and shadow during his years in exile, but he returned with Hun Sen, an indication that he was moving away from the Khmer Rouge and cementing his new 'marriage' with the Phnom Penh regime. (Evidently, Hun Sen, who had flown to Beijing to bring Sihanouk home, had said he could only return on condition the Khmer Rouge guard was excluded.)

At 11 a.m. the 707 circled above Phnom Penh. The red carpet was in place, the military brass band ready. Finally, the one-time king stepped through the doorway, paused and waved with both hands. The crowd emitted a deafening cheer and the media surged forward *en masse*. He slowly moved along the red carpet shaking a hundred hands and paying his respects to the assembled monks, then sat in the shade to watch an exquisite display of traditional Cambodian dance. The accumulated emotion of seeing his 'little children' for the first time in 21 years was overwhelming. Furrows on the 69-year-old face deepened and he constantly dabbed his forehead and cheeks with a white handkerchief. More than once during the one-hour ceremony I wondered if he would collapse.

A one-kilometre long motorcade, a gala reception and an elaborate Buddhist ceremony marked the homecoming of the one-time king who abdicated in favour of his father, expelled the Americans, slept with the Khmer Rouge and was now the (supposedly) neutral leader of the four factions.

However, the return of Khmer Rouge leader Khieu Samphan on 27 November was entirely different, marked by violent demonstrations not seen in Phnom Penh since the anti-Lon Nol student riots of 1974. The former resistance fighter, who had been Head of State during the Khmer Rouge's 1975–79 rule, was beaten by protestors who broke down fences and forced their way into his house, seeking revenge for the deaths of family and friends. Along with Khmer Rouge Defence Minister Son Sen, who had also been in the house, Samphan was hurriedly taken to the airport for a wound-licking flight back to Bangkok, just seven hours after arriving.

By early 1992 the Khmer Rouge were legitimately back in Phnom Penh as members of the Supreme National Council which had established its headquarters here. The 'god-king' was happily ensconced in his beautifully restored palace, entertaining diplomats just as he had done in the flamboyant 1960s when French champagne flowed till the small hours. Diplomatic missions were re-established for the first time since 1975 and flag-flying limos purred up and down Tou Samouth Boulevard. Plans were underway to repatriate refugees, and at last the UN was here: an advance mission (UNAMIC) had been sent to help the factions maintain their ceasefire and prepare for the arrival of UNTAC, the 22 000-strong election and peacekeeping force.

This gave Cambodia a new confidence. But it also sent the dollar plummeting and real estate prices skyrocketing. Restaurants were dominated by soldiers, white Toyota Landcruisers displaying huge 'UN' letters occupied precious parking spots, and prostitutes were increasing significantly. This was only the beginning. The first UN contingent numbered only 268 military and administrative personnel; UNTAC would be more than 80 times larger. Paradoxically, UNTAC was coming to end an era dominated by the Vietnamese, who were said by the West to have 'occupied' Cambodia for 10 years. Yet, UNTAC could be regarded as yet another occupying force, and this was going to be difficult for the Cambodians to accept.

I had been telling family and friends I would stay in Cambodia for at least another two years as it would take that long for elections and a new government to be established, and it was an exciting time in Cambodia's history: the 12-year civil war was drawing to a close, the former monarch was back after 21 years of exile and house arrest, and the UN was sending in its largest ever peace-keeping force. But seeing so many social and cultural changes in Phnom Penh in the first three months of the UN arriving, I was not sure I wanted to live in a city dominated by thousands of UN administrators and soldiers, many of whom seemed to lack the cultural sensitivity these long-suffering proud people deserved.

UNAMIC, the advance mission, was replaced in March 1992 by UNTAC, the transitional authority, and the UN peacekeeping operation began in earnest. The UN was going to take Cambodia to free and fair elections, and optimism was high: the Cambodians expected great deeds from the UN, and UNTAC was exuding confidence. But the optimism trickled away, gradually at first then with accelerated pace from August onwards. First the Khmer Rouge refused to disarm its soldiers and barred the UN from areas under its control. The Government and Khmer Rouge began moving troops and arms around the countryside, as they had done at the beginning of each previous dry season. The Khmer Rouge deliberately attacked UN positions and started holding UNTAC personnel, sometimes as hostages. UNTAC was supposed to create a 'neutral political environment' for the elections, but from November 1992 politically-motivated violence reached alarming proportions. Opposition parties reported attacks against their members and officers, including handgrenade explosions, shootings and murders. Harassment and intimidation by Government agents became widespread.

As 1992 drew to a close, I became less optimistic, more troubled. I was concerned that whatever the UN did—with 22 000 personnel and close to $3 billion—it was not going to solve Cambodia's medium- to long-term problems. Despite the political violence and the Khmer Rouge's non-cooperation, the UN was determined to go ahead with the elections. This meant the UN and the international community could then say they had taken Cambodia to 'democracy', wipe their hands and go home, without due concern for the problems the new government would confront: the Cambodian leaders on all sides had not accepted reconciliation and they were destined to go on fighting, politically or militarily. The UN's transitional period was simply an interlude in a long history of civil conflict. Once the bandaid was removed—once the UN left—the bleeding would begin again.